Tl
Anglo-

The Landscape of Anglo-Saxon England

Della Hooke

Leicester University Press
London and Washington

Leicester University Press

A Cassell Imprint

Wellington House, 125 Strand, London WC2R 0BB, England
PO Box 605, Herndon, Virginia 20172, USA

First Published 1998

© Della Hooke 1998

British Library Cataloguing in Publication Data
A catalogue record for this book is available from the British Library.

ISBN 0 7185 1727 X Hardback
     0 7185 0161 6 Paperback

Library of Congress Cataloging-in-Publication Data
  Hooke, Della.
    The landscape of Anglo-Saxon England / Della Hooke.
      p.   cm.
    Includes bibliographical references (p.) and index.
    ISBN 0-7185-1727-X ISBN 0-7185-0161-6 (pbk.)
    1. England—Antiquities.   2. Great Britain—History—Anglo-Saxon period,
449–1066.   3. Land settlement patterns—England—History.   4. England—
Historical geography.   5. Landscape—England—History.   6. Land use—
England—History.   7. Archaeology, Medieval.   8. Geography,
Medieval.   9. Anglo-Saxons. I. Title.
DA155.H69 1997
936.2—dc21   95–17337
                                                                CIP

Typeset by Ben Cracknell Studios

Printed and bound in Great Britain by Redwood Books, Trowbridge, Wiltshire

Contents

List of Plates

List of Figures

Preface and Acknowledgements

This book is not a history of Anglo-Saxon England: many fine histories are already available. Rather, I would invite the reader to wander along paths that I myself have found of interest. Inevitably, many of my examples will be drawn from areas that I have myself studied and from central and southern England where the documentary record is fullest. The threads we follow are varied but are all drawn upon a canvas which is the landscape itself and, as such, may enhance our understanding and enjoyment of the countryside we see around us today. The image we conjure up, and for the present it can hardly be any more than an image, is tentative and incomplete, for many more threads have been embroidered upon it in the thousand succeeding years; but the early patterns often guided the later and occasionally still show through.

Many individuals have stimulated my interest in this period over the years and have given me continuous support: I am grateful to all of them. Mrs Jean Dowling, in the School of Geography, at the University of Birmingham, professionally retraced a number of the earlier figures but her sudden and unexpected death meant that most of them have had to be my own. I am grateful to the Repographics Unit at Cheltenham and Gloucester College of Higher Education for photographing them so expertly. I should also like to thank several authorities and institutions for permission to reproduce figures: Cambridge University Press for Figure 50, Berkshire County Council for Plate X and Exeter Cathedral Library for Plate VIII while the illustrations from the Cotton Tiberius Calendar have been redrawn from the originals with the permission of the British Library.

Della Hooke

Introduction

The 'Anglo-Saxon period' lasted for some 600 years, a length of time equivalent to a period from the mid-fourteenth century to the present day: far too long a time to fit comfortably into the niche once ascribed to the 'Dark Ages'. These were considered 'dark' on two accounts: first, because so little was known about them, at least for the few centuries following the withdrawal of the Romans, and, second, because the fall of Rome to what were seen as Germanic barbarians represented the loss of the values and achievements of the highly esteemed Classical world.

Archaeology and history together have rendered the epithet untrue but it is only in recent decades that the period has been viewed in its own right, with the Anglo-Saxons relegated to an important but not necessarily dominant role everywhere. In common with Continental nomenclature it is now considered more accurate to refer to this period as the 'early medieval' period. In such a lengthy period many changes obviously took place but, above all, it is no longer possible to point to a definite beginning or a definite end. Bands of marauding Anglo-Saxons cannot have killed off an entire population and immediately replaced earlier traditions with their own; instead, the late Roman and post-Roman period must be fully understood if the early years of the Anglo-Saxon incursions are to be placed into their proper context, for in many areas the flow of life remained relatively little disturbed. At the other end of the period, the great survey carried out by the Norman conquerors in the Domesday Book really summarizes the economic situation as it had developed in late Anglo-Saxon times.

Certainly there was change, and this was one of the most formative periods in English history. The nation of England came into being; this did not occur with the coming of the Anglo-Saxons but over many centuries in which peoples intermarried and tribes amalgamated and in which petty princedoms of various racial backgrounds gradually gave rise to kingdoms, one of which was eventually to become dominant. It was reaction to the threat of yet another outside invasion, that of the Vikings, that helped to unify the Anglo-Saxon peoples, but the newcomers in turn were to take their place in the new England.

An almost complete language change does reveal the impact of Anglo-Saxon culture. Scholars are still at odds as to how many Anglo-Saxons came to these islands to cause such a change. The current uncertainty is reflected in the fact that two of the most recent books on the subject present almost totally contradictory scenarios. One written by a historian based in the north of England believes that there was ample scope for both territorial and social continuity, emphasizing how 'Communities within the old military parts of the province adapted comparatively successfully to the changing circumstances of the fifth century.'[1] One written by an archaeologist based in the South-East, however, concentrates more upon change and notes the numbers of Anglo-Saxons that seem to have been required to produce the effects they did, particularly leading to the fact that 'English became the dominant language in lowland Britain, replacing Celtic dialects there.'[2] There probably were indeed vast differences across the country.

It will be archaeological sources that will eventually help to outline the true picture but at present archaeology is constrained by its own limitations. A lack of known sites, for instance, can suggest diminished population levels, but can archaeologists yet discover the true distribution pattern of settlement sites that made little use of pottery and other lasting artefacts, either because of impoverishment or different cultural backgrounds? The answer ultimately may lie in the landscape, and again archaeological techniques are beginning to build up a picture of field systems and vegetation cover which will in time help to suggest the intensity of land use in specific regions.

Both archaeology and history are now able to tell us much more about life in early medieval England, the former by examining the physical remains and the latter by careful scrutiny of the written document. Archaeology can, for instance, examine the evidence of burials and religious buildings and through these cast light upon men's superstitions and religious beliefs. It is an unbiased guide, as ready to investigate evidence of possible sacrificial, even live, burial, for instance, as that of pious Christian internment. The historian, on the other hand, must consider the bias of contemporary writers and the intended purpose of the documents he makes use of, but he alone can explore the period through the thoughts of those who actually lived in it. Keeping to the religious analogy, he alone can begin to understand the piety of the early Christians, the subsequent weakening (or at least 'amending') of a faith still outwardly expressed in the ever-increasing size and number of its monasteries and churches, and the subsequent rigours of tenth-century reform.

But this book is not about the men who lived in the early medieval period and only indirectly about their social institutions. It primarily concerns the landscape, but a landscape which was even then almost entirely man-made and was greatly affected by regional economic conditions and the administrative framework that had been set up to exploit it. The men are gone but the landscape surrounds us on every side. The early medieval period was but one layer in the palimpsest that we see today, but to understand how today's landscape evolved we need to know more about every stage of its development. In language, nationhood, administrative and ecclesiastical organization, the changes that occurred in this period have left an enduring mark, and this book sets out to examine the evidence from a number of different viewpoints. The early chapters explore the natural landscape with its plants and animals as seen by the Anglo-Saxons. The administrative framework which was developed to exploit the landscape is then examined, especially in Chapters 3 to 5, and particular kinds of landscape are more closely investigated in subsequent chapters, followed by a brief discussion of particular aspects of economic development and culminating in a final chapter which points towards future centuries.

Notes

1. Higham, *Rome, Britain and the Anglo-Saxons.*
2. Welch, *Anglo-Saxon England.*

PART I

The Anglo-Saxon View of the Countryside

CHAPTER 1

The Natural Topography

What did the Anglo-Saxon landscape of England look like? Obviously the answer would depend very much upon which part of the country this question concerned but we can be certain that there were many features which those of us living here today would have found familiar. This is because one of the primary factors affecting our regional landscapes is the underlying geology. Although it is not wise to be too deterministic about the influence of the natural environment, it is difficult to escape from the fact that the predominant rock type helped to set the scene of man's efforts to control and make use of the countryside about him. Use of the rolling downland of the chalk countryside of southern England has changed over the centuries: in Roman times fields of grain covered the upland; in medieval times these had been replaced by unbroken turf pasture; today the scene is again one of undulating ploughland, often stretching as far as the eye can see: a rumpled blanket of yellows and fawns as the grain once again ripens in the summer season. But the gentle upheavals of the chalk escarpments, their steeper scarp slopes giving way to the more gently inclined dip slopes, evoke a picture in the mind which is essentially that of a characteristic type of countryside, whatever its current usage.

Having recognized this fact, it must be said that it is still very, very difficult to paint a picture of Anglo-Saxon England. As will be shown, there is evidence which permits us to make informed guesses about the way the countryside might have looked, but detailed scientific examination of the environment has been made at only a very few places and these are not necessarily representative of areas only a few miles away from the individual sites examined. Such evidence is expensive and time-consuming to obtain and it will be many years before there is enough evidence of this nature to be useful in a general way. Some indication of our present knowledge from this source will appear in subsequent chapters.

Sadly, too, we can never see the landscape as anyone living at that time would have done. Man's attitudes to landscape change over periods of time in ways it is difficult for any one generation to understand – just as attitudes to different kinds of music or fashion change. In the seventeenth century the mountain upland of Snowdonia, for instance, was dismissed by a traveller as 'this horrid spot of hills'[1] and it took the stirrings of the

Romantic movement to create in the general populace a fresh awareness of the beauty of the high hills. Of the views of the local farmer and shepherd at the time we would be sadly unaware if it were not for the Welsh poetry and lyrics referring to their surroundings composed in their own tongue.

Unfortunately, the popular poems and songs of the Anglo-Saxon people rarely found their way into writing. We can be certain that they did exist and there is a story of how Aldhelm, Abbot of Malmesbury, would attract the attention of his wayward flock outside the church by singing such lyrics to them, before moving on to more religious themes.[2] But we cannot know whether his songs were concerned with the surrounding countryside. Sadly, the Christian (Roman) Church discouraged such interest, perhaps because of earlier association with pagan beliefs. The early British ballads, too, are primarily about people, with only incidental references to their surroundings (although Gaelic literature remains rich in observations of nature). The few surviving Anglo-Saxon stories and songs may speak of the wood which 'must on the earth bloom with its fruits', or the hill which 'must stand out green above the land'[3] but it is the feelings aroused by the actions of people that dominate. More usually, written texts were the prerogative of the Church and only Christian matters were considered worthy of the laboured copyings of scribes or of the precious vellum upon which these works were copied.

It is fortunate for us that place-names reveal a great deal about the localities to which they refer. These tell us a little of how the Anglo-Saxons themselves saw their countryside. We shall never know if the Anglo-Saxon farmer felt the same joy in observing pleasant surroundings as most of us do today or what, indeed, would have been beautiful to his eye, but it is possible to suggest, for many regions, what type of countryside would have met him as he went about his daily life.

Place-Names and the Landscape

Although many people probably stayed near their native village for the greater part of their lives, others did travel widely across the country. Itinerant traders would undoubtedly cover many miles and amongst these a very important group were those carrying the salt which was so essential for cooking and curing food. Some salt was obtained from coastal salterns by the evaporation of sea-water but one notable inland salt-producing area was at Droitwich in the West Midlands (now in Worcestershire). Here the brine welled up naturally from underground springs in the Mercia Mudstone and had been worked and traded since at least the Iron

Age. To the compiler of the works ascribed to Nennius in the early ninth century these springs constituted one of 'the marvels of Britain'.[4] Because of the importance of this commodity, many major long-distance routes were known as 'saltways', radiating out in all directions from Droitwich beyond the confines of the Hwiccan kingdom in which they were located.

A traveller passing southwards from Droitwich through the relatively flat midland countryside along one of these salters' routes would have recognized well-known landmarks along his route. Behind him, a few miles to the north, the pointed little summit of Crutch Hill would have been visible on the skyline. Its name was the British word *cruc*, 'a barrow, a tumulus', and this steep little hill must have resembled a man-made burial mound (Figure 1). Droitwich lies near the western boundary of the Hwiccan kingdom in an area where British names had not been entirely overwhelmed by the language of the incoming Anglo-Saxons. With Crutch Hill behind him, he kept the rounded spur of Hadzor to his left. This spur of high land is 'Headdi's *ofer*', the latter a term which recent investigation into place-names has suggested may have been reserved for a particular shape of hill – one of which the end slope or 'shoulder' was convex in shape.[5] The shape is visible from the present M5 motorway passing

Crutch Hill, Worcestershire   *Tysoe, Warwickshire*

Haselor, Warwickshire   *Crookbarrow Hill, Worcestershire*

Bredon Hill, Worcestershire

Fig. 1 Hill-shapes: Old English terms *cruc, hoh, ofer, beorg* and *dun* appear to refer to hills of particular shape.

southwards to Worcester. Another distinctively shaped hill to the south-east of Worcester is again barrow-shaped and bears the name Crookbarrow Hill, combining the British *cruc* with the Old English *beorg*, 'barrow'.

Our traveller would have taken the old Roman road south-westwards at first, heading towards Worcester, the seat of the bishops of the Hwicce

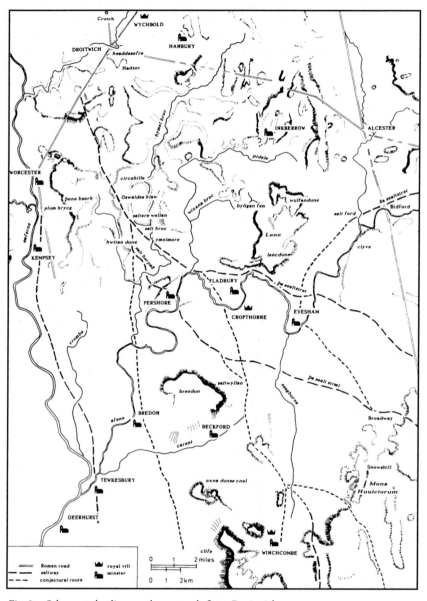

Fig. 2   Salt routes leading south-eastwards from Droitwich.

and a defended *burh* after the ninth century. Before he reached that centre, however, he would veer south-eastwards, still keeping to the relatively low land fringing the Severn valley (Figure 2). His route led him across gently rolling countryside to a low hill which was almost certainly marked with a tumulus, Low Hill (from Old English *hlaw*, 'hill; tumulus, possibly one re-used for Anglo-Saxon burial'). It was to be re-named *Oswaldes hlaw*, 'Oswald's low', after Bishop Oswald, bishop of the Hwicce, sometime in the ninth century.[6] Shortly beyond Low Hill he came to the head of the Saw Brook, then known as *salt broc*, 'the salt brook', where he might quench his thirst or water his pack animals at the *saltere wellan*, 'salters' spring'. One 'salt highway' or 'salt road' continued southwards over the higher land of Windmill Hill (then *hwitan dune*, 'white hill') towards the Abbot of Pershore's market town in the Vale of Evesham. Another followed a lower route to cross the Bow Brook at the 'ford by the wood', a fording point which was to be bridged by late Anglo-Saxon times. The brook was then known as the *hymel broc* after the wild hop (Old English *hymele*) which presumably grew along its banks; marshland near here was known as *hymel mor/ymelmore* in the tenth century. The traveller would have no written map and the physical features along his route, with their individual names, would have been the landmarks for his journey.[7]

Had he chosen the first route, he would still need to ford the brook but his choice might depend upon weather conditions or upon the state of the road, as well as on his ultimate destination. As he travelled southwards on either route the massive Oolitic limestone outlier of Bredon Hill would have been an obvious landmark. The name of Bredon Hill incorporates the British *bre*, Old English *dun,* and *hyll. Bre* meant 'hill' and *dun* seems to have been reserved for a high whale-backed feature such as this (see Figure 1). Whether the other terms added a slight nuance of meaning, or whether they were merely added in a repetitive fashion as each hill-name began to be understood as the proper name for the hill, is far from clear. Away to the west, he could not have failed to see the prominent ridge of hills which bounded the Hwiccan kingdom in that direction. Here a ridge of ancient rocks reared above the flat Worcestershire plain and bore the surviving British name *Malferna*, from *moel, bryn,* 'bare hill' (Plate I). Crowned by two Iron Age hill forts the ridge served as an effective boundary for many hundreds, if not thousands, of years. In Anglo-Saxon times it separated the kingdom of the Magonsæte, established over what was to be much of Herefordshire and southern Shropshire, from that of the Hwicce, which included most of Gloucestershire and Worcestershire and part of Warwickshire (Figure 3).

From Pershore, the traveller might cross the Avon to skirt the eastern foot of Bredon Hill, making his way along a saltway which was still in

Plate I   The Malvern ridge, Worcestershire, which formed the boundary between the Hwiccan and Magonsætan kingdoms, seen across the Central Worcestershire Plain.

use in medieval times, past the *saltwyllan*, 'salt spring', on the Elmley Castle boundary, towards Winchcombe and, ultimately, reaching the Upper Thames valley near Lechlade. Winchcombe itself was a centre established within a *wincel cumb*, 'a crooked coomb', and although the use of the *cumb* term is unusual for such a large feature, the town today can be seen to lie within the great coomb occupied by the headwater streams of the River Isbourne. A *cumb* should be enclosed, as in the sense of the Welsh *cwm* (the term is used by geographers to describe a hollow on a hill-side which once marked the origin of a glacier; this is often 'armchair-shaped' and backed by steeply rising ground), and, indeed, roads must climb steeply up from Winchcombe to leave the town in all but a northerly direction.

These routes were but two of a web of saltways (Figure 4) which can be traced from references to such routes in place-names. Another route from Pershore can be traced through Broadway (the name of which means literally 'the broad road'), following a higher route over the north Gloucestershire Cotswolds to the Thames valley. This climbed the scarp slope by the incised valley of a small stream to skirt the northern spur of Broadway Hill near a point where Anglo-Saxon pagan burials have been located. Here the route climbed out onto the flatter land of the Cotswold dip slope (see Figure 2). The name 'Cotswold' is not recorded before the twelfth century but is undoubtedly a name of Anglo-Saxon origin,

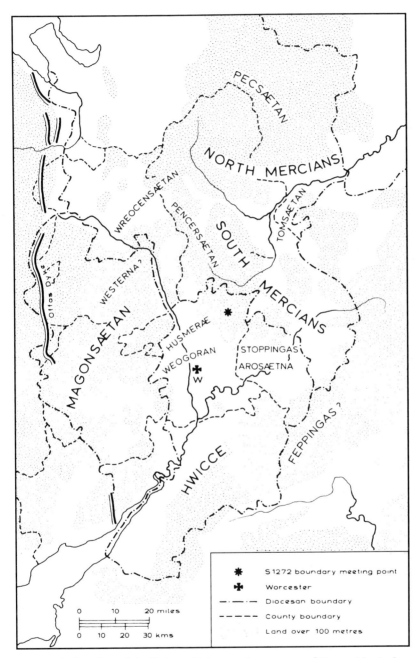

Fig. 3 The kingdom of the Hwicce which was to become part of Greater Mercia. It covered most of the later counties of Worcestershire and Gloucestershire with the western part of Warwickshire. The medieval diocese of Worcester, drawn up in the seventh century, appears to define its boundary.

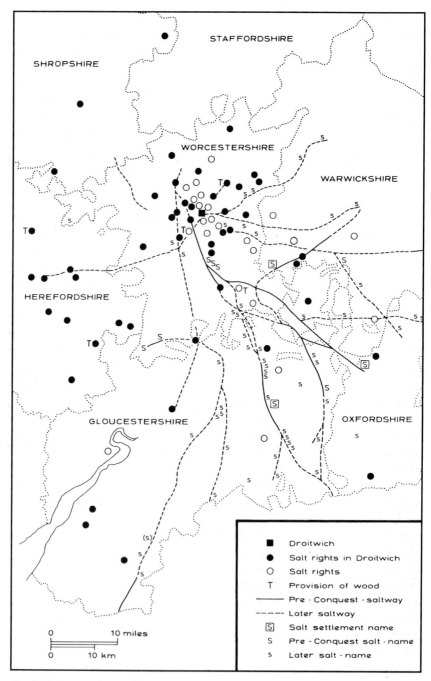

Fig. 4 Saltways radiating from Droitwich. These extended throughout and beyond the Hwiccan kingdom (Hooke, *The Anglo-Saxon Landscape: The Kingdom of the Hwicce*).

apparently referring to an area of high pastureland which was once relatively well wooded.[8] The scarp slope is still heavily wooded, as are the valleys above Winchcombe, but the name today conjures up more an image of the open sheep country which characterized much of this region until the present century, one which has been marked by increased agricultural activity. It was on this last route that the Abbot of Evesham established a market centre at Stow-on-the-Wold in the mid-eleventh century to take advantage of the growing wool trade and the salt traveller, too, would have found it necessary to pass this way before continuing southwards along the ridgeway which carried him over Wyck Beacon, across the Windrush at the Barringtons and across high land again as far as the River Leach.

Of the river-names, 'Avon' and 'Thames' are names of British origin and in this midland region survival of British names was not unusual for large and medium-sized rivers or for commanding topographical features such as the hills of Bredon and Malvern. 'Avon' tells us little about the character of the river for it is derived from a British root *abona*, which meant merely 'river' but this seems to have been applied mainly to ones of some importance.[9] The Windrush is derived from a British word meaning 'fen' combined with *gwyn*, 'white'. The Isbourne, on the other hand, bears an English name for it means simply 'Esa's stream'. The River Leach which drains into the Thames near Lechlade appears to be 'a stream flowing through boggy land', containing a term still surviving in dialect form as *letch*. Some river-names were amazingly old and seem to have been adopted from the Neolithic people who occupied these islands in the prehistoric period; their language was to be overwhelmed by that of Celtic-speaking peoples, perhaps (but there is no dating evidence) before the fourth century BC.

In this way, place-names paint a broad canvas of the nature of the Anglo-Saxon landscape. For the most part, those which have survived are of Old English origin (i.e. the language of the Anglo-Saxons). British names increase westwards and Danish names mark those areas settled by the Danes in eastern England. In the north-west, more names of Norwegian origin are found, as the Viking settlers there tended to come from more northerly regions of Scandinavia. Each language has its own terms for topographical features – like the Old Norwegian *slakki* for a shallow valley – but almost always it can be shown that these terms were used with a precision which conveyed an immediate and special meaning to those who first used them.

When these terms were first used in place-names they certainly referred to specific landscape features but it is not always easy to identify these today. To survive they have usually become associated with settlements, some of which may post-date the coining of the names themselves. In the case of Whichford in Warwickshire, for instance, was 'the ford of the Hwicce' the one across the tiny streamlet which today flows through the village of that name or was it the place where the ancient ridgeway of Ditchedge Lane crossed the deeply incised River Stour on the parish boundary (Figure 5)? This route marked the boundary of the Hwiccan kingdom and the ford may have been well known long before the village came into being.

There is, however, luckily for the historian, a type of document which often records minor place-names and permits named features to be accurately located. From the late seventh century onwards it became customary to record transfers of land in legal documents and as time went by the boundaries of the land concerned might be described in increasing detail, noting significant landmarks. Not all such documented charter grants were accompanied by boundary clauses but those that were provide a rich source of local topographical detail (see Chapter 5).

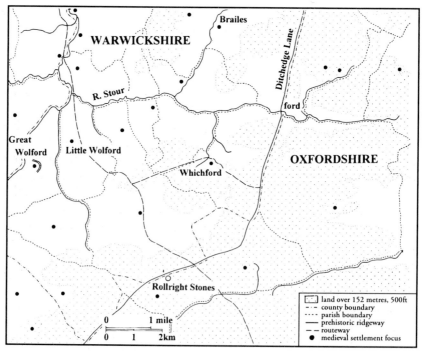

Fig. 5 Whichford and Wolford: routeways and settlements. A prehistoric routeway followed the crest of the Lias escarpment and subsequently formed the boundary between several midland counties. A routeway leaving the Stour valley to run south-eastwards through Oxfordshire is referred to in late Anglo-Saxon charter bounds.

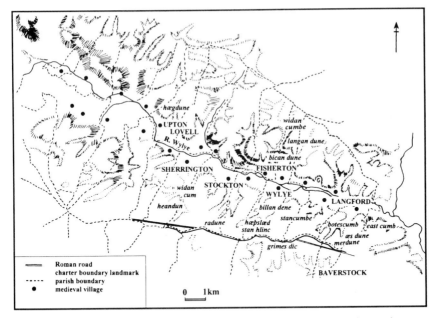

Fig. 6 The Wylye valley, Wiltshire. Numerous natural features are referred to in the boundary clauses of Anglo-Saxon charters and can be related to the local topography.

The River Wylye, for instance, runs ESE through the chalk downlands of Wiltshire. A series of tiny side valleys have been cut by streams draining into the main river from the north and the south: here the landscape comprises 'coomb' and 'down' country typical of chalk countryside. There are a number of boundary clauses referring to estates in this valley and the landmarks they describe can be located with reasonable precision (Figure 6). A number of the streamlets originate in coombs – here the landlocked hollows one would reasonably associate with this term. On the eastern boundary of the parish of Wylye, *stancumbe*, 'stone coomb', lay at the head of the incised little valley below the Iron Age enclosure of Bilbury Rings; the eastern boundary of Sherrington and that of Fisherton de la Mere passed along 'wide' coombs. Larger, longer valleys were described by the term *denu*, as used for the valley which was followed by the western boundary of Wylye or for the valley occupied by the hamlet of Baverstock to the south. The term *slæd*, 'slade', seems to have been reserved for short side valleys which may have been wooded. Between lay various hill spurs described as *dun* features still called 'Down' today, the *dun* term exactly describing the rounded shape of the rolling chalk downland. The *radune*, 'the roe-deer's hill', was the spur of chalk down below Stockton Earthworks (a site of Iron Age and Romano-British

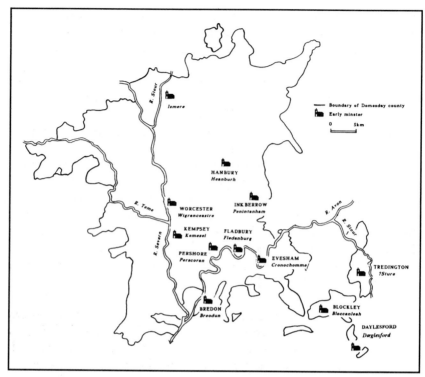

Fig. 7   Early Worcestershire minsters.

occupation) and others included 'ash down' and 'boundary down' in Langford, the 'long down' (now Deptford Down) on the north-eastern boundary of Wylye, *bican dune* on Wylye's north-western boundary and *hægdune* on the western boundary of Upton Lovell. The term *hlinc*, on the other hand, meaning a steep step or lynchet, could be used to describe a steep slope that was entirely of natural origin, like the *stan hlinc*, 'the stony lynch' on the western boundary of Wylye, or one that had arisen along a boundary as the result of ploughing in the fields to either side. This term is still widely used today in chalk districts to refer to a bank that is too steep to bring under the plough.

The naming of places after a major topographical feature, such as a hill or a valley, a river or a spring, represents an ancient tradition of name-giving which was already current in Roman times and many of the earliest Anglo-Saxon names seem to be of this type. Some refer to major archaeological features in the same way. Important early estate centres like those at which early minsters were established frequently conform to this pattern. If one examines the names of the early Worcestershire minsters, for instance, it is found that nearly all of them fall into this category

(Figure 7). The chief ecclesiastical centre and the seat of the Hwiccan bishopric, at Worcester, is a little different in that the name contains Old English *ceaster*, used for a walled town. Recorded as *Wigranceastre* in the early eighth century, the name is, however, partially of topographical origin for it contains a British river-name, *Vigora*, which became a tribal name (that of the *Wiogorna*) and which also survives in the name of a once more extensive area of woodland, the Wyre Forest.

Among the others, Ismere was the site of a minster founded by King Æthelbald of Mercia in AD 736 and although the name was that of a mere, or lake (Old English *mere* with a British word **udso-*, 'water'), on the southern boundary of Wolverley parish, the name was probably an early one for Kidderminster located beside the River Stour, a tributary of the River Severn. Kempsey, beside the Severn to the south of Worcester, was the site of a monastery by the ninth century and its name *Kemesei* is 'Cemmi's *eg*' (Old English *eg*, 'island or land surrounded by marsh'). The church of the present village does indeed stand on an 'island' of terrace gravels between the Hatfield Brook and the main river.

Several minsters were established in the fertile Vale of Evesham. Bredon, founded in the early eighth century, stood beside the Avon on the western flanks of the hill from which it took its name (British *bre*, Old English *dun*, see above); Pershore, one of the earliest minsters to be established, probably *c.* AD 689 by Oswald, prince of the Hwicce, has a name which contains Old English *ora*, 'bank', probably meaning 'osier-bank' and here referring to its location atop a prominent bank overlooking the water-meadows of the Avon. Further upstream, a monastery had been re-established at Fladbury in AD 691–699. This name means 'Flæda's (?Ælflæda's) *burh*' and incorporates the Old English term *burh* which was used for a fortification. In this instance the term may have been used in a manorial sense but, according to charter evidence, a hillfort on Tunnel Hill did form a prominent landmark to the east and this may therefore be a reference to a prominent archaeological, rather than a natural topographical, feature. Only a few miles further upstream, another early minster was established by AD 703 at Evesham within a great meander of the river. The early name of Evesham was apparently *Cronochomme*, 'the *hamm* of the cranes or herons', *hamm* referring to land almost surrounded by water (hence, also, water-meadow).

Other early minsters are known to have been founded within the Worcestershire section of the Hwiccan kingdom. At Hanbury a minster was said to have been founded before the end of the seventh century and this actually stood within the ramparts of an Iron Age hillfort (Plate II). Here the *heanburh*, 'the high *burh*', was obviously a reference to the hillfort itself and again uses a major archaeological feature to coin a place-name.

Plate II   Hanbury minster, Worcestershire: the present church stands on the site of an early Anglo-Saxon minster which was established within the ramparts of an Iron Age hillfort.

To the south-east of Hanbury, a minster was founded at Inkberrow in AD 693 but was said to stand at *Penintanham*, a name which was probably 'Inta's *hamm* by the hill' where the word for hill is *pen*, a British word meaning literally 'head, top'. Here the present village nucleus lies within a loop of the Piddle Brook and one of its tributaries, beneath a spur of high land. It is interesting to note that in two, and probably three, of these cases the name had been transferred from a neighbouring topographical feature to a settlement established in the vicinity.

In those parts of Worcestershire which formed detached outliers within other counties, *Sture*, from the river of that name, may have been the early name of the estate which was later called Tredington (now in Warwickshire), the site of a minster church belonging to the Church of Worcester, and further minsters were established at *Bloccanleah*, Blockley ('Blocca's *leah*' – an early wood name), and *Dæglesford*, Daylesford ('Dægel's ford'), places now in Gloucestershire.

It is a fascinating exercise to examine such place-names in one's own county and to attempt to explain their origins by looking closely at the lie of the land. Because of the work of the English Place-Name Society in collecting place-names and examining their earliest recorded forms this is relatively easy for many counties. To take a modern place-name as it is known today can, however, be dangerously misleading. Great and Little Wolford in Warwickshire, for instance (see Figure 5), lie on either side of the Nethercote Brook, a tributary of the River Stour. It might at first be thought that the names referred to an early ford across the brook linking the two settlements but the earliest recorded form of the name is *Volwarde*, found in Domesday Book, and is apparently a compound of *wulf* and *weard*, '?the wolf's lookout place', perhaps a reference to the ramparts of a hillfort which still surround the church and part of the village of Great Wolford. Where a county has not yet been covered by the English Place-Name Society, parish names can be looked up in Ekwall's *Dictionary of English Place-Names*,[10] now in its fourth edition. This book was compiled some 37 years ago and David Mills has recently offered a partial update for many better-known names.[11] As the example of Wolford shows and the place-name volumes reveal, the true meaning of a name must be sought from the earliest recorded spelling. Over time, names have often been rationalized to a word more familiar to those living at a later date; sometimes deliberately so. In Ireland one local landowner preferred to rename a bay 'Herring Bay' to the rather more poetic but obvious misnomer 'Heron Bay'.

A brief glance at the names of Warwickshire parishes reveals many coined from terms for topographical features.[12] There are, for instance, eight names containing *dun*, seven of them recorded in or before the compilation of Domesday Book in 1086, and nine containing *hyll*, seven of them of this early date. The promontory, or *ofer*, of Haselor, Warwickshire, is undoubtedly the shoulder upon which the church of that parish stands, situated midway between the settlements of Upton and Walcot, and its shape has exactly the convex shape suggested for this feature by Cole;[13] the *hoh* features of Tysoe and Ashow, on the other hand, should resemble the shape of an upturned foot or heel if the current views of place-name scholars are correct (Figure 1). In Tysoe there are several spurs projecting from the marlstone outcrop which marks the south-eastern boundary of the county, one of them the *hoh* associated with the Teutonic god, Tiw. The marlstone edge here formed the south boundary of the Anglo-Saxon kingdom of the Hwicce and a horse figure had been carved into the turf of the scarp face at some date before the Middle Ages.

It was popularly known as 'the red horse of Tysoe', but its site is now lost, possibly beneath woodland. Near the northern boundary of this kingdom another Tiw name occurs for a mere recorded in the eighth century, somewhere near the source of the River Arrow in the Lickey Hills. In addition to these hill names, Oxhill (*Octeselve* in 1086) takes its name from *scylf,* 'a shelf of land', and Knowle from *cnoll,* 'knoll'. The terms *beorg* and *hlaw* can both be used to refer to tumuli but, in the south-eastern part of the county, Grandborough, Shuckburgh and Farnborough may be names referring to the hilly character of the land here, where outcrops of Middle Lias have produced barrow-shaped outlines and where many of the present-day villages occupy elevated positions on such outcrops. Grandborough is 'the green *beorg*', Shuckburgh is 'the goblin's *beorg*' (which sounds more like a tumulus) and Farnborough is 'the ferny *beorg*'. Further north, Harborough is 'the *beorg* of the flocks'.

Some Warwickshire parishes are named after rivers and streams: Brownsover, Arrow, Great Alne and Walsgrave-on-Sowe (*Sowe* in 1043) are names taken directly from the rivers upon which they stand and, in addition, there are five places with *burna* names and six with *broc*. Ford names are particularly frequent, with no fewer than twelve parish names containing this element. Stratford-upon-Avon is 'the ford of the *stræt*', where the Roman road from Alcester crossed the Avon towards the Cherwell valley; Salford Priors is 'the salters' ford' and carried a saltway along the northern bank of the Avon in a E-NE direction (Figure 2).

Names and Superstitious Belief

A number of names refer to springs and wells. In the Celtic world springs were often regarded as sacred, partly, perhaps, in recognition of the need to protect such important features in the landscape as sources of pure clean water (Plate III). Throughout western Britain churches were frequently sited alongside such springs which retained a measure of veneration into later medieval times. The Christian Church must have frowned upon any such pagan belief and regularly preached against well-worship: 'Let no Christian place lights at temples, or stones, or springs, or trees' (St Eligius, AD 640) but itself used their waters for baptism and often compromised by blessing the springs and associating them with a local saint. Often, beliefs associated with springs but displaying obvious pagan links were transmuted into Christian ones and there are several folk tales which tell of a Christian martyr having his head cut off (a link with a pagan Celtic head cult) giving rise to a spring at the scene of the murder. Such tales are related about St Deumanus of Watchet (Somerset), St

Plate III St Uny's spring, St Buryan. Springs and wells were features of considerable importance in Celtic religion, frequently credited with healing properties, and many subsequently became Christian shrines. Many are noted as landmarks in pre-Conquest charters. The well associated with St Uny lies at the north-eastern corner of the parish of St Buryan in West Penwith, Cornwall, not far from the Iron Age courtyard house village of Carn Euny in the adjacent parish of Sancreed.

Kenelm of Clent (Worcestershire), and St Morwen of Morwenstow (Cornwall).

Over the country as a whole, however, many other types of spring-name are recorded. Popular tradition has continued to associate springs with healing, fertility, and divinity, even if this has today often degenerated to the level of the ubiquitous 'wishing-well'. 'Holy wells' (*halig-well*) are not uncommon and place-names recorded in Domesday Book include Holwell in Dorset (*Halegewelle* in 1086), Holywell in Huntingdonshire (*Haliewelle* in 1086) and East and West Holywell in Northumberland (early form as in the Huntingdonshire example). In all these cases the first recorded spelling shows that there can have been no confusion with the word *holh*, used to describe a feature in a hollow or deep valley, or *holegn*, 'holly'. Gelling also notes associations with superstitious or religious beliefs indicated by names containing *hæl*, 'omen', *run*, 'secret, council', as well as with the number seven.[14]

The many bride's wells have been placed by many scholars in this category and associated with fertility (and with St Bride, Brigid of Kildare) and these are not uncommon in the charters: several occur, for instance, on Devon boundaries (Stoke Canon and Culmstock) and another on the boundary of Dyrham in Gloucestershire. They are found throughout the country but Scherr notes the possibility that some of them, at least, may derive their names from *bryd, 'surging, welling'.[15] Other saints frequently associated with springs included St Anne; St Anne's spring, on the slopes of the Malvern Hills in Worcestershire, remains a source of the now well-known Malvern spring water. Others are known as 'Ladywell', after the Virgin Mary, and many local saints had their special sites, like St Chad, bishop at Lichfield, or the Lady Wulfrun who founded Wolverhampton minster. Many such associations may derive only from medieval times because the cult of the saints was strong between the twelfth and fifteenth centuries, but the cults were often based upon much older traditions.

Taking Gloucestershire as a test case, apart from 'the bride's well (or spring)' of Dyrham and the 'seven springs' of Notgrove and Aston, there are few spring-names recorded in the charter boundary clauses in that county which hint at any religious or even superstitious context. Perhaps such springs were seldom located on estate boundaries. The charter names are, however, varied and often illustrative of local conditions. The *blinde wylle*, 'the blind spring', of Donnington is presumably a hidden, secluded or concealed spring and the *holan wylle* of Cold Ashton a spring in a hollow. A large spring in Broadwell gave its name to the parish and 'the stone well or spring' which gave its name to Stowell may have flowed into a stony or stone-built channel. Another group of spring-names are associated with people and include 'the salters' spring' of Maugersbury (on the bank just above the Stow–Burford road, one of the saltways discussed above) and 'the beggar's spring' of Dyrham/Pucklechurch. Others are associated with plants and animals (see Chapter 2), or with the water itself (cold, bright, loud), while the *sponwælle* of Icomb seems to contain the Old English word *spon*, 'wood chip'. The 'winter spring' of a lost Winterwell in North Cerney was probably a spring with a marked seasonal flow (the site is now in a dry valley near Calmsden). The Guitings, Guiting Power and Temple Guiting, in the north-east of the county, derive their names from an Old English word *gyte*, meaning 'a pouring forth, a flood', presumably referring to the nature of the upper Windrush upon whose banks they are situated.

Locations associated with pagan belief, like the mere of Tiw in north Worcestershire, have, however, sometimes given rise to early place-names. A small group of names on the South Staffordshire Plateau may represent lingering paganism in this region[16] (where Penda remained unconverted until his death in AD 655). They include Wednesbury and Wednesfield, the 'fortification' and 'the open land' of Woden respectively. Unexplained earthworks were commonly associated with the god Woden and with Grim. The Wansdyke in Wiltshire is 'Woden's dyke', referring to a linear earthwork of post-Roman date, and the name Grims Ditch has been applied to many such linear earthworks (e.g. Figure 6), Grim, meaning 'the masked one', being a nick-name for Woden 'alluding to the god's habit of going about in disguise'.[17] Similarly, the parish of Grimley in Worcestershire is centred upon a Roman fort; Grimes Graves in Norfolk is the name given to a group of Neolithic flint-mines, and Grimspound is a prehistoric enclosure on Dartmoor. Giants' pits are recorded in midland charters but there are also possible allusions to the monster Grendel, especially found in association with watery features such as pits and meres, in the depths of which he was traditionally supposed to live.

A number of other names may indicate former pagan religious sites, for names containing *hearg* or *weoh* may refer to a heathen shrine. Gelling notes three 'Weedon' names in a broad area of the east and south-east midlands where *weoh* is combined with *dun* to note a shrine in a hill-top situation and the Harrowden names of Bedfordshire and Northamptonshire similarly indicate heathen temples on hills.[18] Prominent landmarks for many miles, it is not surprising that similar locations were frequently chosen for the Christian churches which superseded them. Place-names can be seen to reveal a surprising amount about the natural landscape and also about man's cultural past. The relationship of names to superstitious and Christian belief can only be investigated by archaeology but the relationship between names and topography is open for everyone to explore. The influence of topography has been felt throughout the evolution of man's institutions, often to be expressed in the place-names like a decipherable map to 'hidden treasure': the treasure of understanding man's historical perception of the natural landscape.

Notes

1. Bishop Gibson, 1697.
2. Gallyon, *The Early Church*, p.28.
3. *Gnomic Verses*, trans. Hamer, *A Choice of Anglo-Saxon Verse*, p.111.
4. Hooke, 'The Droitwich salt industry'.
5. Gelling, *Place-Names in the Landscape*; Cole, 'The origin, distribution and use of the place-name element *ora*'.
6. Mawer and Stenton, *The Place-Names of Worcestershire*, p.87.
7. Cole, 'The origin, distribution and use'.
8. Hooke, 'Early Cotswold woodland'.

9. Ekwall, *English River-Names*.
10. Ekwall, *The Concise Oxford Dictionary of English Place-Names*.
11. Mills, *A Dictionary of English Place-Names*.
12. Gover, *et al.*, *The Place-Names of Warwickshire*.
13. Cole, 'The origin, distribution and use'.
14. Gelling, *Place-Names in the Landscape*, pp.31–2.
15. Scherr, 'Names of some English holy wells'.
16. Gelling, 'Further thoughts'.
17. Gelling, *Signposts to the Past*, pp.148–50.
18. Ibid., pp.158–61.

CHAPTER 2

Plants and Animals in Place-Names and Literature

Plants and animals provide the very basis of life, and those that could be eaten or were useful in other ways not surprisingly figure highly in both place-name and literary evidence. Some enjoyed a special significance in superstition but this was to diminish under the impact of the Christian Church, although the use of herbal remedies remained a mainstay of medieval medicine. A Somerset charter of AD 854, in a boundary clause of Taunton, refers to 'the ash-tree which the ignorant call holy'[1] and one is reminded of the importance of the ash as the 'tree of life' in Nordic folklore. To earlier Britons, it had been the oak which had been of special significance and its sanctity was transferred in a small way to Christianity in the many 'holy oaks' which were used as boundary markers, especially on estates held by the church.[2] The *nymet* place-names of south-western England, although taken from a stream-name which has been applied to several different streams, may ultimately derive from Old British *nemeton* 'sanctuary, sacred grove'.[3]

Individual trees have continued to act as well-known local landmarks throughout historical times: the Mitre Oak survived for hundreds of years on the Bishop of Worcester's manor in Hartlebury, Worcestershire, and the Cowley Oak of Malvern Chase (from a local family name) in the same county was 27 feet in girth when measured in 1893.[4] Other venerable old oaks are well known locally and often assumed to be of great antiquity (Plate IV). Trees as boundary markers in Anglo-Saxon charters (see Chapter 4) were often associated with the names of individuals, often local landowners who left no other mark in recorded history. The maintenance of law and order in Anglo-Saxon times was upheld by regular meetings held in the open air and attended by local representatives from the surrounding administrative unit called the hundred. This was a unit based upon a theoretical hundred hides (a land assessment) which also provided a set number of men to serve in the national army. The meeting-places of these units were at accessible locations and frequently marked by an easily recognizable feature such as a barrow, stone or tree and on occasions these gave their names to the hundreds themselves.

Plate IV   Ancient oak tree, Oldberrow, Warwickshire. This is one of many ancient oak trees known locally in the midlands and traditionally ascribed to a great age; this one is often referred to as 'The Domesday Oak'.

An early Worcestershire hundred was known as *Winburgetrowe*, 'Wynburh's tree', after an unknown lady, and it represented the dispersed holdings of the Church of Worcester in the south-east of the original county of Worcester, some of which lay within the counties of Warwickshire and Gloucestershire but remained under Worcester because of the power of the Church. In Gloucestershire, Brentry Hundred is likely to have been named after 'Beorna's tree' in Henbury, where the Bishop of Worcester held his hundred court twice a year in the thirteenth century,[5] but 'the tall tree' of Longtree Hundred in Gloucestershire, which met at a site on high ground on the road between Avening and Tetbury, or of Langtree Hundred in Oxfordshire, seem to have been markers associated with no particular named individual.

One type of tree seems, perhaps surprisingly, to be named frequently in this context: the thorn tree. *Celfledtorn* in Gloucestershire, *Goderestona* in Dorset, *Cicimethorne* in Wiltshire and *Nachededorn* in Berkshire are all examples of hundred meeting-places marked by thorn trees, while in Wiltshire another was in a *Thornegraue*, 'thorn grove', near the Fosse Way. Indeed, the thorn tree occurs as a boundary marker more often than any other type of tree in West Midland charter boundary clauses and in Worcestershire 'Croppa's thorn' also gave its name to an important royal vill, Cropthorne, in the Vale of Evesham. The frequency with which this tree has been noted on boundaries led some writers in the past to suggest that it had been planted deliberately to mark the bounds[6] but its occurrence in this context is far more likely to indicate unexploited or abandoned arable land in such a location. The species of thorn tree is not specified but the two forms of *Crataegus* (hawthorn) are likely candidates. The thorn tree has also been accredited with special sanctity: it has been called 'a trysting tree for fairies' and old superstitions about the ill luck likely to fall upon those who bring hawthorn indoors still prevail. When located at a crossroads, a meeting-place of spirits, it was doubly noteworthy. Given a Christian overtone, the cult of the Glastonbury Thorn remained popular throughout the Middle Ages. One Wiltshire hundred, that of *Alestube* (Elstub), apparently met at a rather unimportant sounding elder-stump in the parish of Enford. This could be taken as a warning, perhaps, not to attach too much significance to a hundred name although the superstitious will remember that the elder tree, too, was associated with witches.

With plants that could be eaten or were of practical use one is on much surer ground. The excellence of the wood of the 'maple and oak, the tough yew and the dark oak' (here, in an Anglo-Saxon 'riddle', probably used to make a scabbard) finds its way into literature[7] and wood was indispensable for both domestic utensils and tools in Anglo-Saxon England, as well as being used for quality objects such as the lyre and maplewood cups found with princely burials at Sutton Hoo.[8] But lesser plants also had their uses. A study of South Staffordshire place-names[9] notes the bog myrtle, *myrica gale*, Old English *gagel*, giving its name to Gailey near Penkridge, and this had a wide variety of uses as bedding, sweet-smelling faggots and as a moth and flea repellent. It also provided a yellow dye or could be used to flavour ale and beer. *Wir*, as in Great and Little Wyrley, seems to have been another name for the bog myrtle. *Humulus lupulus*, Old English *hymele*, the wild hop, gave rise to the place-name Himley, 'the *leah* where *hymele* grows', in central Worcestershire and also gave rise to a stream-name near by. The wild hop was common in well-wooded areas and in the Middle Ages was used to flavour beer while the young shoots might be cooked and eaten as a vegetable. Marchington is said to be derived from Old English *merece*, 'wild celery, smallage', a plant used for flavouring.[10] Another plant commemorated in Staffordshire parish-names is the wild plum, Old English *plyme*, found compounded with 'hill' in Blymhill.

Berries were undoubtedly collected from the wild just as they are today. The blackberry has been eaten since Neolithic times and the Old English word for a bramble, *brembel, bremel,* occurs in place-names like those of Bramher in Sussex, Bramerton in Norfolk, or Bramshaw and Bramsholt in Hampshire. The raspberry has also been called the 'hindberry' as it is eaten by deer in the woods and Imberberrie in Sussex is 'raspberry hill'. The plums of Blymhill have already been noted and other names referring to this fruit are Plumstead in Kent, Plumtree near Nottingham and Plymtree in Devon, but the fruit could have been wild or cultivated. The *surapel*, 'sour apple', is likely to have been the wild crab-apple and occurs frequently as a boundary landmark in charters, but apples have been used as estate place-names at Apley in Lincolnshire, Appleford in Berkshire, Appletreewick in the North Riding of Yorkshire and many other places. The sloe-tree, Old English *sla(h)*, does not seem to have been commonly used for early parish-names but certainly occurs in boundary clauses (Slaugham in West Sussex, 'homestead where sloes grow', is recorded *c.* 1100).

That the Anglo-Saxons had great faith in herbal cures is illustrated by one of the 'Leechbooks' preserved in a mid-tenth-century manuscript.[11] Much of the content of such works was derived from older Classical sources but some was of English origin. No doubt it was the idea of 'sympathetic magic' which gave rise to the belief that the adderwort, *polygonum bistorta,* known to the Anglo-Saxons as *nædre wyrt*, would provide a cure for adder bites for its contorted rhizome resembles a coiled snake (Figure 8). This herb was also said to be conveniently 'produced in the place where the adder is' (for reliability, it should be gathered in April).[12] Some herbs were accredited with a multitude of uses, like betony, *stachys officinalis*, known to the Anglo-Saxons as *biscopwyrt*, 'bishopwort':

This wort, which is named betony, is produced in meadows, and on clean downlands, and in shady places; it is good whether for the mans soul or for his body: it shields him against monstrous nocturnal visitors and against frightful visions and dreams; and the wort is very wholesome, and thus thou shalt gather it, in the month of August without [use of] iron: and when thou have gathered it, shake the mold, till nought of it cleave thereon, and then dry it in the shade very thoroughly, and with its roots altogether reduce it to dust; then use it, and taste of it when thou needest.[13]

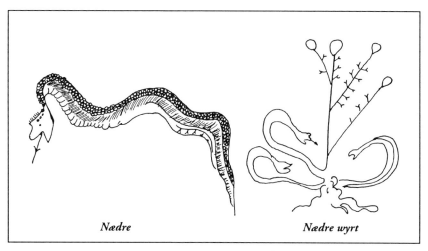

Fig. 8   Adder and herb: *Nædre* (adder); *Nædre wyrt* (adderwort).

And need of it one might have on many occasions for not only did it protect against nightmares but provided a cure:

> If a mans head be broken. For sore of eyes. For sore of ears. For dimness of eyes. For bleared eyes. For strong blood-running from the nose. For tooth-ache. For sore of side. For sore of the broad of the loins. For sore of belly. In case a mans inwards be too costive. In case blood gush up through a mans mouth. In case a man have a mind not to be drunken. In case a pustule is going to settle on a man. In case a man be inwardly ruptured. In case a man become tired with much riding or walking. In case a man may be out of health or feel nausea. That a mans meat may easily digest. In case a man cannot retain his meat. For sore of inwards, or if they be swollen. For taking of poison. For bite of snake. Again, for bite of snake. For bite of mad dog. In case a mans throat be sore or any part of his neck. For sore of loins and if a mans thighs ache. For the hot fever. For foot disease.[14]

Alas, this cure-all was a fraud, 'with no outstanding virtue of any kind'.[15] Never mind, the Leechbook lists many other herbs which could be tried for such things as an adder bite, including *gentianella amarella*, the fieldwort, the Anglo-Saxon *feld wyrt* (gentians *did* grow in England and this one is said to have grown upon Salisbury Plain); *plantago major*, the great plantain, known traditionally as *wegbræd*, 'waybread'; *potentilla reptans*, the creeping cinquefoil, earlier known as *fifleafe*, 'fiveleaf'; *melilotus altissima* or *heort clæfre*, 'hart clover'; or *verbena officinalis* or *æscþrotu*,

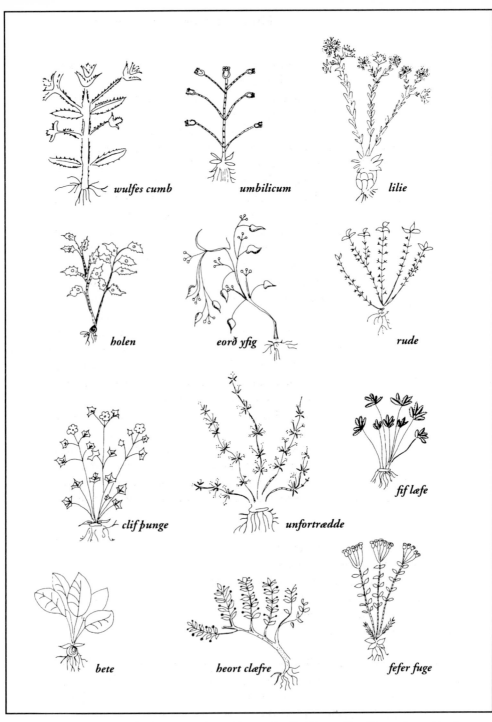

wulfes cumb

umbilicum

lilie

holen

eorð yfig

rude

clif þunge

unfortrædde

fif læfe

bete

heort clæfre

fefer fuge

Fig. 9   Some of the herbs named and illustrated in 'Bald's Leechbook', now housed in the Manuscripts Department of the British Library.

'ashthroat', to mention just a few (Figure 9). More generally, the *eorð yfig*, 'earth ivy' (*glechoma hederacea*), bitter enough to be used instead of hops in the making of ale in medieval England, was useful for the 'bites of creeping things'. Hopefully nature carried out its own cure while these were being tried. Some herbs were, of course, efficacious, and Western medicine is only now beginning to realize what natural properties they often possessed, but in Anglo-Saxon England such healing must have been largely a case of trial and error with more than a pinch of faith required.

Sometimes particular plants, other than the more obvious trees, occur in conjunction with boundary landmarks. Cress springs and streams are common, like, for instance, those found on the boundary of Crediton in Devon or Stoke Prior in Worcestershire, while in Cornwall a charter of Trethewey in St Martin-in-Meneage, a parish on the Lizard peninsula, refers to 'the pool of wild garlic' (Cornish *kenin*), a plant which still grows profusely in the area but which was not favoured by the Anglo-Saxon farmer who knew it as *crawan leac*, 'crow's leek'. The thistles and woad mentioned in several Worcestershire charters may have been used directly for wool making – the thistles to nap the cloth and the woad to dye it. More often the references are to plants which conveyed the nature of the surrounding countryside: to the reeds, sedges and rushes associated with damp places, the broom, heather and furze of heathlands, or to planted crops of barley, rye, wheat and flax. These and others will be discussed further in subsequent chapters.

Literary and charter sources also contain references to the animals and birds with which the peasant farmer would have been familiar. A particular English (and British) fascination was with riddles. These may owe less to Classical sources than the herbariums and be more truly 'English' in character:

> My neck is white,   my head is tawny
> and so are my sides.   I am swift in my stride.
> I bear weapons of battle.   On my back there is hair
> and the same on my cheeks.   Over my eyes
> two ears stand up.   I walk on my toes
> in the green grass . . . [16]

This is the badger, Old English *brocc*, which figures in several place-names. Brockhall in Northamptonshire is 'badger hole or sett' and Broxted in Essex is 'the badger's head', probably referring to a hill of similar shape. Charters show that places with badger holes were sometimes well-known local landmarks and a Worcestershire charter for Tapenhall in North Claines refers to *brocc holes weg*, 'the way to the badger holes'.

Fox holes noted on the boundaries include those on the boundaries of Donnington in Gloucestershire and Bengeworth in Worcestershire and gave their name to a hundred division, Fexhole, in Warwickshire. Foxes were found everywhere and, in Devon, the Crediton charter refers to 'the head of the fox coomb' and that of the South Hams to 'the vixen's dyke', while the Worcestershire charter of Broadwas notes the 'fox batch'. The fox was an unwelcome visitor and Foxcote in Gloucestershire may have been 'fox-infested cottage', Foxton in Cambridgeshire and in the North Riding of Yorkshire 'village where foxes abounded'. Similar names recorded by this period include Foxearth in Essex and Foxhall in Suffolk, both referring to the burrows, and Foxley, 'fox wood', in Northamptonshire and again in Wiltshire.

While the fox was a pest, the wolf was a more dangerous predator. It was traditionally thought to be of an evil nature, its faults grossly exaggerated, and it was deemed sinful by the Christian Church to eat any animal killed by wolves. This may have arisen from a fear of catching a disease like rabies, although the accidental eating of food already touched by a dog could be exonerated by the singing of psalms. Wolves may have been captured in the pits recorded on the boundaries of Broadwas and Bredicot in Worcestershire, and others are noted in several Gloucestershire localities, as at Olveston (associated with a ridge), Bishop's Cleeve (associated with a wood) and Ewen (associated with quarries), and elsewhere in the country. In Devon, for instance, they were associated with pits and a coomb in Crediton and with a spring in the South Hams. Wolf skins were a valuable commodity but a more prized coat was that of the beaver, still present in Anglo-Saxon England. This animal gave its name to a stream, the *beferburna*, near Worcester, while beaver pits were noted on the boundary of Pucklechurch in Gloucestershire. Other beaver place-names have been noted as far apart as Nottinghamshire, Wiltshire and Yorkshire.

Animals noted in Gloucestershire charter boundaries are fairly representative of the species most frequently noted in early minor place-names. In addition to the fox, wolf and beaver noted above, other wild animals include the deer, especially the hart and the hind, and the cat (probably wild) – animals associated with partially wooded countryside. Pigs were also pastured in woods but it is not easy to tell whether the Gloucestershire place-names refer to the domestic pig or the wild boar. Domestic animals include the sheep (and the ram), cattle (the calf, the bull, the oxen) and the hound (probably a hunting dog). The ubiquitous mouse is also frequently named. Worcestershire charters add the goat, the horse, the weasel, the hare and the otter.

Insects, too, gave rise to place-names although, as with animals and birds, it is not always easy to distinguish such references from personal names since the Anglo-Saxons appear to have used both animal and insect names as descriptive personal names or nicknames. In Worcestershire, for instance, a 'beetle wood', *ceafor leage*, is recorded on the boundary of Upton Snodsbury but Ceafor appears as a personal name in the parish-name Charingworth in Gloucestershire, *Chevringavrde* in 1086, meaning 'the enclosure or farm of Ceafor's folk'.[17] Of all insects, it is the bee which appears most frequently and this is perhaps not surprising since its honey provided the main source of sweetening for early medieval food and for mead. Bees were deliberately reared on many estates and several place-names incorporating *beo* refer to places with bee-keepers. Honey was also collected from wild bees and it may have been this which gave rise to the numerous 'honey brooks' recorded.

No-one familiar with the countryside could have remained unaware of the bird life and references to species of birds are common in place-names, both parish-names and minor names in charters. These too, from their preferred habitat, indicate something about the nature of the surrounding countryside. Larks frequent open country and are often associated with moorland or open downland pastured by sheep. In Gloucestershire a *lafercan beorh*, 'lark barrow', is noted in the high Cotswolds on the boundary of Cutsdean and another on the high eastern boundary of Evenlode. A similar association with a barrow is noted in the Vale of Evesham in Worcestershire. The hawk, in contrast, was a bird which nested in partially wooded regions and is noted in Gloucestershire on the boundaries of Cold Ashton, Olveston and Woodchester near the wooded scarp slope of the Cotswold escarpment and also on the boundary of Deerhurst estates to the west of the River Severn. *Wrænnan leage* in Pucklechurch was the 'wren's wood'. A pool associated with 'hens' (?the moorhen) is noted in Pucklechurch and others are noted in Worcestershire, where other birds mentioned are doves, crows, finches, ducks and swallows. In this county several names referring to the *cran* may be to cranes or be a reference to the heron, still known as 'crane' in some dialects today.

Several of these birds are described in the Anglo-Saxon riddles, displaying a keen awareness of their individual traits:

> I'm a wonderful thing;   I vary my voice:
> I bark like a dog,   I bleat like a goat,
> I quack like a goose,   I shriek like a hawk;
> I imitate the eagle,   the gray one, the cry
> of the fighting bird;   sometimes the kite's voice
> is familiar to my mouth,   or the sea-mew's song,
> where I happily sit . . . [18]
> (The jay or the magpie.)

Or

> *Đeos lyft byreð   lytle wihte*
> *ofer beorghleoþa   þa sind blace swiþe*
> *swearte salopade   sanges rope*
> *heapum ferað   hlude cirmað.*
> *tredað bearonæssas   hwilum burgsalo*
> *niþþa bearna   nemnað hy sylfe*

translated as:

> Over the hillsides   this air upholds
> bright little creatures,   swarthy and dark-clad;
> bold of song,   they fare in flocks
> and loudly chirp.   They tread the headlands,
> sometimes men's houses.   They name themselves.[19]

(The swallow? – gnats, midges, starlings, jackdaws, house-martins and other solutions have been suggested.)

It might be thought that some of these references were purely allegorical, like the eagles which frequented high places (Figure 10): an eagle's ridge is noted on the Crediton boundary in Devon and other eagle names in that county include Ernsborough, Easdon, Yes Tor and Yarnscombe. In other counties ravens may have been associated allegorically with special sites like the hillfort of Ramsbury in Berkshire. However, these may well have been references to the real birds that frequented such places. Although most of

Fig. 10 An Anglo-Saxon eagle. The eagle was the symbol of St John and is found on a fragment of the Lindisfarne Gospels rescued from a fire in 1731 and now preserved in Cambridge Corpus Christi Library (MS 197B0).

the eagle places were in high open country, especially hills, cliffs and valleys, a likely habitat for the golden eagle, some were in woodland, indicated by combination of the bird name with such features as *leah* and *wudu*, 'wood', or *sceaga*, 'small wood'. Gelling[20] notes that these were surely fish or sea eagles which once nested much further inland if lakes and rivers provided a suitable habitat. She notes that it is the 'eagle white behind' (i.e. white-tailed) which appears as a battlefield scavenger in the tenth-century poem celebrating the Battle of Brunanburh: the victors left behind them

> the dark-coated, swart raven, horny-beaked, to enjoy the carrion, and the grey-coated eagle, white-tailed [as above], to have his will of the corpses, the greedy war-hawk, and that grey beast, the wolf of the wood.[21]

The mature sea eagle has such a white tail. Recently the bones of such a bird have been found by David Miles in excavations of an Anglo-Saxon site at Barton Court in the Thames valley of Oxfordshire, only some twenty miles away from where the eagle is recorded in the place-name Earley, 'eagle wood', near Reading. Miles notes that the bird would have been highly visible, 'cackling and emitting short yaps like a puppy which can be heard up to 2km away' and choosing the crowns of large trees for its nest.[22] The raven was one of the other battlefield scavengers noted above. This bird, Old English *hræfn*, occurs with *leah*, 'wood', in the place-name Raveley in Huntingdonshire, and with *dæl*, 'valley', in Ravendale, East Humber (and perhaps in Ravensdale, Derbyshire).

Apart from the *wrenna*, *lawerce*, and *hræfn*, easily recognizable as the wren, lark and raven, many other common birds are still known by their Old English names: the *spearwa*, *swealwe*, *crawa*, *ðrysce* and *goldfinc* are clearly the sparrow, swallow, crow, thrush and goldfinch, but just as we have coined names which express a bird's individual characteristics the Anglo-Saxons knew one bird as the *ðisteltwige* because it ate thistledown, and it is not certain whether this was an alternative name for the goldfinch or the linnet. Similarly, was the *rindeclifer* (incorporating Old English *rind*, 'bark', perhaps with *clifer*, 'claw') the woodpecker or the nuthatch?

The swan was as attractive to the Anglo-Saxon poet as it is to us today:

> Silent is my garment   when I tread the earth
> or dwell in the towns   or stir the waters.
> Sometimes my trappings   lift me up over
> the habitations of heroes   and this high air,
> and the might of the welkin   bears me afar
> above mankind.   Then my adornments

resound in song   and sing aloud
with clear melody   – when I do not rest
on land or water,   a moving spirit.[23]

In place-names it is difficult to distinguish *swan* from *swan*, 'a herdsman, a peasant', but when the word occurs in the names of streams and lakes, as in Swanbourne in Buckinghamshire, it is most likely to refer to the former.

Some beasts were undoubtedly mythical and the dragon or serpent was often seen as the guardian of treasure, like the dragon in the Anglo-Saxon poem of Beowulf. It guarded a cave filled with 'ancient treasures, which in days gone by some men carefully hid there, great relics of a noble race, precious stone', and when attacked by Beowulf 'came raging once more, the dread evil creature, flashing with surges of flame, to seek out his foes, the hated men'. It was the hero's last battle for, although the dragon was killed, he was himself 'hurt sore unto death' and having viewed the treasure of gold and jewels taken from the dragon's lair 'his soul passed from his breast to seek the splendour of the saints'.[24] This connection with treasure explains names like Drakelow in Derbyshire, *(æt) dracan hlawen* in AD 942, for the term *hlaw* seems often to have been used for a tumulus re-used for pagan Anglo-Saxon burial[25] and the tumulus might be expected to contain treasure, guarded by this creature:

draca sceal on hlæwe,
frod, frætwum wlanc

'dragon must live in mound,
Old, proud in his adornments;'[26]

The serpent, Old English *wyrm*, may be commemorated in the name of Worminster near Glastonbury in Somerset; similar names include Wormley in Hertfordshire. For Christians, the dragon or serpent was seen as a power of evil, the devil, the tempter and the enemy of God, linked with death and darkness, but in more ancient religions it was closely linked with fertility and the renewal of man and earth. This conflict is illustrated in early church sculpture, as on the twelfth-century font in the church at Avebury in Wiltshire (Figure 11), where the bishop is found striking a winged serpent with his crozier, or on the Norman font at Hook Norton in Oxfordshire, where a two-headed serpent represents the spirit of evil consuming itself. It was St Michael, as well as St George, who was said to have slain dragons in this strife between the two factions, and hill-top churches dedicated to him, like the one on Glastonbury Tor, have been

A horrid beast, I lie in the ghastly gloom of a cavern, aroused, I rise fluttering into the lofty air and fly with my crest displayed, the fair air whirling. My crawling body is stronger than that of all snakes or of any monsters dragging their excessive weights. Though uncouth and savage, I feed through a tiny mouth, my chest through narrow pipes is filled with breath, and not to my teeth do I owe my sinister power, nay, the seat of my impetuous strength is in my tail.

(*Aenigmata Eusebii*, XLII, trans. E. von Erhardt-Siebold)

Swa is dryhten god   dreama rædend
eallum eaðmede   oþrum gesceaftum
duguða gehwylcre   butan dracan anum
attres ordfruman   þæt is se ealda feond.
þone he gesælde   in susla grund.
ond gefetrade   fyrnum teagum
biþeahte þreanydum

Similarly the Lord God, the giver of joys,
is benignant to all other creatures,
to all their multitudes, except to the dragon alone,
the source of poison, that is the ancient enemy
whom He bound in the pit of torments
and fettered in fiery chains
and loaded with afflictions.

(The Bestiary. A. The Panther (fo. 96a);
The Exeter Book II, ed. Mackie pp. 64–5)

Fig. 11   Dragons depicted in verse and on the fonts at Avebury (Wiltshire; twelfth century) and Hook Norton (Oxfordshire; Norman).

seen as an expression of the vanquishing of an older faith. Superstitions concerning these animals have, indeed, lingered on in local folklore to the present day.

Mythical beasts abound in Anglo-Saxon sculpture and a ninth-century cross-head from Cropthorne in Worcestershire (Plate V) depicts 'a dragonesque creature with the head, claws, and wings of a bird and a tail terminating in a large leaf', birds with hooked beaks, and a beast with 'a long tongue protruding from its mouth and looped round its foreleg'.[27] The cocks and hens which figure on the architectural friezes at Breedon church in Leicestershire may date from the end of the previous century and are outstanding in their sophistication (see Chapter 9). But Anglo-Saxon man was probably more of a pragmatist and his main interest was undoubtedly in those animals and birds which could be of direct use to him and many animals were hunted for food. This will be discussed further in subsequent chapters.

Plate V   This ninth-century cross-head survives in the church of Cropthorne, Worcestershire, which once served a royal vill. Its decoration is said to depict 'a dragonesque creature with the head, claws, and wings of a bird and a tail terminating in a large leaf', birds with hooked beaks, and a beast with 'a long tongue protruding from its mouth and looped round its foreleg' (Romilly Allen 1906, p. 183).

Notes

1. Sawyer, *Anglo-Saxon Charters*, S 311; Birch, *Cartularium Saxonicum*, B 476.
2. Hooke, *Anglo-Saxon Landscapes of the West Midlands*, pp.167–74.
3. Gover, *et al.*, *The Place-Names of Devon, Part 2*, p.348.
4. *Victoria History of the County of Worcester*, Vol. 2, p.320.
5. Smith, *The Place-Names of Gloucestershire*, III, p.126.
6. Grundy, 'Saxon charters of Worcestershire', p.105.
7. Riddle 13, *Anglo-Saxon Riddles*, trans. Baum, p.17.
8. Wilson, 'Craft and industry'; Bruce-Mitford, *The Sutton Hoo Ship-Burial*.
9. Hooke, *The Landscape of Anglo-Saxon Staffordshire*, p.43.
10. Ekwall, *The Concise Oxford Dictionary*, p.314; *Oxford English Dictionary* Si-St 259.
11. *Herbarium Apuleii Platonici*, B.L., Cotton Vitellius, C.iii; Cockayne, *Leechdoms*; Cameron, 'Bald's *Leechbook*'.
12. *Herbarium Vi*, in Storms, *Anglo-Saxon Magic*, p.89; Cockayne, *Leechdoms*, p.243.
13. Ibid., p.71.
14. Ibid., pp.3–5.
15. Grigson, *The Englishman's Flora*, pp.346–8.
16. Riddle 29, *Anglo-Saxon Riddles*, trans. Baum, pp.26–7.
17. Smith, *The Place-Names of Gloucestershire*, I, pp.242–3.
18. Riddle 68, *Anglo-Saxon Riddles*, trans. Baum, p.53.
19. Riddle 19, ibid., p.21; *The Exeter Book*, II, ed. Mackie, p.148.
20. Gelling, 'Anglo-Saxon eagles',
21. 'The battle of Brunanburh', *Anglo-Saxon Poetry*, trans. Gordon, p.328.
22. Miles, 'Appendix' to Gelling, 'Anglo-Saxon eagles', pp.178–9.
23. Riddle 21, *Anglo-Saxon Riddles*, trans. Baum, p.22.
24. 'Beowulf', *Anglo-Saxon Poetry*, trans. Gordon, pp. 45ff.
25. Hooke, 'Burial features'.
26. *Gnomic Verses*, trans. Hamer, pp.110–11.
27. Romilly Allen, 'Early Christian art'.

PART II

The Organization of
the Country

CHAPTER 3

The Kingdoms and Estates of the Anglo-Saxons

By the Anglo-Saxon period the landscape of England had already been intensively farmed for thousands of years. Clearance was widespread across eastern England, at least, in the prehistoric period and virgin woodland had rapidly disappeared from the scene. Under Roman rule, agriculture had been extended over the higher chalklands and limestones of southern and eastern England as population levels rose and as the army and towns required grain and other commodities for non-farming populations. When the Roman Empire fell, marginal lands were the first to go out of production, many areas probably already suffering from soil impoverishment. Indeed, abandonment of marginal land may have begun under the declining fortunes of the Empire as early as the fourth century. There is evidence of decay in many towns of Britain by the end of that century: some were virtually abandoned and in most regions villas were no longer being built.

The material trappings of Roman civilization seem to have been cast away rapidly as markets collapsed following the inevitable disruption in trade brought about by the fall of the Empire. A dramatic drop in the general standard of living seems certain: landowners were unable to sustain the standards which had characterized the period of optimum achievement under Roman rule. Less is known about the lower classes but it is likely that landowners would employ less labour and this section of the community may well have been forced into poverty and vagabondage. All sections of society were affected but 'those who survived were those who held on to what they already had, the land'; the farmers themselves probably moved more towards animal husbandry, the traditional type of farming.[1] There is no evidence that domestic stock deteriorated in quality.[2] In the west, Roman civilization had been little more than a veneer and if arable land were to be abandoned, recourse could readily be made to the traditional economy of stock rearing. Trade between the Mediterranean and western Britain continued and there seems to have been less social disruption in these regions.

Narrative sources of the period indicate that these difficult times were, however, traumatic for the British population as opportunistic raiders from several places intensified their attacks. Picts and Scots were among them but it was the Anglo-Saxon tribes from the North Sea littoral who made the greatest impact. Themselves the victims of a disintegrating economy in Europe, these peoples may have been forced to steal what they had hitherto obtained through legitimate trade. There is evidence, too, of a worsening climate at this time: areas along the North Sea coast on the Continent were subject to inundation and their inhabitants forced to seek a living from land elsewhere. There is evidence that some of these people may have been assimilated at first as peaceful farmers in some parts of southern England but many regions staggered under the import of piratical raids and plundering hoards. The amount of devestation caused should not be under-estimated for the destruction, even on a limited number of occasions, of the crops and herds of folk who had no other means of survival could easily lead to starvation and death, a fact brought home vividly in many areas of the world today.

One of the closest narrative sources, that of the British writer Gildas compiled in about AD 540, presents one view of events as he knew it. He likens the attacks to

a fire heaped up and nurtured by the hand of the impious easterners spread from sea to sea. It devastated town and country round about, and, once it was alight, it did not die down until it had burned almost the whole surface of the island and was licking the western ocean with its fierce red tongue.

So a number of the wretched survivors were caught in the mountains and butchered wholesale. Others, their spirit broken by hunger, went to surrender to the enemy; they were fated to be slaves for ever, if indeed they were not killed straight away, the highest boon.[3]

The tide of Anglo-Saxon incursion spread inexorably across Britain from its eastern shores after the middle of the fifth century, its power waning, however, as it spread westwards. The British population was not wiped out, whatever the narrative sources suggest. Although large numbers of Anglo-Saxon immigrants followed the initial raids and settled across England they formed only a small proportion of the surviving population. The bulk of the population, especially in the west, must surely have remained of Romano-British stock. Even the rulers and leaders of the western kingdoms in the seventh century included many of British extraction. In the Herefordshire and south Shropshire region, the first

Plate VI   Offa's Dyke. View in southern Shropshire, to the north of Knighton.

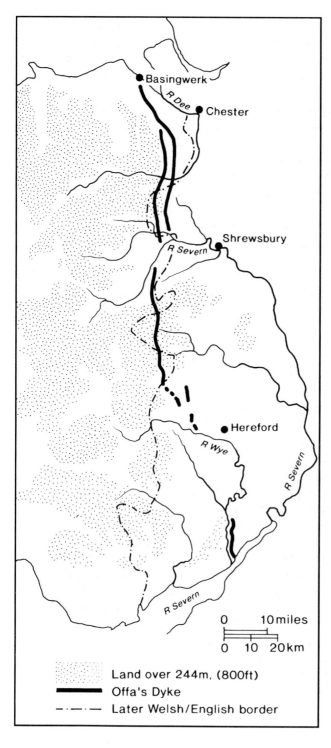

Fig. 12 Offa's Dyke, constructed under the leadership of the Mercian king, Offa, in the eighth century, perhaps when the leaders of Powys were attacking his kingdom (after Hill, 1981).

recorded king of the Magonsæte was Merewalh, whose name means 'illustrious Welshman' and there seems to have been a strong British component, too, in the kingdom of the Hwicce which extended over most of Worcestershire and Gloucestershire and the western part of Warwickshire.

Yet Anglo-Saxon culture permeated society to such an extent that the language of even the general populace was eventually to change to that of the newcomers: Old English. British words as place-names survive in increasing numbers westwards but it seems that in time their original meanings ceased to be understood. By the time of the Norman Conquest most of the lords and landowners had Anglo-Saxon names and it is likely that the bulk of the population considered itself to be of one race. Indeed, by the eighth century pockets of people still significantly British in some way were regarded as strange enough to be described by the term *walh*, 'Welshman, foreigner'.[4]

In the Welsh Borderland, however, the two races remained culturally distinct. In spite of initial good relations between Anglo-Saxon rulers and the kings of Gwynedd, and the assimilation of the Magonsæte into Mercia, the leaders of Powys were raiding across Mercia in the eighth century, a situation which led to the construction of Offa's Dyke by the English in an effort to demarcate an effective boundary (Figure 12; Plate VI).[5] (Noble believed that the dyke represented a patrol line set back from an older frontier.)[6] Welsh remained the dominant language to the west of this boundary until further efforts were made by the English to conquer Wales in the late thirteenth century. The way in which the English tongue was foist upon, but in time accepted, by the Welsh may offer a comparable situation to that which had existed earlier after the Anglo-Saxon take-over. In Wales, in particular, English was to become the official language of the land-owning minority. Place-names, however, did not generally alter. (In medieval Fifeshire English gradually supplanted Gaelic amidst the middle classes in a similar way because it was the language of merchants and tradespeople.) Cornishmen, too, continued to rebel against Anglo-Saxon dominance. Although most of Devon was to fall under the sway of the English by the seventh century, Cornwall was not fully assimilated until the tenth century; its language was spoken until recent times and Cornish place-names survive throughout the county. In situations of conquest, it seems likely that the Anglo-Saxons might wish to replace British with Anglo-Saxon place-names as a means of expressing power and possession but one has to remember that several hundred years were to elapse between the date of the first Anglo-Saxon migrations and the recording of most place-names, ample time for any community to adopt the language of what it sees as the superior order if it so wishes, especially in a climate of new aspirations and opportunities, and of changing settlement patterns.[7]

Indeed, many of the settlements bearing Old English names may only have been established in middle and later Anglo-Saxon times (see Chapter 6). It is not surprising, therefore, that any earlier British settlements were to diminish in importance, their names ignored and eventually forgotten. A parallel may be seen in some Third World countries today where the villages of subordinate groups are rarely identified by name. In Thailand, many such settlements are referred to only as, for instance, the Karen village or the Lahu village (the names of two northern hill tribes), however many of these there might be – presumably they are of little interest beyond the immediate locality. This situation may have much in common with the *walh* settlements of later Anglo-Saxon England. It is interesting that it seems to have been in those regions which had earlier been heavily 'Romanized' that people once again appear to have been prepared to accept most readily the new language and its accompanying traditions.

There is also growing evidence of integration between native and newcomer in some regions. At Orton Hall in Cambridgeshire and Barton Court Farm in Oxfordshire the Anglo-Saxon buildings appear to respect the layout of Romano-British buildings and at Catholme in Staffordshire an Anglo-Saxon settlement seems to lie between Romano-British farmsteads. The early Anglo-Saxon settlement of Mucking occupies a site on the barren northern shore of the Thames estuary as if this was the only land left available. The argument for continuity and close peaceful contact between the indigenous population and the invaders is, however, still weak. In time, bone and genetic evidence from cemeteries which seem to hold both Romano-British and Anglo-Saxon burials may help to answer questions about intermarriage. At Frilford, in the Upper Thames Valley above Abingdon, bangles and rings, fashionable among British women, accompanied some female burials in early cemeteries where the men had Anglo-Saxon grave-goods. At Wasperton in Warwickshire, however, a burial ground in use from the late Roman period continued in use and stratigraphically later graves contained Anglo-Saxon grave goods. It seems that the population here gradually adopted the fashions of the Anglo-Saxon race. Similar integration is suggested by the burial evidence at Bishops Cleeve, Gloucestershire, and other cemeteries in the midland region may display the continued use of British burial rites into the fifth and sixth centuries, of British methods of wool production and, in some cases, possible skeletal evidence of a British presence in the Anglo-Saxon cemeteries of this period.[8] 'At the level of the basic subsistence economy and social unit', some degree of continuity may be suggested. Indeed, it

Fig. 13 The seventh-century kingdoms.

is not unlikely that a rural populace, though genetically British, would in time cease to regard itself as culturally British and would come to think of itself as Anglo-Saxon.[9]

The warring bands of the fifth century and the more peaceful immigrant farmers seem to have taken several centuries to become the dominant force throughout England and to evolve an established social hierarchy. It was not until the seventh century that the individual kingdoms had clearly parcelled out the land between them (Figure 13).[10]

There was little stability of government and they continued to fight against each other for several more centuries, with one or other kingdom being most powerful at a given time. Only under the threat of a completely new take-over by the Vikings (Danes and Norwegians) did England finally rally its resources under the then-dominant rule of Wessex.

Territorial Organization

The kingdoms must in many regions have incorporated much of the territorial organization of Roman Britain and also assimilated the smaller tribal groupings of the newcomers themselves. In some regions even older tribal groupings appear to have come to the fore once the civic administration of Roman Britain had foundered, for Roman divisions, too, had been laid upon the foundation of the Iron Age tribal areas. There are hints that the Anglo-Saxon kingdom of the Hwicce owed much to one sector of the Dobunnic grouping of the late Iron Age.[11] Here the Dobunnic tribe had fallen into factions when threatened by Roman domination and earlier loyalties may have surfaced again with the Roman withdrawal to influence kingdom divisions. Although the Hwicce themselves, and their kingdom, may have been Anglo-Saxon in origin, the latter may well have been based upon an existing territory. The same may be true of other early Anglo-Saxon kingdoms but unless one can penetrate back beyond the political boundaries of the later seventh century it is difficult to postulate their make-up. This may be possible in the case of Kent where a Celtic (Belgic) Iron Age principality became a Romano-British *civitas* centred upon *Durovernum Cantiacorum* (Canterbury)[12] and it seems that Trinovantium territory underlay the kingdom of Essex.[13]

There is, however, evidence which helps us to identify folk groups within the main political kingdoms, groups which were ultimately to become wholly absorbed and to lose their individual identity. The kingdoms absorbed these smaller and, in some cases, probably older folk groupings as they began to stabilize their boundaries but the lands of these folk can often be suggested. In Staffordshire the lands of the *Pencersæte* and *Tomsæte* can be recognized within Mercia, the former occupying the valley of the River Penk, the latter the valley of the River Tame.[14] In Worcestershire it is possible to suggest a possible territory for the *Husmeræ* whose territory was focused upon the valley of the River Stour in the north-western part of the later county (Figure 14).[15] Opinions differ about the racial composition of such groups but it seems likely that a stronger British element might be envisaged in the more westerly parts of England. On both sides of the Pennines in the north of England, for instance, it has been possible to suggest the territories of earlier British polities which were to become subsumed into the later kingdoms.[16]

Others seem to have been Anglo-Saxon tribes, although not necessarily the original invaders they were once thought to have been. They may stem from a renewed period of expansion by small groups under a leader and their settlement is often found to be secondary to that of the earliest regions of Anglo-Saxon pagan burial. Many such groups bear *ingas* names, denoting loyalty to a named leader. In Warwickshire the *Stoppingas*, to judge from their name and the location of their lands, were an Anglo-Saxon tribe who were allotted land across the headwaters of the River Alne (Figure 15). This grouping looks suspiciously secondary to the older Roman centre of Alcester which may itself have lain within the lands of the *Arosæte* of the Arrow valley, but a group of estates around and to the south of the old town certainly passed into the hands of Anglo-Saxon rulers. Rich cemeteries have been found at Bidford, where the Arrow flows into the River Avon. In the kingdom of the East Saxons the *Berecingas* occupied the south-western corner of Essex, the *Hæferingas* the land around Havering and the *Uppingas* a nearby upland area. Similar groups have been noted in Sussex, notably the *Hæstingas* and the *Meallingas*. The

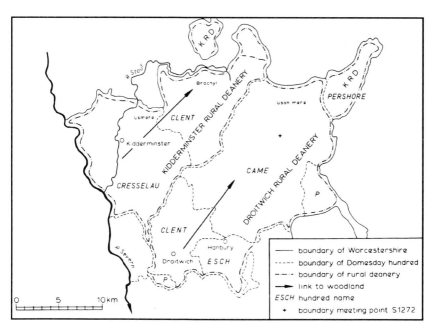

Fig. 14 North-west Worcestershire: the territory of the Husmeræ (Worcestershire), reconstructed from the evidence of pre-Conquest charters and later administrative boundaries (Hooke, 'Pre-Conquest estates in the West Midlands').

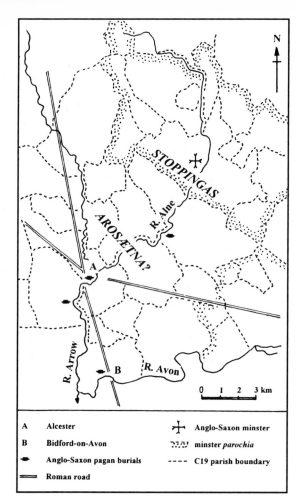

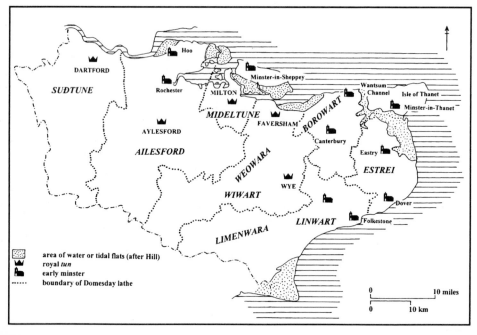

A   Alcester

B   Bidford-on-Avon

⬥   Anglo-Saxon pagan burials

═══   Roman road

✠   Anglo-Saxon minster

⋰⋱⋰   minster *parochia*

- - - -   C19 parish boundary

Fig. 15 (left)   The territory of the Stoppingas (Warwickshire), based upon the probable extent of the *parochia* of the early medieval minster as reconstructed from medieval ecclesiastical evidence. This appears to represent a block of land across the headwater region of the River Alne on the fringes of the Warwickshire Arden.

Fig. 16 (below)   The Kentish lathes (after Brooks 1989).

Fig. 17 (opposite)   Known royal vills as listed by Sawyer (1983).

⬚   area of water or tidal flats (after Hill)

♛   royal *tun*

🏰   early minster

⋯⋯   boundary of Domesday lathe

Hæstingas seem to have been a semi-independent tribal group who were merged into the Sussex kingdom after their defeat by Offa of Mercia in AD 771.[17] Identifiable groups often took the name of their geographical location. The *Wilsæte* were the folk of the Wylye valley in Wiltshire, the *Wreocensæte* the folk who lived below the Wrekin. As the kingdoms became established, however, these *regiones* lost their individual identities.

Within the kingdoms much of the administration was carried out from royal vills. These were often in heartland regions at the focus of a unit later found to be assessed at 50 or 100 hides. The hide was a fiscal assessment based, according to Bede, upon the notional amount of land needed to sustain one family (probably an extended family with slaves and retainers).[18] In Kent the unit of assessment was to be the sulung. Within eastern Kent, Brooks has identified four regions, known as lathes, dependent upon the royal vills of Canterbury, Lympne, Aylesbury and Wye (Figure 16).[19] The assessments themselves are ancient and the earliest charters show such units in force. But the hide cannot have referred to an exact and consistent area of land, even of the arable apportionment, until a much later date. By the time that hidages are systematically recorded, as in Domesday Book, the old patterns of land holding have become exceptionally confused and it is a difficult task to reconstitute any earlier groupings. These estates would have paid their revenues to the royal vill in a render known as the king's *feorm*, upon which renders in kind the first tax assessments must have been made. Some settlements are documented as having been royal vills[20] (Figure 17) and many others can be identified through the known distribution of royal estates.

In the early days it was customary for the king and his retinue to travel throughout his kingdom and each district of this nature would have contributed towards the upkeep of the royal court and the board and lodging of its retainers. At first the renders were frequently in kind, paid at the focal estate centre, but these were often later replaced by money renders. There are residual payments of this nature noted in some of the early charters. Westbury minster in Gloucestershire was in the late eighth century paying 'two tuns full of pure ale and a coomb full of mild ale and a coomb full of Welsh ale and seven oxen and six wethers and 40 cheeses and six long *peru* and 30 "ambers" of unground corn and four "ambers" of meal, to the royal estate'.[21] The community at Berkeley in Gloucestershire was only relieved of their part of the king's food-rent in AD 883 and this seems to have consisted of a render of clear ale, beer, honey, bullocks, swine and sheep.[22]

At central places within the most densely settled areas, and often upon royal estates, minsters were being established by the late seventh century to administer to the parochial needs of the people. These were monastic communities served by a number of priests. Some did not last for many centuries and were taken over by their most successful counterparts. On occasions these seem to have continued to draw renders of the kind outlined above. The minster at Bath, for instance, drew six porpoises and 30,000 'herrings' from its Tidenham fisheries.[23]

How much do Anglo-Saxon arrangements owe to the British past? Costen believes that 'It would be absurd to suggest that the English failed to utilise the pre-existing structure which they found'[24] and notes how the Laws of Ine show that Welsh society continued to exist alongside the new English society in the seventh century. Suggesting a measure of continuity in estate organization, he points out that the royal *tun* of Cannington, for example, appears to have succeeded the nearby hillfort site as an estate centre. How far this reflects direct continuity is questionable but nodal areas of settlement and cultivation must often have remained pivotal to later estate formation in parts of western Britain.[25] In Hampshire, Klingelhöfer finds no evidence for such continuity but suggests new valley-based territories he calls 'archaic hundreds' (Figure 18).[26]

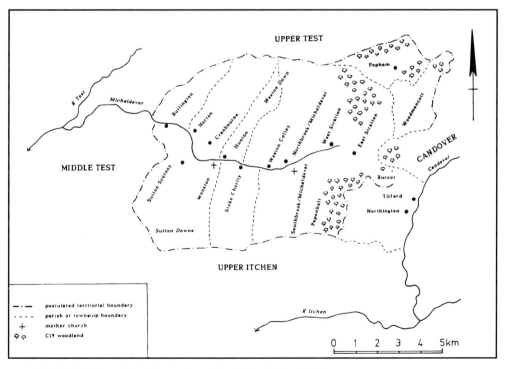

Fig. 18   A Hampshire valley territory (after Klingelhöfer 1992).

Administrative arrangements in other parts of western Britain seem to have been not dissimilar, although the written records are fewer or later in date. In Wales the royal vills (the *maedrefi*) were located within divisions known as *commotes*; these were subdivisions of kingdoms or *cantrefi*, each of which was notionally supposed to consist of a hundred townships (*trefi*).[27] In Cornwall the place-name *lys* indicates the location of a royal court, as in the name Liskeard. Although Christianity had to be introduced afresh to the Anglo-Saxons, who were pagan when they first came to this country, a separate strand of British Christianity had revived or been reintroduced into western Britain by the end of the fifth century. At the Synod of Whitby in AD 664 England chose to accept the teachings of the Roman rather than the Celtic (British) Church. Many monasteries of British foundation were simply assimilated into the Anglo-Saxon church although those in Cornwall were not finally granted recognition until the tenth century.[28]

Initially it seems likely that relatively large estates might provide the upkeep for a royal vill and perhaps for an associated minster. Place-names suggest a specialization in providing food materials in keeping with local resources. Thus settlements called Cheswick, Old English *chese* and *wic*, might be places where riverside water-meadows supported dairy herds; Hardwick might represent a settlement of shepherds caring for their *heorde*, flocks, and a Berwick might derive from *bere-wic*, 'barley farm'. These large estates, sometimes known as 'multiple estates', often possessed outlying holdings in waste and woodland which all provided towards the central coffers.[29] It is likely that the early groupings called hundreds developed from such territories assessed at approximately a hundred hides each, each centred upon a focal receiving point. Similar groupings in Danish regions later became known as *wapentakes*.

A feature of many folk divisions which has also been recognized in many of the royal multiple estates is links to distant pastures and hunting grounds. A hint of this early type of administrative arrangement is found in the charter evidence and in even later documentary evidence. Essentially, estates in rich 'heartland' regions were linked to others in more remote regions. This seems to have made the maximum use of resources within a given territory. Probably the best-known examples of such an arrangement come from Kent, where estates in the Coastal Foothills or the rich inland Vale of Holmesdale enjoyed rights in the woodlands of the Weald. How much of this system is inherited from a Roman or pre-Roman past is debatable[30] but at least part of this kingdom was traditionally taken over rapidly by the Germanic peoples with a degree of complicity on the part of the British rulers. The amount of disruption to existing administrative arrangements might, therefore, be considerably less than in many other parts of the country. Here the

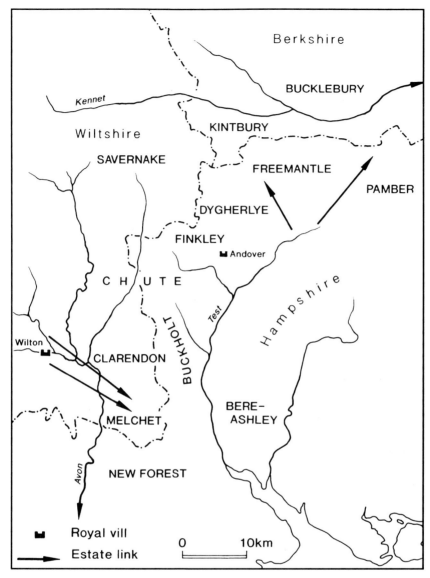

Fig. 19   Woodland links in south-central England based upon charter and
Domesday evidence.

Germanic settlers, many of them of Jutish origin, also adopted the
Romano-British name for the province, *Cantium*, probably meaning
'corner land, land on the edge'.

The system is, however, found elsewhere in the country. Links between
the woodlands of Arden, in north-western Warwickshire, and the early
developed lands of the Feldon, in the south-east of that county, remained
in force into medieval times. In Wiltshire, an estate at South Newnton,
close to the ancient royal centre of Wilton in the Wylye valley, was granted

by King Edmund in AD 943 together with a meadow beside the Wylye and an estate at Frustfield in the south of the county.[31] The latter has been identified as part of the large parish of Whitparish, later part of the Forest of Melchet. Wilton still enjoyed timber rights and pasture in Melchet in 1086 (Figure 19). A second example is that of Overton, in Hampshire, located in the valley of the Test, which was confirmed to the Bishop of Winchester together with its woodland at Tadley, near the northern boundary of the county, in AD 909.[32] Tadley was later to be included within the Forest of Pamber. In the territory of the Middle Saxons (Middlesex), Keith Bailey notes similar links.[33]

The majority of such links identified in southern and central England appear to have been between estates in more developed regions and areas of woodland. The advantages of such a system will be explored in Chapter 7 but the arrangements were probably begun to exploit wood-pasture, perhaps on a seasonal basis. It seems likely that they originated long before Anglo-Saxon times, in a period when woodland was perhaps even more scarce. Once again, they are paralleled in the Celtic world beyond Anglo-Saxon influence. In Wales similar links were preserved between the royal centres in riverine and coastal locations and their summer pastures, the *hafodydd*, in the hills. The evidence of summer pasturing in north-eastern England is examined in Chapter 8.

Early territorial groupings were to become fragmented as the Anglo-Saxon period progressed, accompanied by changing attitudes to land ownership. Whereas all land was originally held from the king in exchange for services, actual ownership seems to have been a relatively late concept. It emerged with the growth of a middle tier of society which was sufficiently well established to fill the role of landed thegn. The kingdoms themselves were only becoming stabilized by the sixth and seventh centuries and most early land grants were of sizeable tracts of land, often given to the church or to prominent lay landholders. These in turn often leased out parcels of their estates to lesser lords. Thus larger territories and multiple estates appear to have become increasingly fragmented as the Anglo-Saxon period progressed. It is only by the ninth century that smaller estate units begin to figure prominently in the charter grants. By about this date a network of small estates existed over the more prosperous regions of the country, many to become the manors recognized at the time of the Norman Conquest.

The Anglo-Saxon Kingdoms

The Anglo-Saxons first concentrated their power on a kingship basis in south-eastern England and Kent quickly became an independent unit.

Its king, Æthelberht I, who reigned from AD 580/93 to AD 616/18,[34] indeed claimed to be 'Bretwalda', chief king, but the extent of his influence remains uncertain. His marriage to the daughter of a Christian Merovingian king also reintroduced this faith into his kingdom and the Roman church at Canterbury is said to have been repaired for her use. It was also to Kent that, upon the instigation of Pope Gregory, Saint Augustine came in AD 597 whereupon he succeeded in converting the king himself, establishing a monastery at Canterbury. Literacy was revived and laws encoded. Conversion of the kingdom on this occasion was not permanent but was reconfirmed upon the arrival of Theodore, sent by the Pope in AD 668 to become Archbishop of Canterbury. Theodore's influence was long-reaching for he organized bishoprics throughout the country and united the British and Anglo-Saxon Churches.

It was a north-eastern kingdom, Northumbria, which was, however, dominant in the early part of the seventh century. Here King Ida claims to have established a dynasty in about AD 547, building his fortress upon the great rock of Bamburgh to rule over Bernicia, a kingdom which was eventually to extend northwards into present-day Scotland as far as the Firth of Forth. To the south lay the kingdom of Deira, apparently coextensive with earlier Brigantian territory, and beyond that Elmet, a territory with a pronounced British underlay. The first two of these kingdoms became united under Æthelfrith in AD 604 but the Britons remained in control of Elmet as late as *c.* AD 620.[35] It was Æthelfrith's successor, Edwin, who was eventually to be recognized as overlord of all England apart from Kent (whose princess he thereupon married – his second wife) and who became the first Christian king of Northumbria.

In this period, however, kings had to prove their worth in battle. It was an heroic age: retainers had to be provided with hospitality and rewarded with booty: 'It is for a king to be in the hall bestowing rings'.[36] Minstrels sang of the prowess of their leaders in the mead hall and recounted their achievements against their enemies: the poem of Beowulf notes 'the sound of the harp, the clear song of the minstrel'. The bonds this feasting and companionship gave rise to are well illustrated in the poem of 'The Wanderer', where a solitary exile, his lord now dead, 'must needs stir with his hands for a weary while the icy sea across the watery ways, must journey the paths of exile' as he thinks with yearning 'of retainers in hall and the receiving of treasure'.[37] This is a reminder of the necessity for a king to show conspicuous wealth and to reward his followers.[38]

The nature of such kingship is exemplified in the fortunes of the Deiran royal family during the seventh century: of eight males, three were killed in battle, two were murdered, one was poisoned and two died in childhood as exiles in a foreign land:

the normal expectation of a Northumbrian king in the seventh century was to be killed in battle. Only by success in war could he fulfil a king's duty to keep fast hold of his kingdom, and the success which initiated his reign was usually followed by the failure which cost him his life.[39]

Edwin was the only one of his dynasty to achieve distinction as a king, possibly because he was the only one to reign long enough (seventeen years). Even he was killed in battle in AD 633. Several times the male line became extinct and even Oswine, who ruled until 651 and of whom it was said:

He was both handsome in appearance and tall of stature. Pleasant in speech and of courteous manner, he was generous to all, to nobles and common people alike. And so it came about that all men loved him for the royal dignity displayed in his character, his appearance and his noble deeds, and from almost every kingdom men of even the noblest birth flocked to serve him,

fared little better. His reputation served him little for he was murdered in 651, betrayed by the man whom he believed to be his most faithful friend.[40]

It was in Northumbria, however, that Christianity was to flower. It was enriched by the British Christianity brought here by the Irish monks from the island of Iona who founded the monasteries of Lindisfarne in AD 635, of Melrose and elsewhere. Richly illuminated manuscripts like the Book of Durrow and the Lindisfarne Gospels contain pages full of curling designs and spirals, rhythmical patterns and half-hidden animal heads in myriad colours (Figure 20). Many of the designs are reminiscent of Celtic metalwork but reappear in stone on great carved crosses which marked Christian places of assembly. One of the largest of these is the Ruthwell Cross, standing eighteen feet high on the shores of the Solway Firth but now given sanctuary within the church there. Such crosses must have been a common sight in this, Northumbria's 'golden age', and abound in the churches of Yorkshire and Durham.

Northumbria was to send missionaries down into Mercia but the two kingdoms were contending for overlordship and were in a state of almost perpetual war throughout the seventh century. Although Edwin had first married Cwenburh, the daughter of a Mercian king, it was another Mercian king, the pagan and savagely aggressive Penda, who was to murder their son and kill Edwin himself, later killing Edwin's successor Oswald in battle at *Maserfeld* where it is said 'the battlefield

Fig. 20   Ruthwell Cross, Northumbria, and an illustration from the Lindisfarne Gospels: cross-carpet page introducing the Gospel according to Saint John (LG fo. 210b).

had lain all white with the bones of saints'.[41] Oswald's successor, Oswy, was to wreak revenge, for near a flooded tributary river of the Humber he took on an army much larger than his own and secured a victory in which Penda himself was killed. The northern kingdom was, however, to be continually weakened by civil strife which allowed its southern neighbour to become pre-eminent.

Mercia's period of supremacy came in the eighth century when Æthelbald, possibly the nephew of Penda, claimed supremacy over the 'South English'. It was not until the reign of Offa, after Æthelbald's murder in 757, that this was stabilized sufficiently for the Mercian king to claim to be Bretwalda with any degree of confidence, occasionally even using the title *rex Anglorum* (king of the English). His leadership of the English was acknowledged by Charlemagne and the papacy and in his reign of 39 years he was able to issue a Code of Laws, reform the coinage and introduce a currency that remained in use until the thirteenth century. By constructing the great frontier work of Offa's Dyke through the Welsh Borderland he kept the Welsh of Powys at bay but was not able to maintain continuous rule over the kingdom of Kent. Coenwulf, who took over the throne on the untimely death of Offa's son, also had trouble with the south-eastern kingdoms and in 825 Ecgberht of Wessex killed the next Mercian king, Beornwulf, at the battle of *Ellendun* (Wroughton) in which Mercian supremacy was brought to an end.

The end of the eighth century witnessed the increasing upheavals caused by another wave of invaders – the Vikings. It is likely that Britain had traded peacefully with the Scandinavian world for many centuries, and certainly the grave goods found in the seventh-century burials of Sutton Hoo suggest a dynasty in East Anglia with a strong Scandinavian element present. But in AD 789, according to the Anglo-Saxon Chronicle, piratical raids took everyone by surprise and coastal monasteries were sacked and looted, monks and nuns taken for ransom.

> 793. Here terrible portents came about in the land of
> Northumbria, and miserably afflicted the people: these were
> immense flashes of lightning, and fiery dragons were seen flying
> in the air, and there immediately followed a great famine, and
> after that in the same year the raiding of the heathen miserably
> devastated God's church in Lindisfarne island by looting and
> slaughter.[42]

However exaggerated this may be, attacks by the 'Danes' were as terrifying as had been those of the Anglo-Saxons before them. The raiders were well armed with excellent swords used as slashing instruments, javelins, lances and axes. They raided spasmodically just as the Anglo-Saxons had done just a few centuries before and, like their predecessors, moved on to settlement and conquest. Similarly, too, there was little unity or organization behind the initial invasions, which were part of a widespread expansion by the seaways of Europe. In the middle of the ninth century professional armies were mustered and Danish armies began to over-winter in England after 835.

Until the 'Great Army' landed in 866 the English were able to cope with these attacks but by 867 the 'Danes' had conquered Northumbria,

East Anglia and most of Mercia. Wessex was occupied from Chippenham but in 871 Alfred, succeeding to the kingdom of Wessex unexpectedly in the early part of the campaigns, rallied English opposition and in 878 forced the Danish leader Guthrum to accept a treaty in which the boundary between English and Danish law was fixed across midland England, part of it following the Watling Street. Scandinavian settlement was widespread and its influence can be seen in the place-names across eastern England.

In his campaigns against the Danes Alfred had organized the *fyrd* as a national army and fortified central *burhs* in southern England. His successes gave him uncontested right to be regarded as king of the English, a title he himself never claimed. England had progressed to nationhood at last. The peace was, however, again broken in the late 970s by difficult Anglo-Scandinavian relationships, even by renewed attacks. England was once again brought 'to its knees' [43] and a Danish king, Knut, had himself elected king at London. The image of the Vikings as mere terrorists and brigands is, however, refuted by the ability they showed to organize trade in their territories and the stability of England under Knut, who reigned over a peaceful and sophisticated kingdom until his death in 1035.

The physical remains of these political vicissitudes are few. We may look at the great rock of Bamburgh in Northumbria and understand at once why Ida long ago chose it as the site of his stronghold; we can gain an impression of the beauty and solitude that drew hermits like Cuthbert to such lonely places as the island of Lindisfarne, but the physical expression of administrative or ecclesiastical power is today expressed by features of rather later origin. In a few places, however, remnants of great earthen dykes bear witness to the necessity for early rulers to defend their territories. The Devil's Dyke near Cambridge still rises in places to a height of nearly 10 metres (30 feet) above its forward ditch. Most of these date from the troubles of a long distant past but the last great earthen dyke to be constructed in this way, Offa's Dyke in the Welsh Borderland, is perhaps the most impressive (Figure 12). It is reasonably well preserved in a few places but for much of its length it is a low abraded bank and ditch which today forms no obstacle for the cattle and sheep who wander across it at will; in places it has disappeared altogether. But in its sheer length and in its location following the ridges and the crests of hills, it is a striking reminder of Offa's might and also of his role in the Carolingian renaissance of the Continent. Other boundaries may be physically slight or unmarked – and Offa's Dyke was not to become a lasting major political boundary – but the administrative divisions they represent are a major influence in our lives today. These will be discussed further in the next two chapters.

Notes

1. Costen, *The Origins of Somerset*, pp.53–6.
2. Bourdillon, 'Countryside and town'.
3. Gildas, *The Ruin of Britain*, p.27.
4. Cameron, 'The meaning and significance of Old English *walh*'.
5. Hill, *Offa's and Wat's Dykes*.
6. Noble, *Offa's Dyke Reviewed*. These views are summarized by Gelling, *The West Midlands*, pp.102–13.
7. Hooke, 'The Anglo-Saxons in England'.
8. Ford, 'Anglo-Saxon cemeteries'.
9. Esmonde-Cleary, *The Ending of Roman Britain*, pp.203–5.
10. Bassett (ed.), *The Origins of the Anglo-Saxon Kingdoms*.
11. Hooke, *The Anglo-Saxon Landscape*, pp.16–18.
12. Brooks, 'The creation and early structure of the kingdom of Kent'.
13. Bassett, 'In search of the origins of the Anglo-Saxon kingdoms'.
14. Hooke, *The Landscape of Anglo-Saxon Staffordshire*, pp.16–17.
15. Hooke, 'Pre-Conquest estates'.
16. Phythian-Adams, *Land of the Cumbrians*, Chapter 4; Faull, 'Place-names and the kingdom of Elmet'; Fleming, 'Swadal, Swar (and Erechwydd?)'; Hooke, *Anglo-Saxon England*.
17. Welch, 'The kingdom of the South Saxons'.
18. Charles-Edwards, 'Kinship, status, and the origins of the hide'.
19. Brooks, 'The creation and early structure of the kingdom of Kent'.
20. Sawyer, 'The royal Tun in pre-Conquest England'.
21. Sawyer, *Anglo-Saxon Charters*, S 146; Whitelock, *English Historical Documents*, I.507–8 (possibly a later forgery).
22. Sawyer, ibid., S 218; Birch, *Cartularium Saxonicum*, B 551.
23. Sawyer, ibid., S 1426; Robertson, *Anglo-Saxon Charters*, p.117.
24. Costen, *The Origins of Somerset*, pp.86, 90.
25. Hooke, 'Territorial organization . . . central places, central areas'.
26. Klingelhöfer, *Manor, Vill, and Hundred*; Hooke, 'The administrative and settlement framework'.
27. Jones, 'Post-Roman Wales', pp.299–302.
28. Olson, *Early Monasteries in Cornwall*; Hooke, 'Saxon conquest and settlement'.
29. Jones, 'Celts, Saxons and Scandinavians', pp.49–52.
30. Everitt, *Continuity and Colonization*, pp.32–9, and *passim*.
31. Hooke, 'The use of early medieval charters'.
32. Ibid.
33. Bailey, 'The Middle Saxons'.
34. Brooks, 'The creation and early structure of the kingdom of Kent', p.67.
35. Williams *et al.*, *A Bibliographical Dictionary*, pp.22–3; Dumville, 'The origins of Northumbria'.
36. *Gnomic Verses*, trans. Hamer; Hunter Blair, *Northumbria*, p.36.
37. 'The Wanderer', *Anglo-Saxon Poetry*, trans. Gordon, p.73.
38. Webster and Backhouse, *The Making of England*, p.38.

39. Hunter Blair, *Northumbria,* p.40.
40. Ibid., p.51, citing Bede, *A History of the English Church,* III.14.
41. Hunter Blair, *Northumbria,* pp.44–5.
42. *Anglo-Saxon Chronicle* 793, trans. Swanton, pp.54–6.
43. Wilson, 'The Viking adventure', p.178.

CHAPTER 4

The Demarcation of Boundaries

Remove not the ancient landmark, Which thy fathers have set.
(Proverbs 22.28)

Boundaries are one of the most permanent and ancient features in the English landscape.
(W. G. Hoskins).[1]

Man is a territorial animal and few primitive tribes have been unaware of the extent of the land over which they claimed rights. By prehistoric times Britain was a sophisticated society. There may have been frontier regions which fell first to one group and then another, and whole territories could undoubtedly change hands, but by Anglo-Saxon times, at least, it is unlikely that there were any unclaimed zones. The wildest moorland was of value for summer grazing and although the boundaries of kingdoms might fluctuate local folk groups would certainly know their territories. Nevertheless, frontier regions do often seem to have consisted of relatively little-developed terrain and fixed boundary lines may well be a late feature in such regions.

It is noticeable how frequently the boundaries of kingdoms seem to have been drawn through relatively empty regions. In some cases, woodland may have been allowed to regenerate in such locations and this situation is paralleled along the borders of some early kingdoms on the Continent in what was later to become Germany.[2] The great Wealdan forest separated the South Saxons from the kingdom of Kent and from an early kingdom in the Surrey region. Further to the south-west, the woodlands of Selwood on the Wiltshire/Somerset border long formed the frontier between the British and the Anglo-Saxons before the latter's final thrust into the south-west peninsula.

This does not mean that intercommoning could not take place along such frontier zones and this may have been the normal practice before kingdom boundaries were finally fixed. A Worcestershire charter refers to two Mercian folk groups having rights over land on the Birmingham Plateau although ultimately much land to the north of this spot was to lie firmly within the Hwiccan kingdom (see Figure 3 on p. 7).[3] The Forest of Wychwood on the south-eastern border of the Hwiccan kingdom (Figure 47, p.143) is also somewhat anomalous, its name suggesting connections with the Hwicce although it was to lie outside their kingdom in the territory of the West Saxons.

The Age of Boundaries

In Anglo-Saxon England a hierarchy of boundaries can be recognized, some of them probably ancient, some evolving as the period progressed. The comment by W. G. Hoskins at the head of this chapter reflects the tendency throughout the 1960s and 1970s for scholars to seek out continuity in the territorial divisions of the English landscape. As parish boundaries have persisted in use for nearly a thousand years, with very little change up to the last century, so there was an attempt to look for their origins in a pre-Anglo-Saxon past. This effort was largely fruitless, for as one moves back in time so the evidence becomes flimsy or non-existent, leaving too much room for speculation. In spite of suggestions that some Anglo-Saxon estate units which later became parishes may have perpetuated the boundaries of Roman villa-estates,[4] not one villa-estate has yet been successfully identified and additional Roman settlement sites are continually being found which now cloud the apparent correspondence between villa location and parish area. Yet there are regional groupings of estates which still tempt one to envisage a pre-Anglo-Saxon origin in their formation. The Roding estates of Essex, for example, taken over by 'the people of Hroþa', is one such grouping.[5]

It is unlikely that early boundaries would not influence later ones. A change in the ruling power rarely involves the total destruction of a country's economic framework, whatever subsequent adjustments may be made, for the land must continue to produce sufficient food to maintain both its indigenous inhabitants and any newcomers. For the same reason few conquerors would entirely kill off the farmers and slaves who worked the land. Certainly in the case of the Anglo-Saxon conquest, the numbers who entered the country in the fifth century in the early years of the seizure of power must be counted in tens, not hundreds, of thousands and must have formed no more than a fraction of the indigenous population.

In 1972 Desmond Bonney argued that the choice of Grim's Ditch, a linear bank and ditch earthwork which he believed to be of pre-Roman date, as a parish boundary, in preference to a nearby Roman road, indicated the apparent antiquity of this stretch of boundary (Figure 6 on p. 11). The earthwork and the road follow the crest of the watershed between

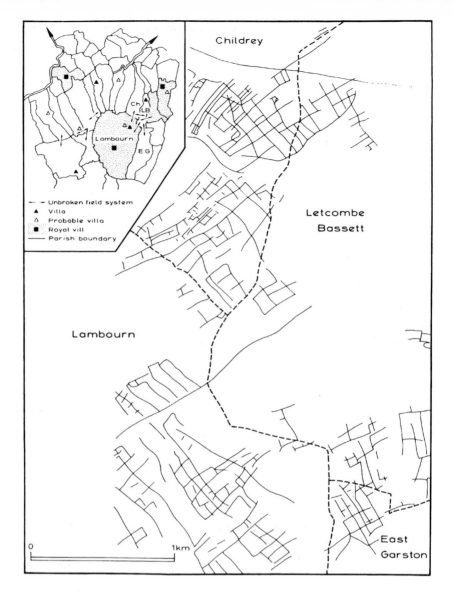

Childrey

Letcombe
Bassett

Lambourn

East
Garston

0   1km

the valleys Wylye and Nadder in present-day Wiltshire. Bonney's argument was that the Roman road was ignored as a boundary 'because it came not as an initial feature but as a later intrusion into an area already densely occupied and with an established layout of territorial and tenurial units'.[6] The earthwork appears to have separated two Iron Age settlement areas focused upon the valley regions although many of the settlements themselves lay on the slopes of the intervening ridge. It is not unlikely that such a marked topographical divide might continue to act as a boundary over a very long period of time but the argument tells us little about the antiquity of the individual units within the valley area.

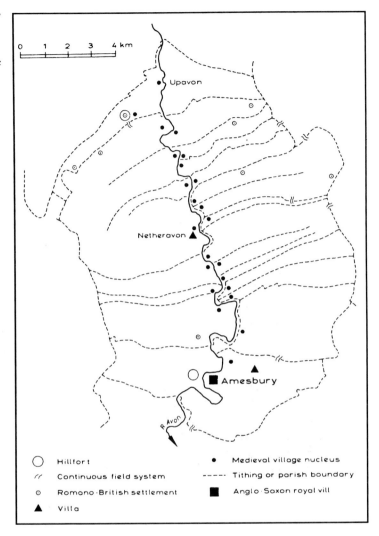

Fig. 21 (left) 'Celtic' fields and parish boundaries in south-central England: there appears to be little correspondence between the two; fields systems and Roman settlement sites actually straddle later boundaries.

Fig. 22 (right) Anglo-Saxon estates in the Avon valley, Wiltshire, showing the typical estate pattern of a riverine area of the chalk downland but one in which again estate boundaries cut through early field systems.

Upavon

Netheravon ▲

○ ■ Amesbury

R. Avon

○	Hillfort	●	Medieval village nucleus
⟨⟨	Continuous field system	-----	Tithing or parish boundary
⊙	Romano-British settlement	■	Anglo-Saxon royal vill
▲	Villa		

There are indeed persuasive arguments for rejecting the hypothesis that the boundaries of minor estate units can be traced back into Roman times. Unwin has shown the apparent discontinuity which existed in parts of eastern England where parish boundaries carve through Roman field systems on a totally different alignment.[7] This has also been found to be the case in the Wylye valley area noted by Bonney and in the Vale of the White Horse, formerly in Berkshire but now in Oxfordshire (Figure 21). In both these areas parish boundaries not only cut their way through field systems known to have been in use in Roman times (as late as the late fourth century AD), but actually bisect settlement sites. Sometimes the distribution of known Roman villas in relation to parish boundary patterns still presents a tempting picture of large valley territories maintaining some sort of administrative cohesion into Anglo-Saxon times (Figure 22), but it is difficult to find evidence to corroborate this. Looking at the places in which so-called 'Celtic' fields (now known to have continued in use or even to have been laid out in Roman times) are cut by boundaries makes it difficult to recognize functioning boundaries, even those of major administrative divisions, which can be pushed back in time although allowance must be made for the abandonment of marginal land.[8]

There are some areas in the Vale of the White Horse where the boundaries of another kind of early field system, one of large square fields, continued to be respected by Anglo-Saxon estate boundaries (see Chapter 6), suggesting that at whatever date the estate boundaries were drawn up a functioning field system remained under the plough. Similar patterns of large square fields are now being detected in many different regions but seem to vary in date. In parts of eastern England, in Essex, Williamson[9] has argued that the fields are earlier than a Roman road, known as the Pye Road, which bisects them, but in the Vale such fields seem to be restricted to the land around Roman villas. In the Wylye valley where few Roman villas have been located, the more irregular smaller fields termed Celtic fields seem to have continued in use throughout the Roman period even on the lower slopes. The square fields, however, seem to have been in use in many regions and seem to have influenced the line of later boundaries on many occasions where the area of arable did not change and was being cut through by estate boundaries (Chapter 6, Figure 40). This tells us little, however, about the date of the individual boundaries themselves. A similar stepped pattern would result if an open field system was being partitioned late in the Anglo-Saxon or even post-Conquest period.

An argument for the estate boundaries having been demarcated in or by pagan Anglo-Saxon times draws upon an apparent tendency for pagan Anglo-Saxon burials to have been placed upon or very close to boundaries, either as secondary burials within suitably situated prehistoric barrows or in unmarked graves, a correlation again noted by Bonney in Wiltshire.[10] Such an argument must distinguish between the normal burial of the dead adjacent to settlement sites and a special fashion of interring particular people upon the boundaries of the land they held. Charles-Edwards[11] has shown how under Irish law in the late sixth or early seventh century, minor boundaries might be marked with a *fert*, or grave mound, which effectually marked an hereditary right to land upheld by the presence (even in death) of a man's ancestors. Such a fashion could well have been represented in many early tribal societies before it was destroyed by Christianity and it may have persisted at least into the seventh century in areas where paganism was only slowly eradicated amongst the Anglo-Saxon elite. This is an attractive argument and there have been attempts to examine it as thoroughly as possible.[12] Unfortunately there is insufficient data for a sound statistical analysis of burial/boundary location to be made and the argument remains open.

Land Divisions

In the hierarchy of boundaries that existed in Anglo-Saxon England, those of the kingdoms must be considered first. These were perhaps the most fragile boundaries of all. Certainly it is not unreasonable to expect that many of these may have been rooted in antiquity, especially in the most heavily settled parts of the country. It is well known that Iron Age tribal divisions formed the basis of the Roman *civitates* and, although the exact lines of their boundaries cannot yet be accurately drawn, it seems that tribal loyalties carried through on many occasions into post-Roman times, perhaps assisted by the re-emergence of a Celtic/British royal elite in some regions, or by the maintenance of Roman administrative traditions in others. As Anglo-Saxon power became established across the country, kingdoms coalesced, incorporating any underlying British strata. Earlier boundaries might be followed or disregarded dependent upon individual circumstances. On the Wiltshire–Gloucestershire border Barker has tried to show how a possible territory dependent upon Roman Cirencester became subdivided under Anglo-Saxon rule.[13]

The kingdoms themselves remained unstable for a very long period of time, as shown in the previous chapter. Frontiers changed but these often entailed the wholesale take-over of recognized territories. Since Archbishop Theodore established bishoprics to serve the kingdoms of the late seventh century the boundaries of the dioceses, as they become known in medieval times, have frequently been taken to be our surest indication of the extent of the seventh-century kingdoms. Detailed local studies may, however, suggest places in which frontiers have or had been subject to substantial readjustment. Very few boundary descriptions of the Anglo-Saxon dioceses survive although that between the see of Hereford and the see of Worcester was so described, probably during the episcopate of Bishop Athelstan (1021–56), and this probably reflected the eastern boundary of the Magonsæte, a kingdom established over land in latter-day Herefordshire and southern Shropshire.[14] Identification of the boundary line is not without its difficulties but in part it follows the crest of the Malvern hills and a further lower ridge of upland to the north, a line perpetuated in the later division between the counties of Herefordshire and Worcestershire (see Figure 3 on p. 7).

   The boundaries of the folk-groups which became part of the larger kingdoms can also only be suggested with a strong degree of caution and only then if they can be detected from later boundary evidence. Sometimes focal settlement regions can be suggested upon the basis of place-name evidence[15] and it always worth considering the possible antiquity of a boundary line which follows a marked physical division for a long distance or which served as the boundary of a later hundred or even ecclesiastical division (see Figure 14 on p. 47). Hundreds were administrative units which emerged in the tenth century as judicial units. In the north-east of England similar groupings were termed *wapentakes*, a word of Scandinavian origin. Such divisions may have been based upon earlier territorial units, especially those centred upon a royal vill, but they were often subject to change, and regroupings are known to have taken place. In their fullest early recorded form they often appear to relate to tenth-century patterns of land ownership. The ecclesiastical parish groupings known as rural deaneries are not recorded before the twelfth century but, again, some of them may have incorporated earlier divisions.

   It is, however, the boundaries of the smaller administrative units that are perhaps the most intriguing, especially those of parishes. Today these meet us as a complicated web of lines and patterns upon the modern map – at least, where they have not been shamefully omitted even on large-scale maps by modern map-makers. As Angus Winchester notes, 'Once established, the network of parish boundaries formed an invisible web which both bound families into communities and divided communities one from another.' [16] They formed the administrative unit used in a great deal of our historical documentation, and, as such, form the basis of almost any detailed local historical study. To our ancestors they were of vital importance, for membership of a legally recognized community gave the security formerly only available to those within a kin group: all marriages, births and deaths were recorded within the church registers, and poor relief was only available to those able to show that they belonged to a particular parish.

   But how did parish and township boundaries arise? Under Anglo-Saxon leadership the larger territories were to become fragmented. Although subdivision may have begun in the pagan Anglo-Saxon period, it seems to have been in the ninth, tenth and eleventh centuries that the individual estates became more or less stable units. In part this reflects a changing attitude to ownership in the early medieval period made possible by an increasingly stable political and administrative background, with the concept of ownership of land replacing a less permanent arrangement.

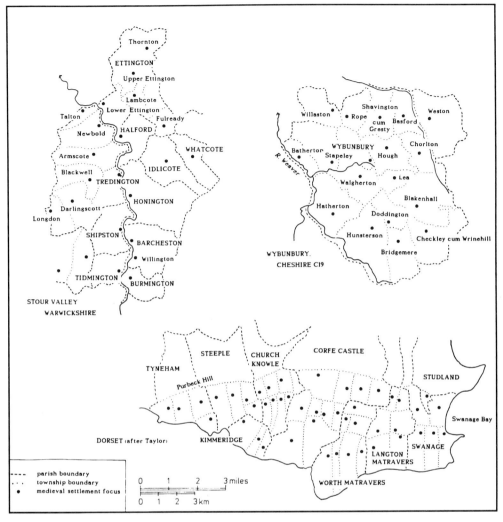

Fig. 23 Townships and parishes. In many parts of the country the ecclesiastical parishes contained a number of separate 'township' estates.

The Church was in the vanguard of such a movement. Busily accruing estates unto itself it was also encouraging the production of written statements that could be used as legal documents to prove possession. Lay lords were also building up large estates but the Anglo-Saxon pattern of land ownership reflected in estate place-names seems to be of that of the lesser lords who were the actual local tenants of individual estates and the lords of local communities.

The parish is an ecclesiastical unit: it represents the land of a community paying tithe to a local church. This unit might include a number of separate township communities and in regions of low economic revenue several might have to band together to find the necessary dues. The township seems to have been the smallest community division of those represented regularly in late Anglo-Saxon charters – apart from some tiny vills which may have been little more than individual farmsteads. Such a unit was viable enough to lease out to a subtenant and most ecclesiastical parishes comprised a number of individual townships (Figure 23). Sometimes the boundary of the ecclesiastical parish was simply drawn around any existing Anglo-Saxon estates but subdivision within a parish could also take place at a later date. As time passed, many of these minor subdivisions lost, or never achieved, any lasting independence as there was an increasing tendency for most legal and social transactions to be based upon the parish unit.

Initially, finance to uphold Christian provision seems to have been drawn towards the primary minster foundations. In the seventh and eighth centuries the Christian Church was based upon a system of such minsters or monasteries with a group of priests centred upon each, catering to the needs of a surrounding territory. Very often the early minsters would be established at a focal point within part of a folk territory, frequently at a royal centre. The territory of a minster may on occasions be represented by a *parochia* which can be reconstructed from later evidence. When a minster was established at Wootton Wawen in the Hwiccan part of Warwickshire in the eighth century, the land was said to have been granted 'within the boundaries established by the ancient possessors'[17] (see Figure 15 on p. 48) but it is not certain how much this was a figure of speech to lend authenticity to the claims of the church. The territory, however, can be suggested by the extent of the later recorded *parochia* of this monastery which had lapsed by the time of the Norman Conquest. As the period progressed new minsters were also established, some of dubious religious significance for the endowment of a monastery became a means of perpetuating family claims to land and power.[18]

The later Anglo-Saxon period was a time of enormous expansion in church foundation and church building. Particularly in the tenth and eleventh centuries, local lords were founding churches upon their estates within the regions served by the minsters, churches which vied with the minsters for financial support. At first built in timber, the best supported churches were only to be rebuilt in stone as the centuries progressed and few examples of the earlier churches survive or are necessarily documented. Although priests are recorded on some manors in Domesday Book, implying the existence of a church, this is not a complete record of the churches in existence. At first it seems to have been those churches established upon the fringes of a *parochia* which broke away from the main unit. The territory accredited to a minster established at Crediton in Devon in an eleventh-century boundary clause may be a case in point

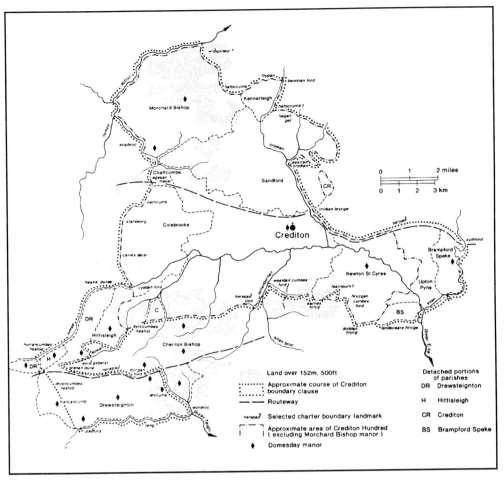

Fig. 24 The *parochia* of Crediton minster showing those manors noted separately in Domesday Book and some of the features noted as landmarks around the minster estate (S 255 in Hooke 1994).

(Figure 24).[19] The land of Crediton Hundred actually indicates the territory over which Crediton had pastoral rule at the time of the Norman Conquest, but omits a number of manors in the east which had been taken to Exeter and a string of tiny manors along the southern fringe of the *parochia* which were at Domesday held by individual local lords. These were tiny estates, many assessed at no more than a single virgate, which lay on the flanks of Dartmoor and had for some reason broken away from the main Crediton lands. In Hampshire, too, Patrick Hase was able to show that it was often marginal estates in woodland country that were among the first manors to become independent of the mother church.[20]

The early timber churches rarely survive. Greensted timber church near Epping in Essex, formerly thought to be a rare survival of the sort of wooden church that could have been found in some regions in late Anglo-

Fig. 25   The church of St Andrew, Greensted, Essex, (after Kerr and Kerr 1982, p.143); massive timbers in the north and south walls are split tree trunks from an earlier building. The standing building is now known to date from after the Norman Conquest.

Saxon England, is now known from dendrochronological evidence to be post-Conquest in date. Not the first church building on the site, this may be the eleventh-century building which was possibly a resting place of the body of St Edmund who had been murdered by the Danes for refusing to deny his faith. Nave walls of vertically split logs were mortised into wooden beams, a typical Anglo-Scandinavian building technique (Figure 25). Other churches had by then long been rebuilt in stone, like All Saints' church at Wittering in Cambridgeshire or St Laurence's chapel, Bradford-on-Avon, Wiltshire, the latter a tenth-century building which may have been intended to house the body of Bishop Aldhelm (Plate VII).

By the tenth century the Church had established a system of tithe payment to ensure its maintenance. The ecclesiastical parishes were the units which were recognized as dependent upon a particular church, whether this was the original minster church or one of a later foundation. While the early minsters often lost their right to tithe they jealously preserved their rights to burial dues and church-scot. In the more heavily developed regions, parishes were fully demarcated by the time of the

Plate VII   St Laurence's chapel, Bradford-on-Avon, Wiltshire, a tenth-century building which may have been built to house the body of Bishop Aldhelm.

Norman Conquest but in some more remote regions parish foundation was still going on into the twelfth century. In the Weald, in particular, Everitt[21] argues that many of the churches seem to have only been established at a relatively late date with permanent settlement here only a feature of the later Anglo-Saxon period. Whatever the date of parish formation, the boundaries of the ecclesiastical parishes naturally followed those of pre-existing estates and thus provide information about the pattern of later Anglo-Saxon land division.

By the later Anglo-Saxon period the multiple estate, comprising a number of related settlements bound together to support an estate structure with a focal vill, was, in most regions, long since a thing of the past. Fragmentation had progressed and there was an increasing tendency for each estate to be regarded as a viable economic unit in its own right. Even where great landowners, such as a particular church, held numerous adjacent estates, these were increasingly administered as separate units. In Worcestershire, for instance, Bishop Oswald in the tenth century was regularly leasing out properties belonging to the Church of Worcester.

Parish Patterns

To maintain a viable farming unit certain resources were essential: sufficient arable land for crop-growing and sufficient pasture for domestic stock including plough animals, with meadow hay to carry animals through the winter. Timber and wood for fuel were other basic requirements. An effort to incorporate these resources within the boundaries of an individual manor accounts for many of the boundary patterns we perceive today. In chalk and limestone regions parishes often stretch upwards from a river valley to the crest of an adjacent ridge, taking in meadowland beside a river, arable land on sloping hillsides and pastureland above on the more marginal land. This pattern is clearly visible in the Wylye valley of Wiltshire (see Figure 6 on p. 11) and in the Vale of the White Horse, now in Oxfordshire (Figure 26), but is repeated in many such scarpland regions of southern and eastern England. In the Vale of Pickering in Yorkshire, the parishes to the south of the River Derwent carve up the northern slopes of the Wolds in the same way.

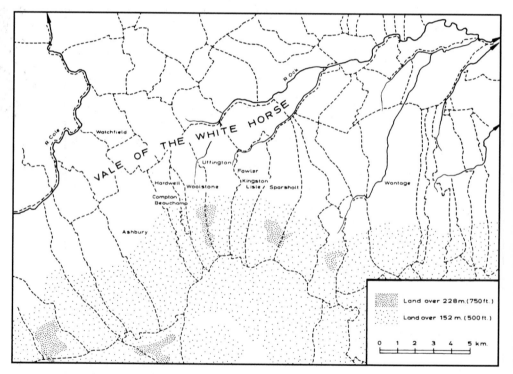

Fig. 26   Estates in the Vale of the White Horse, Oxfordshire.

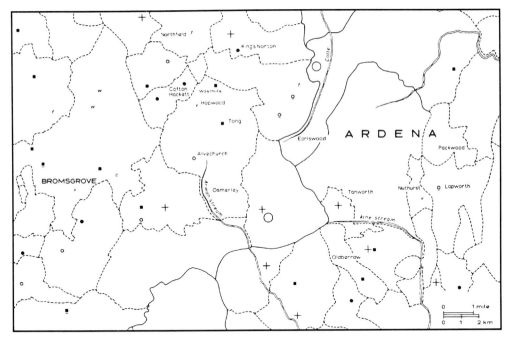

Fig. 27 Parish patterns in the Warwickshire Arden (from Hooke, *The Anglo-Saxon Landscape: The Kingdom of the Hwicce*).

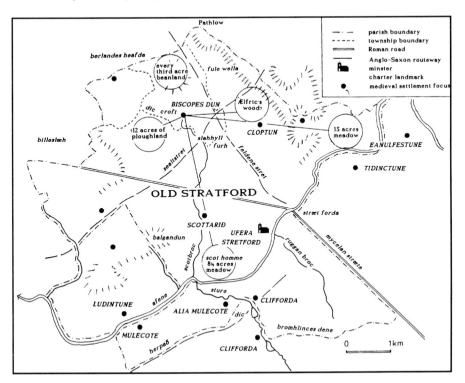

Fig. 28 Shottery estates, Warwickshire.

On the low-lying claylands of central England an 'organic' pattern of estates often emerges, less subject to the constraints of the terrain. Winchester notes a similar pattern in the Eden valley of Cumbria and suspects less seigneurial planning in the pattern. Signs of regular planning have often tempted scholars to envisage some kind of overall control but environment can also be an important factor in estate patterns, as shown above. 'Organic' patterns also typify the Warwickshire Arden (Figure 27) where Roberts suspected late parish formation.[22] Here irregularities of shape sometimes arose from the regrouping of smaller parcels of woodland and waste around settlements to support late church foundations; others represented irregularly-shaped areas of land only latterly taken into surrounding manors. Some of these patterns will be discussed further in Chapter 7.

As subdivision occurred, if a particular estate lacked an essential resource, attempts might be made to allocate an additional plot of land which supplied this requirement. Such an allocation could usually only be made within a territory under similar ownership and there are many instances of such land allocations in pre-Conquest charter grants. Leases of separate townships within the Bishop of Worcester's manor of Old Stratford in Warwickshire were being made in the tenth and eleventh centuries and one recorded grant is that of Bishopton in AD 1016 (Figure 28). Added to the lands of Bishopton itself was '15 acres of meadow on the river-furlong opposite Tiddington and 8½ acres on Shottery water-meadow, and 12 acres of ploughland between the river and the dyke at the stone-digging, and a messuage in Warwick, and the wood of Ælfric'.[23] Apart from the property in Warwick these additions all seem to have lain within the bishop's pre-existing manor of Old Stratford, which he had held since at least the ninth century. In such a way parishes acquired detached portions which were only tidied away during nineteenth- and twentieth-century reorganization.

Where parishes or townships have carved up a central area of rough grazing, moorland or heathland, between them, a particular pattern of boundaries is common. It is likely that the central area may have been held in common before the boundaries across such terrain were stabilized and the boundaries often radiate outwards from a central point in a star shape. In Warwickshire such a pattern is found upon Dunsmore, an area which remained open heathland until the time of parliamentary enclosure in the eighteenth century (Figure 29). A little to the north, a similar pattern of boundaries carves up a patch of boulder-clay-covered plateau to the north of Monks Kirby. Only on the undeveloped land could the boundaries be drawn freely; on the surrounding lowland their irregularity suggests that they were demarcated through already farmed countryside. Sometimes a surprising number of boundaries converge upon a single

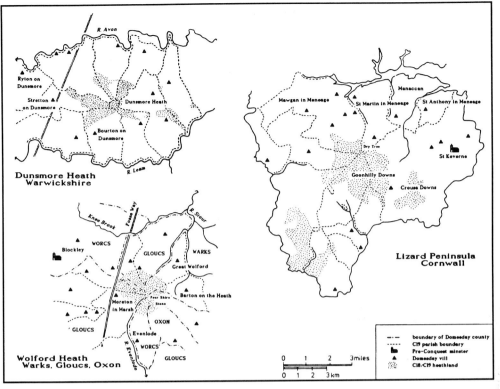

Fig. 29 Converging boundaries, showing areas of pasture divided up between surrounding parishes.

point where such an area of rough grazing has been partitioned in this way. In Wiltshire eight townships converge on the downland between the Wylye and Nadder valleys, meeting at a remote high point on the Roman road between Chicklade and the Deverills. Five of these boundaries were also the boundaries of hundreds (see Figure 6 on p. 11).

On the Lizard peninsula of Cornwall a monastic estate was centred upon the British monastery of St Keverne but in the tenth century this was being split up between lay tenants. The territory, lying in a region known as Meneage (a name incorporating the Cornish term *manach*, 'monk, monkish') reached the sheltered creeks of the Helford River on the north, incorporated dissected farmland lying mostly below 100 metres to the south of this, and then extended onto the unimproved moorlands of the Goonhilly and Crousa Downs, areas of barren heathland produced upon outcrops of igneous serpentine and gabbro. Upon Goonhilly Downs, five parish boundaries and at least two further township boundaries converged at 'Dry Tree' (possibly named from a gallows) where a barrow, *cruc drænoc*, was one of many tumuli upon the high moorland and where the spot is now marked by a large standing stone, re-erected this century (see Figure 29).

Moorlands and marshlands were areas of intercommoning where boundary demarcation was often late and disputed. Winchester notes the continuing disputes throughout the sixteenth and seventeenth centuries over the ownership of open waste which continued on the wetlands of the Weald Moors in Shropshire, an area which had undoubtedly been one of intercommoning in the Anglo-Saxon period (Chapter 8). Similar disputes took place between the parishes which made use of the hill grazings on the Long Mynd in the same county. In the Welsh Borderland some mountain tops were only roughly partitioned until the eighteenth century and heaps of stones were often put along the boundary on the open uplands in an effort to mark the lines where other distinctive landmark features were few.

Sometimes, a patch of land, usually heathland, remained unclaimed or its ownership contested long enough for it to become known as 'No Man's Land', although the pattern of parish boundaries recorded later shows that this rarely remained the case for many centuries. One of the earliest records of such land occurs in twelfth-century documents

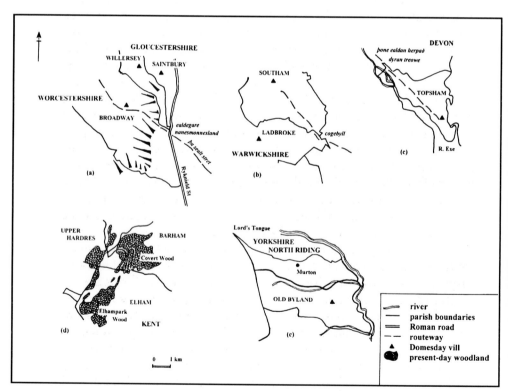

Fig. 30   Parish patterns: irregular boundaries.

describing the lands held by Evesham Abbey on the border of Worcestershire and Gloucestershire. Where the boundaries of the parishes of Saintbury, Willersey and Broadway met at the top of the Cotswold scarp, charter boundary clauses refer to the *ealdgare quod indigene nanesmonnesland uocant secus buggildestret,* 'the old gore which the natives call "No-Man's-Land" beside Burghild's street',[24] which was probably a patch of uncultivated common (Figures 30a and 35a on pp. 78, 98). In this instance the parishioners of Willersey, the estate obtained by the church of Evesham, were successful in incorporating this small area within their parish lands. Similarly, an area of heathland which now bears the name 'No Man's Heath' is found on the Warwickshire–Leicestershire border lying along the parish boundaries of Newton Regis. Such names occur across the country: in Cornwall 'no-mans'-lands' are found on the boundary of St Issey and Wadebridge and along the parish boundary of Norval and St Martin to the north-east of Looe, both adjoining road junctions.[25]

Several Old English words indicate disputed territory where boundaries were not resolved: Old English *(ge)flit,* 'strife, dispute' is not infrequent and usually refers to quite a small tract of land in dispute between neighbouring territories. Flitteridge is a ridge within the Sussex Weald, probably swine pastures claimed by a number of different communities, but Flitwick in the parish of Wootton Rivers in Wiltshire may be 'farm in disputed ownership'. Hooper notes a 'Flittermere Pond' between the parishes of Great Gidding and Lutton on the Huntingdon/Northampton boundary where the boundary shows an odd kink in its route, here marked by a hedge, placing the pond safely within Huntingdon.[26] Old English *þreapian* meant 'to contend, dispute' and its Middle English form occurs in the name of Threapwood near Wrexham which Winchester notes was a tract of woodland on the Anglo-Welsh border which was 'reputed to be part of no county, parish or township, paying no land tax or rates, and beyond the jurisdiction of justices of the peace in either county. It was a genuine "no man's land"'.[27] Old English *ceast,* 'strife, contention', again in its Middle English form, occurs within the name Chesland Wood, found near the parish boundary of South Wraxall in Wiltshire. That such disputes continued to arise is shown by the name Callingwood in Staffordshire which contains an Old Norman French word *calenge,* 'challenge'. It seems that many of these references were to blocks of woodland and may have referred to parcels that were once appendant to other estates in the way once common in the Weald or the Warwickshire Arden. Minor disputes are even recorded at the time of eighteenth-century enclosure awards. In Worcestershire the boundary between Hanbury and Feckenham was uncertain in several places as late as 1832.[28]

Adjustments to the local terrain have sometimes resulted in very strange parish shapes. Extensions onto a heath or into a wood might give rise to a curious 'pan-handle' effect. Beresford notes one such projection known as 'Lord's Tongue' in Murton township in the parish of Old Byland in Yorkshire.[29] In woods, especially, subdivision between estates might give rise to an interlocking pattern of boundaries (Figure 30d and see, further, Chapter 7).[30] While on occasions the boundaries were obviously attempting to reach towards some obvious physical feature such as a pond, which would probably have been a useful watering place for stock, it is sometimes difficult to understand today what may have given rise to such early diversions from the obvious line. In south Warwickshire a protruding area of Southam parish was known as 'the cock's bill' in the tenth century (Figure 30b).[31] One of two such protrusions in the vicinity, there is no variation in the terrain and it seems likely that the boundary was veering around early fields which have now left no visible trace.[32] Sometimes such meanderings in the line of a boundary are easily explained: a boundary may veer away from a stream to accommodate a mill site, for instance, although it is more common for a boundary to continue to follow the original meandering course of a stream that has later been straightened. On occasions, a tongue of land may run outwards along a strip of road (Figure 30c).

Boundary Features

The boundaries of these administrative units of early medieval England were obviously drawn with a careful eye on the local topography. Rivers and streams were particularly effective as boundary markers in that they were obvious features in the landscape, even in well-wooded regions. In Celtic law major rivers fulfilled this function so adequately that such a river was known as a recognized 'stay' of a boundary: a conclusive boundary marker the correctness of which would not be questioned.

In practice, such features were often unavailable but a walk along any stretch of parish boundary may help to suggest why that particular line was taken: even in relatively featureless country a slight valley feature may have been followed or a barely perceptible ridge of slightly higher ground. Early medieval man had no written map and the boundary had to be related to real features, even if these now no longer exist. Only across areas of open heathland or pasture could boundary lines follow relatively straight lines and a particularly irregular boundary was probably making its way through a man-made landscape of fields and farms (see Chapter 6).

Many boundaries chose to follow roads for considerable distances. As noted earlier in this chapter, much has been made of the use of roads to argue for a chronological sequence of boundaries, the argument often hinging upon whether they were drawn along roads known to be of Roman date or whether they ignored these, in which case the boundary might be considered earlier in date than the road itself. This is a dangerous argument for boundaries were concerned with the delimitation of such land as pasture, arable or meadow and the existence of a Roman road might be totally irrelevant. Nevertheless they did often choose to follow Roman roads in areas of open pasture where other distinctive features were few. Where a number of boundaries follow a routeway for a long distance then it may well be suspected that the routeway itself is ancient. On the boundary of Warwickshire and Gloucestershire a route along the edge of the ironstone escarpment known as Ditchedge Lane is followed for many miles by both the county boundary and by hundred and parish boundaries (see Figure 5 on p. 10). It runs past the prehistoric stone circle of the Rollright Stones and is indeed likely to be an ancient ridgeway. The boundaries of the estates in the Vale of the White Horse, on the other hand (see Figures 26 and 41 on pp. 74, 123), cut across the ancient ridgeway there although it is referred to in boundary clauses as it is crossed. Here the estates were running beyond the ridgeway to the downland watershed and the road was not conveniently placed to act as a boundary.

Today most parish boundaries are demarcated by the walls or hedges in general use in the surrounding countryside and few stand out in any obvious way. The line of the boundary may be old but in heavily farmed countryside field boundaries are regularly hedged and ditched. In some regions, where land ownership now often runs across parishes, the modern trend of hedgerow removal has indeed removed the boundary line as a visible feature. This is particularly evident on the North Berkshire Downs (now in Oxfordshire) which fringe the southern side of the Vale of the White Horse. Although a turf balk may still mark a former parish boundary this is of little visual impact among the acres of swaying corn.

There is documentary evidence that some boundaries in Anglo-Saxon times were marked by living hedgerows (see Chapter 5) and Dr Max Hooper evolved a method of assessing the approximate date of a hedgerow by noting the number of different kinds of shrubs it contained.[33] Obviously this method would be affected by local traditions of planting mixed-species hedges and, perhaps, by local soil type but in general it was found that an additional shrub species might be expected to colonize a hedgerow every hundred years. Thus a surviving Anglo-Saxon hedgerow would be species-rich, with perhaps ten or eleven different species represented. In Worcestershire, an attempt by the present author[34] to examine every hedge recorded in pre-Conquest documents showed few ancient hedgerows surviving in arable regions but rather more in pastoral regions. In the latter, the hedgerow has continued to play a useful part in the farm economy, providing shelter and protection to domestic stock and preventing animals from straying. Thus more species-rich hedges were noted to the west of the River Severn, near the Herefordshire–Worcestershire border. The most impressive, however, was a hedgerow atop a pronounced bank which separated a former area of common waste in Kempsey parish from the abbot's wood in the neighbouring parish of Pershore. Here ten species were regularly recorded in sample 30-yard lengths (oak, hawthorn, elm, blackthorn, rose, elderberry, ash, hazel, field maple, gorse). Although there were ditches on either side, the deepest lay to the west as if it had been aimed at preventing animals grazing on the common from entering the abbot's woodland.

It is likely that this kind of hedge-dating exercise might be of particular interest in those parts of the country less affected by farming change. Some of the Devon hedgerows are amazingly impressive and it was in this county that Hooper was able to identify the likely boundary of a farm holding called Chumhill in the parish of Bratton Fleming.[35] The name of the holding is derived from an Old English place-name meaning 'Ceomma's spring' which suggests that it was a pre-Conquest estate and it was found that a multi-species hedge separated it from the rest of Bratton parish – the existence of eleven species of shrub would suggest an age of over 1000 years.

Some of the turf-covered boundary banks of Cornwall may be even older for some bear a close relationship to pre-Roman field systems. Certainly such banks of stone and turf, often covered with a rich variety of living plants and shrubs, lay along the lines where tenth-century documents referred to dykes as, for instance, along parts of the northern boundary of the parish of St Keverne in the Lizard peninsula and along the boundaries of the estate of Trerice in St Dennis. Recent archaeological research in Derbyshire has also proved the antiquity of some stone walls, a number of which at Roystone Grange were apparently erected by Roman times.[36] One 'old wall' along the boundary of Ditchampton near Wilton in Wiltshire apparently marked the boundary of this township by AD 1045.[37]

Notes

1. Hoskins, *English Landscapes*, p.37.
2. Metz, 'Das "gehagio regis" der Langobarden'.
3. Hooke, *The Anglo-Saxon Landscape*, pp.85–6.
4. Fowler, 'Agriculture and rural settlement', Fig. 1.9, p.41.
5. Bassett, 'In search of the origins of the Anglo-Saxon kingdoms', pp.21–3.
6. Bonney, 'Early boundaries in Wessex'.
7. Unwin, 'Townships and early fields'.
8. Hooke, 'Regional variation'.
9. Williamson, 'Settlement chronology'.
10. Bonney, 'Early boundaries in Wessex'.
11. Charles-Edwards, 'Boundaries in Irish Law'.
12. Goodier, 'The formation of boundaries'.
13. Barker, 'Institution and landscape', pp.38–40.
14. Sawyer, *Anglo-Saxon Charters*, S 1561; Finberg, *The Early Charters of the West Midlands*, pp.225–7.
15. Hooke, *The Landscape of Anglo-Saxon Staffordshire*, pp.14–25.
16. Winchester, *Discovering Parish Boundaries*, p.3.
17. Sawyer, *Anglo-Saxon Charters*, S 94; Birch, *Cartularium Saxonicum*, B 157.
18. Wormald, 'Bede, Beowulf and the conversion'.
19. Hooke, 'Saxon conquest and settlement'.
20. Hase, 'The development of the parish'.
21. Everitt, *Continuity and Colonization*, pp.196–258.
22. Roberts, 'Settlement, land use and population', pp.110–34.
23. Sawyer, *Anglo-Saxon Charters*, S 1388; Kemble, *Codex Diplomaticus Aevi Saxonici*, K 724.
24. Sawyer, *Anglo-Saxon Charters*, S 80; Birch, *Cartularium Saxonicum*, B 125.
25. Gascoyne, *A Map of the County of Cornwall 1699*.
26. Hooper, 'Hedges and history'.
27. Winchester, *Discovering Parish Boundaries*, p.38.
28. Feckenham Inclosure Award, Worcester County Record Office.
29. Beresford, *History on the Ground*, pp.34, 54.
30. Everitt, *Continuity and Colonization*, p.284.
31. Sawyer, *Anglo-Saxon Charters*, S 892; Napier and Stevenson, *The Crawford Collection*, pp.19–22.
32. Hooke, *The Anglo-Saxon Charters-Bounds of Warwickshire*.
33. Hooper, 'Dating hedges'.
34. Hooke, *Anglo-Saxon Landscapes of the West Midlands*, pp.248–51.
35. Hooper, 'Hedges and history'.
36. Hodges, *Wall-to-Wall History*.
37. Sawyer, *Anglo-Saxon Charters*, S 1010; Kemble, *Codex Diplomaticus Aevi Saxonici*, K 778.

CHAPTER 5

Boundaries: The Written Record

Ðis synd þa land gemære æt eowlan gelade of eowlan gelade and lang bladene of bladene and lang riþiges þ on fugel mære midne of fulgel [sic] mere þ on þone oþerne fugel mere of fugel mere þ on gild beorh of gild beorh and lang sealt stræte to þan stane of þan stane to þan oþeran stane þ swa to þan þriddan stane 7 to þan feorðan stane of þam stane to þære grenan stige of þære stige to lafercan beorh of lafercan beorh on þone ealdan weg þ ofer þone broc þ eft on þone ealdan weg of þam ealdan wege þ forð on lang dune a bi heafdan þ hit cymð to þan ealdan slo of þan slo to þan lytlan beorhe of þan beorge on þ sic ond long sices ofer þone broc to heort wellan of heort wellan to hwete wellan 7 þreo æceras earð landes of hwete wellan a bi þan earð lande to þan 'to' brocenan beorge of þan beorge forð on geriht on þæt sic of þam sice be þan heafdan þ hit cymð to mules hlawe 7 þreo æceras þonne adune and lang þære furh þæt cymð to bladene swa and lang bladene þ hit cymð eft to eowlan gelade.

(Boundary clause of Evenlode, AD 969).[1]

These are the land boundaries at Evenlode: from Evenlode along (the) Bladen; from (the) Bladen along the streamlet so that to the middle of bird mere; from bird mere so that to the other bird mere; from bird mere so that to *gild* barrow; from *gild* barrow along (the) salt road to the stone; from the stone to the other stone so that thus to the third stone and to the fourth stone; from the stone to the green uphill path; from the uphill path to lark barrow; from lark barrow to the old way; so that over the brook so that again to the old way; from the old way so that onwards along the hill always by the headlands so that it comes to the old slough; from the slough to the little barrow; from the barrow to the watercourse; along the watercourse over the brook to hart spring; from hart spring to wheat spring; and three acres of ploughland;

from wheat spring always by the ploughlands to the broken
barrow; from the barrow straight on to the watercourse; from
the watercourse by the headlands so that it comes to Mul's
low (mound or tumulus); and three acres; then down along
the furrow so that it comes to (the) Bladen; thus along (the)
Bladen so that it comes again to Evenlode.

From the late seventh century onwards scribes were formulating official
documents to record the transfer of privileges relating to a particular estate
in order to make a long-lasting legal record. It has already been noted that
the Church was in the vanguard of such a movement. Following the
established principles of Roman law, documents were drawn up which were
based upon the style of Roman land documents, thus continuing a European
style of estate survey.[2] It seems that such a document replaced an earlier
tradition of laying a sod from the land concerned upon the holy altar before
witnesses.[3] Such a transfer of land might alleviate the financial burdens tied
to an estate and in many cases allow the new holder to bequeath it to
whomsoever he wished. Because of this, even the king found it necessary to
grant a Devon estate to himself to hold in his private possession.[4] Ultimately
all land rights were vested in the Crown but throughout the seventh, eighth
and ninth centuries an increasing number of estates were being granted to
the Church and others to lay lords. Normally these grants ensured that such
land was freed from tax burdens but the king usually reserved the right to
bridge- and fort-building and to call for military service from the estate. In
subsequent centuries many estates were leased to individuals and their heirs,
often for a term of three lives.

Few early charters survive in their original form and most have been
transcribed many times, occasionally with accidental changes to the text.
The charter shown in Plate VIII is an authentic tenth-century document
referring to the grant of land at Tywarnhayle in Perranzabuloe, Cornwall,
by King Edgar to Eanulf, his faithful *minister*.[5] Some were lost and
attempts were made to reconstruct a convincing document, as in the loss
of Devon charters after the destruction of the cathedral library by the
Vikings in the tenth century.[6] On other occasions, churches have claimed
early dates for documents which were compiled much later but the content
of which they believed (or hoped) to be true. A few are downright forgeries.
Debates about authenticity have continued for many decades and the
comments of historians who have investigated individual texts are listed
in a handbook compiled in 1968 by Peter Sawyer which is now being
brought up-to-date by Susan Kelly.[7]

The survival of charter evidence for England is not even and
unfortunately most of the earlier records of land transfer in eastern England

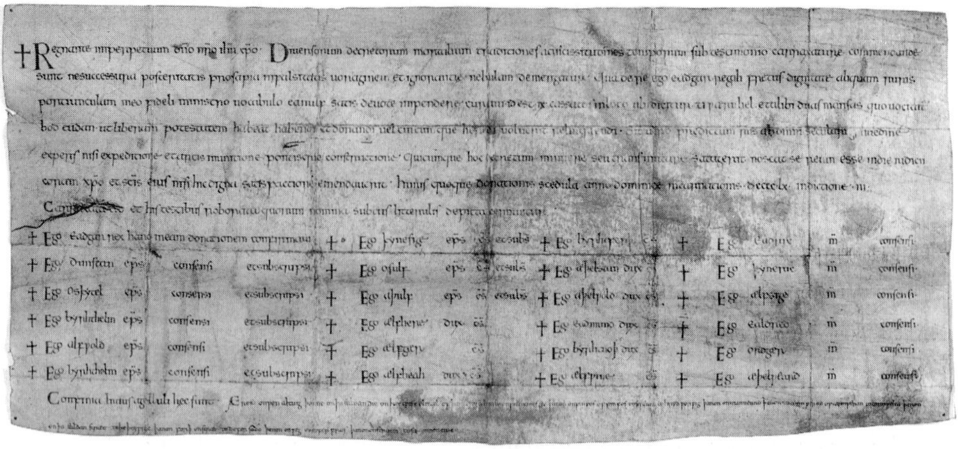

Plate VIII   Charter of Tywarnhayle, Cornwall. This records a grant by King Edgar to Eanulf, his *minister*, in AD 960. It concerns an estate at Tywarnhayle in the parishes of Perranzabuloe and St Agnes, Cornwall. It is reproduced here by kind permission of Exeter Cathedral Library.

were destroyed by the Danish invasions. There are far fewer charters, too, for the north of England. Some cathedral scriptoria were obviously more productive than others in compiling and saving such documents and for this reason there is a vast amount of richly detailed material available for the estates which belonged to the churches of Worcester, Canterbury, Abingdon and Winchester. As David Hill notes, 'Kent has the best coverage, whereas shires such as Lancashire or Herefordshire have practically none.'[8] An overwhelming proportion of the charters concern gifts to or by the Church and were initially preserved in the great cathedral libraries or the scriptoria of monasteries. We have very little knowledge of the history of estates which did not pass through the hands of the Church. For this reason 'when we quote charter evidence on practically any subject we are probably quoting a tenth-century charter, and . . . a charter from a particularly limited part of the country. An awareness of the bias in the evidence will help to offset it.'[9]

The nature of the evidence also varies temporally as well as spatially. A charter names the grantor and the grantee, and normally indicates the size of the estate, frequently mentioning appurtenances to which the grantee will obtain rights. These usually include rights in woods, fields, meadows and pasture but might include special rights such as hunting or in fisheries where these were applicable. A substantial number of charter grants are accompanied by boundary clauses which allow the boundaries of an estate to be identified on the ground. The bounds accompanying early charters, however, are often sparse in detail, giving little more than a few boundary markers at cardinal points on an estate boundary. Many of the early Kentish charters are of this type. As time progresses not only does the number of charters increase but the amount of detail included within the boundary clauses also increases and some of the tenth- and eleventh-century boundary clauses are brimming with topographical detail. Many of the later charters concern smaller areas of land, especially as many estates were then being leased out by church landowners to individuals for a limited period (usually for the lifetimes of three people).

Many charters give some topographical information in explaining the location of a particular estate. Thus a grant of *UUestanæ in Tenid* by Hlothhere of Kent to Abbot Beorhtwald of Canterbury in AD 679[10] refers to Thanet which was at that time an island, cut off by the Wantsum channel and its marsh-fringed banks from the Kentish mainland. An example of an early Kentish charter which is accompanied by only the simplest indication of its boundary is that of land beside the River Lympne which was used for the collection of salt (about which, more later), granted by King Æthelberht of Kent to Abbot Dunn and the church of St Mary at Lyminge in AD 732. The bounds of this land are given: 'the king's land on the east, the River Limen on the south, and Huda's creek on the west and north'.[11] This type of boundary clause does not necessarily imply that the boundaries of land units were still vague at this point in time: it merely reflects the undeveloped nature of boundary recording in the early diplomatic tradition.

For an estate at Evenlode in Gloucestershire, a parish lying in the wide vale which separates the Gloucestershire from the Oxfordshire Cotswolds, there is both an early simple charter boundary clause and a later fuller one. The first accompanies a lease of the estate by King Offa of Mercia to Ridda, *minister*, made in AD 775. After the death of Ridda's wife and daughter, the 8-hide estate was to revert back to the monastery of Bredon (in south Worcestershire). It was said to lie on the east bank of the Evenlode, then known as the *Bladen*, and to be bounded by '*cenepes* marsh' on the east, 'hart spring' and 'Mul's low' on the south, the river *Bladen* on the west and '?Ælfhere's mere' and 'Cetta's tree' on the north.[12] This offers more landmarks than some early charters but a later lease of AD 969 by Bishop Oswald of Worcester, quoted at the head of this chapter, notes 31 landmarks along the same boundary (Figure 31).[13]

In the tenth-century bounds the *Bladen* is still given as the only boundary marker on the west because it provided a definitive boundary on that side of the estate. Indeed, the place-name, *Eulangelade/ Eowlangelade* means 'Eowla's river-crossing'. The more detailed bounds, however, show that the Evenlode boundary followed a tributary streamlet,

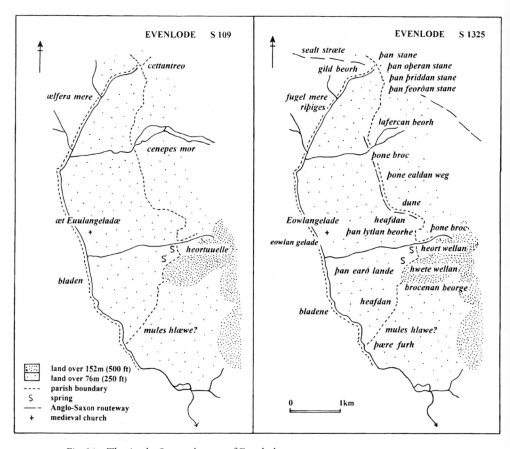

Fig. 31   The Anglo-Saxon charters of Evenlode.

a *riþig*, and then passed by two meres, then both called 'bird mere'. These were apt names because this part of the estate was long an area of marshland and heath, frequented only by fishers and fowlers and presumably rich in bird life. There was also a barrow here on the heathland and from this the bounds ran, interestingly, 'along the salt road to the stone, from the stone to the other stone so that thus to the third stone and to the fourth stone'. At the time of the Norman Conquest the boundaries of Worcestershire (an outlier of the main county comprising the parish of Evenlode), Gloucestershire (originally the separate county of Winchcombeshire), Warwickshire and Oxfordshire met on the heath, their boundaries radiating outwards in the manner discussed in the previous chapter (see Figure 29 on p. 77), and this reference to the four stones at this point may suggest that these midland counties had come into being as early as the mid-tenth century. Today the boundary meeting point is marked by a large stone block erected in the eighteenth century. The barrow is also of interest, for it seems to have been the lost *Ildeberg,* 'hill or barrow of the guild or guildsmen', at which a court was held in which Abbot Walter proved his right to the possession of disputed land in Bengeworth in Worcestershire.[14] Such courts were frequently held in accessible places in the open countryside, often on or near boundary meeting points (see Chapter 3) Here a major saltway was reached by the northernmost corner of the estate, providing easy access.

From this point the boundary swung in a southerly direction across the high land with an uphill path, a 'lark barrow', an old way and a brook being noted along its course. The way was in fact followed by the boundary for some distance as it swung south-eastwards along a hill and can still be followed as a narrow lane running towards the adjacent estate of Chastleton. The bounds were to leave the way, dipping down to cross a tributary stream of the Evenlode at the 'hart spring' noted in the earlier charter. Here, however, a further spring is also mentioned: the 'wheat spring'. There was ploughland, too, in this corner of the estate. A 'broken barrow' further along the south-eastern boundary may refer to a barrow that had already been looted but no sign of either this or 'Mul's low' below appears to have survived. The final stretch of the boundary was cutting through the adjoining arable lands of Evenlode and Adlestrop, indicated by reference to a furrow, headlands and to ?acre-strips, as it plunged downhill back to the Evenlode.

There are many hundreds of boundary clauses of this nature and many have still to be 'solved'. Few charters survive in their original form, having been copied again and again by generations of scribes, but some originals can still be seen in the British Library in London. At the Dissolution many monastic records found their way to the manuscript collection of Sir Robert Cotton (1571–1631), together with two of the earliest manuscripts of Bede and a number of versions of the Anglo-Saxon Chronicle. Many manuscripts were destroyed in a disastrous fire in 1731 but the surviving records became one of the foundation collections of the British Museum in 1753. They are now preserved within the archives of the British Library although there are other major collections, as in the Bodleian Library, Oxford, or individual cathedral libraries. There they can still be read and handled and it is a thrilling experience to see a document which was compiled on parchment, some as many as 900 years ago (see Plate VIII). The original documents are in Latin with the bounds in Old English, written in the handwriting of the time, and familiarity with the palaeography is necessary to read them. The later copies are of course in the various scripts of later periods and, in some few, attempts were made to translate the Old English bounds into Middle English, sometimes with very misleading results.

In the nineteenth century several scholars began to transcribe the documents and to publish them as collections. J. M. Kemble in his work *Codex Diplomaticus Aevi Saxonici,* produced between 1839 and 1848, edited the scripts in an effort to correct the style to that felt to be then acceptable and, for this reason, the texts transcribed by a later scholar, W. de Gray Birch, in his *Cartularium Saxonicum* of 1885–99, are usually more reliably true to the originals. Both of these works are available in good reference libraries and have been reprinted in America in recent years. There are other more accessible texts available in county collections and here G. B. Grundy working in the 1920s and 1930s was certainly the most prolific writer. Although his translations do not always meet the standards of modern scholarship, his efforts to identify boundary landmarks and to 'solve' the boundary clauses have made the work that much easier for subsequent scholars. Where more detailed research has taken place, however, some of his proffered solutions must now be declared suspect.

The practical use of a boundary description to clarify a contested boundary is shown in a document of AD 896 in which it is recorded that Bishop Wærferð of Worcester claimed that he had been dispossessed of 'well-nigh all the woodland belonging to Woodchester' (now in Gloucestershire) by the inhabitants of Bisley, Avening, *Scorranstane* and Thornbury. He ordered his yeoman, Ecglaf, to ride the boundary of the estate with the citizens' chaplain, Wulfhun, *7 be hine þa gelædde ealle þa gemæru swa he him of þam aldan bocum rædde hu hit ær Æþelbald cyning gemærude 7 gesealde,* 'and he showed him all the bounds as he read to him out of the old books, according as King Æthelbald had originally defined and granted it'.[15] Some of the landmarks appear to repeat those of an earlier eighth-century grant by Æthelbald to the church of St Peter, Worcester, but this may have been fabricated to substantiate the later claim.[16]

Again in the early eleventh century Wulfstan and Wulfric claimed part of an estate in Worcestershire which Athelstan, Bishop of Hereford, claimed to have bought previously. The estate lay in the parish of Inkberrow in the east of the county. To settle the dispute it is recorded that a day was

appointed . . . for going to the estate, and the same people who had traced the boundaries for him [should do so again], and they said [that] if the boundaries were the same as when they were first traced, the bishop was the rightful owner of the estate. Then the bishop and the man who sold him the estate and those who had been his witnesses came thither, and Wulfstan and his son and those who were their companions came, and they all rode round the boundaries, as they had been first traced for the bishop, and all who were there said that the bishop was the rightful owner of the estate. Then the man who sold him the land acknowledged it to be so.[17]

These records show that the perambulation of an estate to identify boundary landmarks was a very real activity and this practice was of course continued throughout historical times by the tradition of 'beating the bounds' in Rogation Week, the time between the fifth Sunday after Easter and Ascension Day. Once again, it was the Church which upheld ancient tradition in making sure that the bounds of its parish were known to each successive generation. Local officials would similarly record the boundaries of individual townships and stewards those of a particular manor but in many cases these smaller units became subsumed into the parish and the practice allowed to lapse. For this reason it is now often difficult to trace township boundaries unless these remained viable units until mapped by much later cartographers and the boundaries of Domesday manors can rarely be identified.

Although many Anglo-Saxon boundaries were described in detail, the practice died out after the Norman Conquest. Writs replaced charters and written boundary descriptions were rarely preserved. Many enclosure awards of the mid-eighteenth century and later carry written descriptions of boundaries but these are rarely as instructive about the actual countryside as the documents produced 700–800 years earlier. These later records often identify land by naming the current owner. Although some earlier maps purport to show parish boundaries, the earliest Gascoyne's *Map of the County of Cornwall* published in 1699, few are accurate enough for the purposes of estate identification while some, like Greenwood's early nineteenth-century map of Devon, are positively misleading.

It was only in the mid-nineteenth century, in 1841, that the boundary surveyors of the Ordnance Survey began systematically to ascertain and map parish boundaries, tracing them on the ground. Although estate, parish and sometimes township boundaries find their way onto historical maps, this was the first deliberate attempt to clarify actual boundary lines. Many of the books and maps produced survive and are stored by the Ordnance Survey at Southampton.[18] Coverage of the country is now far from complete and by far the easiest method of checking the line of a boundary before any nineteenth- and twentieth-century changes is to examine the Tithe Index maps preserved in the British Library. On these the boundaries of titheable areas are shown on the first-edition one-inch Ordnance Survey map: in practice this usually means the bounds of parishes. In 1836 the payment of annual tithe, by then often payable to private individuals who had bought up monastic rights at the Dissolution, was extinguished where previous commutation had not already taken place and tithe maps produced after the act are often the earliest accurate records of individual parish boundaries. Some counties, like Devon, have an almost unbroken cover and copies are preserved in county record offices.

Boundary Features

As the larger territories were broken up into smaller units, the new boundary lines were frequently drawn with close attention to the actual terrain, although this is not always self-evident from the boundary descriptions themselves. Rivers and streams were frequently used as boundaries, especially in wooded regions where they were often the only distinctive landmarks. They had the virtue of being clearly visible and relatively stable features and where a local stream- or river-name was not known, the Anglo-Saxons had many terms to differentiate kinds of watercourses. While a *burna* tended to be a substantial stream or small river, a *winterburna* was one with a marked seasonal flow; really small watercourses might be described by the term *sic*, implying little more than a ditch, and a drainage channel in a marsh might be termed a *sihtran*. At the head of a stream Worcestershire charters often refer to 'batches' and along some boundaries one can follow a natural slight valley above the present-day spring line which carries the boundary line further along this related feature. A frequent sign of the permanence of a boundary line is shown when a boundary today continues to follow the original winding course of a subsequently straightened stream or follows river meanders long since abandoned.

Although reference is often made to a stream which marked the course of a boundary, sometimes the valleys themselves are described and distinctive terms were used to describe different kinds of valleys: *denu*, 'dean', for those which were long and winding, *cumb*, 'coomb', for the enclosed basins which mark the upper parts of streams in chalk and limestone country, as described in Chapter 1. On higher land the boundaries frequently mention other distinctive physical features such as edges or ridges and the spurs or summits of hills.

The written descriptions of the boundaries pick up a series of individual landmarks in the way illustrated at the beginning of this chapter and are at first often confusing. Indeed, some nineteenth-century historians dismissed the boundary clauses with disdain, regulating them to the realms of 'mere topography'. They are, however, full of detail, permitting one to build up a fragmented picture of the Anglo-Saxon countryside as it was seen by its inhabitants. Fragmented, because only the boundaries are discussed in this detail, but it will be shown in successive chapters that such information can be interpreted to give a much fuller picture. Where charters are available in large numbers, this information can be studied closely. A search through historical maps and related records may produce now often forgotten field-names and minor place-names which actually represent the survival of names recorded in boundary clauses. Once a line has been relatively closely identified, fieldwork may help to locate other features, especially those relating to unchanging local physical features. Even if few landmarks can be identified on the ground, fieldwork will provide an understanding of the nature of the countryside involved and perhaps provide clues to the relationship between the boundary and the natural topography.[19] Obviously there have been many changes in land use over the centuries which must be taken into consideration.

While the 'solution' of boundary clauses is an enthralling study it does require an inordinate amount of patience and skill. While Hoskin's claim that 'the average time taken to "solve" a charter is about two years' may be a little exaggerated, it is certainly true to say that some boundary clauses 'are rich and offer enough fieldwork for years'.[20] For some areas the present writer has built upon the work of Grundy and others and has offered 'solutions' to the charters of a whole county. Staffordshire, Worcestershire, Devon and Cornwall have been published and Warwickshire is now complete;[21] Gloucestershire is well on the way. No doubt others with more local knowledge will be able to add to these proffered solutions in time.

Along a boundary, quoted landmarks can be either linear features or mere points. Some were, and still are, obvious in the landscape but others were surprisingly ephemeral, given the fact that future identification might be required. Trees were frequently noted as boundary markers – numerous species ranging from the long-lived yew to the rather less significant hawthorn. Yet even tree species were frequently to regenerate themselves by seedlings and suckers and it is perhaps surprising how often the same species of tree can be noted today very close to the point at which such a tree was recorded nearly a thousand years ago. Even in the Warwickshire Feldon, a region of intensive arable cultivation since at least the late Iron Age and one where, over much of the region, woods were virtually eradicated by late medieval times, thorns still grow near the 'thorn clump' of a Long Itchington charter and at the *hlangan* thorn tree on the boundary of the nearby estate of Lower Radbourne. Even such features as badger holes and fox holes can sometimes be traced today as these animals continue to frequent the same spots of rough countryside, often sloping ground that was too steep to warrant clearance and cultivation.

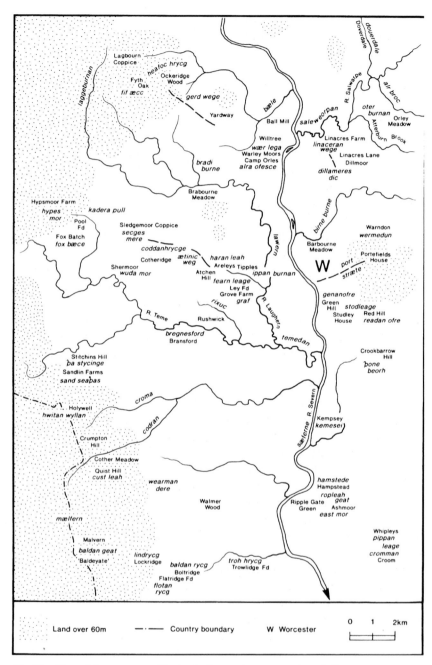

Fig. 32   Natural features named in Anglo-Saxon charters: an example from west Worcestershire.

There are other isolated landmarks of botanical interest, like the 'ash-apple-tree' recorded in a Worcestershire charter of Pendock.[22] The 'ash-apple-tree', here associated with a wood or clearing (*leah*) is strikingly reminiscent of the Whitty Pear, *Sorbus domestica*, the true service tree, not a native of Britain but unaccountably found growing wild in the heart of the Wyre Forest in Worcestershire in 1678. It had perhaps been introduced into this country by the Romans who used its fruit to make an alcoholic drink.[23] Its fruit strongly resembles that of the common crab-apple while its leaves are almost identical with those of the rowan or mountain-ash. Is this 'The ash-tree that bears apples, by the river Wye' recounted among 'The Wonders of the Island of Britain' in the 'History of the British' compiled by Nennius in the ninth century?[24] The 'rough-barked maple-tree' of Stoke Prior, Worcestershire, produces the fissured bark which this tree acquires with age. Those interested in survivals of paganism will be interested by the references to the 'ash which the ignorant call holy' on the boundary of Taunton in Somerset.[25] Attention to local detail is shown in such landmarks as *þa ifihtan ac*, 'the ivy-covered oak-tree', again in Stoke Prior, or the place called *wata cumb þer stondað apeltreo 7 mapeltreo togædere gewæxan*, 'Wat's coomb where stands the appletree and maple-tree grown together', on the boundary of Bishop's Cleeve, Gloucestershire.[26]

The majority of boundary clauses begin at a cardinal point on the estate boundary, often a corner but occasionally mid-way along one side, especially if this happens to lie on a road running from the major settlement. The majority run in a clockwise direction but there are aberrations. They seem to have been drawn up by those most conversant with the local terrain although the advice and practice of a particular institution may lead to similarities in technique and recording that can sometimes be detected: a tendency to make greater use of compass direction, for instance, or the use of particular prepositions in the clauses.

In some areas it is possible to produce a surprisingly full map of the physical features named in boundaries. Figure 32 shows an area of Worcestershire. It was important to the boundary surveyors that the features chosen as landmarks should be either linear features running along the boundary or small and precise enough to serve a useful function as markers, so that one finds reference to rather more minor features than occur in place-names. The charter descriptions are particularly important in that such features can be accurately located and examined in the field, permitting a close investigation to be made of the way particular terms were used. In some clauses the features named were intervisible and as one walks along a particular boundary the features unfold one by one in sequence. This is particularly the case along part of the boundary of Oldberrow in the Warwickshire Arden where the apparently unnatural

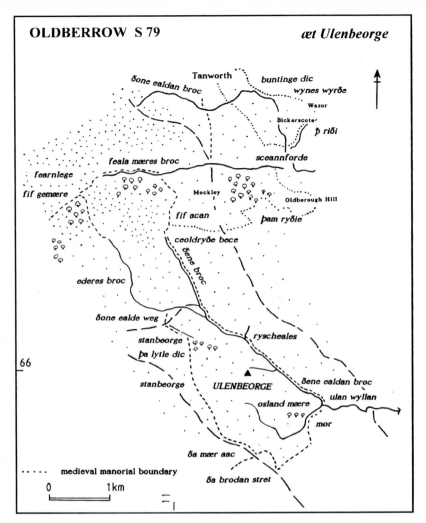

Fig. 33   Oldberrow boundary clause drawn up by the Church of Evesham to substantiate their claim to the estate. Oldberrow was taken from Worcestershire into Warwickshire in 1894.

line of the southern boundary of the parish (Figure 33) is found to actually follow an area of former marshland described in the charter as a *mor* before following a hill crest from 'stone barrow' to 'stone barrow' (although *beorg* here may mean 'hilltop').[27]

Another boundary clause which leads one easily through the country-side is that of Stoke Prior in Worcestershire (Figure 34). Here the eastern boundary of the parish runs in a southerly direction to an abrupt little hill now known as Two Tree Hill. In Anglo-Saxon times this was known as *werdune*, 'watch hill', although it is uncertain why this was so. The bounds continue 'from the front of watch hill to the middle part of watch hill', and when these are followed it is found that the boundary does indeed

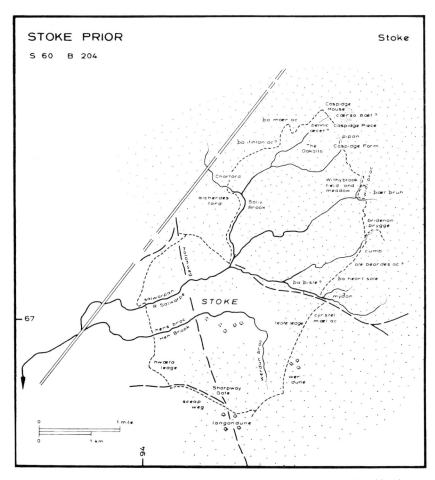

Fig. 34 The Anglo-Saxon boundary of Stoke Prior in Worcestershire produced by the
Church of Worcester in an attempt to strengthen its claim to the whole estate. The charter
claims to date from AD 770 but this is highly unlikely; it survives in a late eleventh-century
manuscript.

climb the northern tip of a hill which then swings away south-westwards
as a long ridge. The boundary, however, leaves the ridge part way along
and the bounds tell us that it ran 'from the middle part of watch hill to
watch hill brook; from mid watch hill brook to the middle part of long
hill' where it in fact crosses a brook and makes its way to the prominent
landmark of Piper's Hill on the Hanbury/Stoke Prior boundary.[28]

The boundary clauses are full of interesting snippets of information
and every region brings its own delights. While the landmarks relating to
land use are perhaps of the greatest importance to the landscape historian
and will be examined in subsequent chapters, the unusual ones are also

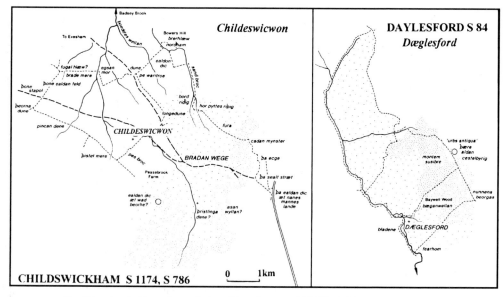

Fig. 35a   Anglo-Saxon boundaries of Broadway and Childswickham.

Fig. 35b   Anglo-Saxon boundaries of Daylesford.

of interest. These include references to such diverse features as burial places, prehistoric and Roman settlement sites and hitherto unsuspected routeways: all of archaeological significance. One such intriguing site is that of 'Cada's minster' located on the Cotswold scarp near or within Willersey Iron Age hillfort (Figure 35a). No church site is known there today but the location obviously suggests the presence of a Christianized pagan shrine in the Anglo-Saxon period, perhaps similar to the features recently identified at Uley Bury a few miles to the south-west.[29] On a different note, the *waritroe* (for *treow*) on the Childswickham boundary in the same general area is a reference to a gallows tree.

In their boundary clauses the Anglo-Saxons frequently referred to features of an earlier period and were obviously familiar with their use. Some hillforts are referred to as *urbs antiqua*, 'old fortification', and one wonders if even then this carried the sense of 'old town', a feature of hillforts not recognized again until relatively recent times. One such hillfort stood on the Adlestrop boundary, on the Gloucestershire/ Oxfordshire boundary, and an early eighth-century charter of the adjacent estate of Daylesford was referred to as the *þære aldan cestelbyrig*,[30] *ceastel* implying the use of stone in the ramparts (Figure 35b). On the summit of Bredon Hill, overlooking the Vale of Evesham on the Gloucestershire/Worcestershire border, the bounds of Kemerton ran 'to the summit of the aforesaid hill Bredon on the top of which is the fortification anciently called *Bænintesburg*,[31] a name which survives in that of the Banbury Stone referring to an enormous block of Oolitic limestone standing within the ramparts of the hillfort. In both these cases the British word for hill, *bre*, was incorporated into the hill name: the Chastleton example being *mons susibre* in the eighth-century charter, the latter combined with the Old English word for a hill, *dun*, and 'hill' in the present-day name Bredon Hill.

The Gloucestershire examples both occur in early clauses of a relatively simple nature but two Berkshire clauses containing reference to hillforts derive from a time when greater accuracy was being attempted. The western boundary of Uffington in the Vale of the White Horse, described in the mid-tenth century, ran through the middle of Uffington Castle, the great Iron Age hillfort near the White Horse on the ridgeway which follows the crest of the North Berkshire Downs (see Figure 41 on p. 123). The bounds were said to run 'into Ashbury's south gate and thus out at the north gate', Ashbury then being the name given to the hillfort.[32] Similarly, the eastern boundary of East Woolstone, the adjacent estate, in AD 958 was described as running 'to the north gate, then to the south gate', passing through the fort in the opposite direction.[33] The 'gates' were, in fact, cut through the Iron Age defences in Roman times.[34]

Other archaeological features used frequently as boundary markers included barrows, to describe which several terms were available. As several scholars have noted, the British term *cruc* and the Old English term *beorg* could be used to refer to either a tumulus or a barrow-shaped natural hill (Chapter 1, see Figure 1 on p. 3) but where it is used in the former sense it almost always seems to describe a tumulus that was recognized to be ancient in Anglo-Saxon times. Old English *hlaw*, on the other hand, translated here as 'low', seems more often to have been used to describe a burial mound that was either erected or reused by the pagan Anglo-Saxons.[35] Both terms occur frequently in place-names as well as in charters. Several charters refer to 'heathen burials' but no such site has ever been excavated and to hazard a guess about the specific implications of this term would be mere supposition: some have thought that it might refer to the site of a pagan Anglo-Saxon burial in a flat grave, especially as the word *byrgels* or *byrgan* is often associated with a personal name, while others have tentatively identified some sites as groups of ancient barrows.[36]

Roads were often followed by boundaries and, as such, appear frequently in the boundary clauses. A made-up road appears to be suggested by the use of the term *stræt* while a *herepað* was also a major highway. In the Midlands many roads used by salt traders (see Figure 4 on p. 8 and Chapter 1) can be reconstructed from such evidence. Such routes often

Plate IX Stepping-stones, Meavy, Devon, the *cleaca* of the Anglo-Saxon charter?

crossed rivers and streams by fords but substantial bridges were being built in this period at a few major river crossing points. Most bridges referred to in the Worcestershire charters were often simple plank features across minor streams. A Devon charter contains what may be a surprising reference to *cleaca*, 'stepping stones', at a site where the River Meavy flowing down from Dartmoor runs through Meavy parish is still crossed by stepping stones today (Plate IX).

Literary associations are few. A Cornish charter for Lesneage in St Keverne refers to *hryt eselt*, 'Eselt's ford', in what may be a reference to the 'Eselt' of the Cornish legend of Tristan and Isolt, a legend known to be ancient,[37] but it may be more fanciful to see an early reference to the English outlaw Robin Hood in the reference to *hodes ac*, 'Hood's oak-tree', on the boundary of Dormston in mid-Worcestershire, a figure who does not otherwise appear in legend until the fifteenth century.[38]

It is not, however, in such isolated references that the real interest of the charter bounds lies. As shown in the case of the Evenlode charter discussed above, and as will be explored in subsequent chapters, they are a very rich source of topographical detail that can tell us a great deal about early medieval land use.

Notes

1. Sawyer, *Anglo-Saxon Charters*, S 1325; quoted from Birch, *Cartularium Saxonicum*, B 1238.
2. Stenton, *The Latin Charters*, pp.174–233.
3. Earle, *A Hand-Book to the Land-Charters*, pp.xv-xvi, 49–51.
4. Sawyer, *Anglo-Saxon Charters*, S 298.
5. Ibid., S 684; the original is in the library of the Exeter Dean and Chapter, 2522.
6. Chaplais, 'The authenticity of the royal Anglo-Saxon diplomas'.
7. Sawyer, *Anglo-Saxon Charters;* revised Kelly (1994).
8. Hill, *An Atlas of Anglo-Saxon England*, p.23.
9. Ibid., p.25.
10. Sawyer, *Anglo-Saxon Charters*, S 8; Birch, *Cartularium Saxonicum*, B 45.
11. Sawyer, ibid., S 23; Birch, ibid., B 148; Brooks, 'Romney Marsh', pp. 96–7, Fig. 8.5.
12. Sawyer, ibid., S 109; Birch, ibid., B 209.
13. Sawyer, ibid., S 1325; Birch, ibid., B 1238.
14. Round, 'Introduction to the Worcestershire Domesday', pp.253–4.
15. Sawyer, *Anglo-Saxon Charters*, S 1441; Birch, *Cartularium Saxonicum*, B 574.
16. Sawyer, ibid., S 103; Birch, ibid., B 164 (possibly a fabrication).
17. Sawyer, ibid., S 1460; Kemble, *Codex Diplomaticus Aevi Saxonici*, K 898, trans. Hooke, *Worcestershire Anglo-Saxon Charter-Bounds*, pp. 330–1.
18. Aldsworth, 'Parish boundaries on record'.

19. Hooke, *Anglo-Saxon Landscapes of the West Midlands*.
20. Hoskins, *Fieldwork in Local History*, p.36.
21. Hooke, *The Landscape of Anglo-Saxon Staffordshire*; *Worcestershire Anglo-Saxon Charter-Bounds*; *The Pre-Conquest Charter-Bounds of Devon and Cornwall*.
22. Sawyer, *Anglo-Saxon Charters*, S 1314; Hooke, *Worcestershire Anglo-Saxon Charter-Bounds*, pp.264–8.
23. Hickin, *The Natural History of an English Forest*, pp.14–20.
24. Nennius, *British History*, lxxiii, 70, p.16.
25. Sawyer, *Anglo-Saxon Charters*, S 311; Birch, *Cartularium Saxonicum*, B 476 (spurious).
26. Sawyer, ibid., S 60, S 1549; Birch, *Cartularium Saxonicum*, B 204; Heming, *Hemingi Chartularium*, pp.245–6.
27. Sawyer, ibid., S 79; Birch, *Cartularium Saxonicum*, B 124 (bounds probably ninth century).
28. Sawyer, ibid., S 60; Birch, ibid., B 204; Hooke, *Worcestershire Anglo-Saxon Charter-Bounds*, pp.65–9.
29. Hooke, '"Cada's minster", Broadway, Worcs.'; 'Two documented pre-Conquest Christian sites'; Woodward and Leach, *The Uley Shrines*.
30. Sawyer, *Anglo-Saxon Charters*, S 84; Birch, *Cartularium Saxonicum*, B 139 (bounds later than charter grant).
31. Sawyer, ibid., S 57; Birch, ibid., B 232.
32. Sawyer, ibid., S 1208; Birch, ibid., B 687; Gelling, *The Place-Names of Berkshire, III*, pp.686–9.
33. Sawyer, ibid., S 575; Birch, ibid., B 902; Gelling, ibid., pp.682–4.
34. Miles and Palmer, 'White Horse Hill'.
35. Hooke, 'Burial features'.
36. Kemble, 'Notices of heathen internment'.
37. Padel, 'The Cornish background of the Tristan stories'.
38. Hooke, *Worcestershire Anglo-Saxon Charter-Bounds*, pp.194–6; Holt, *Robin Hood*.

PART III

The Anglo-Saxon Landscape

CHAPTER 6

The Landscape of Settlement and Farming

Erce, Erce, Erce, mother of earth,
May the Almighty, the Lord everlasting, grant thee
Fields growing and flourishing,
Fruitful and reviving,
Store of gleaming millet-harvests,
And broad barley-crops,
and white wheat-crops,
And all the crops of the earth.[1]

To envisage the landscape of those regions which were most densely settled in Anglo-Saxon times we have to unpeel many layers of medieval and post-medieval development. Change has been enormous in modern times, particularly under the impetus of the expanding populations which followed the Agricultural and Industrial Revolutions. One has only to look at the first-edition Ordnance Survey maps produced in the 1830s or thereabouts to see how settlements and towns were then much smaller. In the rural countryside it was not only that the villages and hamlets were smaller but the houses themselves were smaller; they were often built in the materials of the locality so that they fitted more closely into the rural scene.

The geometric-shaped fields which characterized many crop-growing regions after Parliamentary Enclosure have also to be removed. Earlier, many parts of England would have been farmed under an open-field system which involved, in each township, the cultivation of strips of land dispersed amongst a small number of large fields which belonged to the entire community. Hedges were often absent although the large open fields themselves might be bounded in this way. If we were able to go back further in time, to the thirteenth century for instance, the amount of land cultivated under this system in the Midlands, eastern and south-central England would probably cover a greater area, for the enclosure of land in Tudor times for large-scale stock-rearing had not then taken place.

The open fields themselves, in some form, would have been present in many regions by the later Anglo-Saxon period and amidst them would have been the hamlets which preceded the later medieval villages. This in itself would have been a different landscape scene to that found earlier in the Anglo-Saxon period for this, too, was a period of profound change in many regions. At first farmsteads seem to have been scattered across the landscape as they had been in Roman times but the red-tiled villas of much of Roman Britain had long since crumbled into decay. Instead, houses would have been built largely of timber and thatch. In upland regions widespread use was made of turf as a building material: for peasant dwellings the use of stone for other than wall foundations seems to have been a thirteenth-century development.

Changing Settlement Patterns

Many regions have so far failed to provide the concrete evidence required to understand early settlement patterns. In some regions this is because the type of houses built left little permanent trace once abandoned. In regions where pottery was widely used and can be relatively closely dated, settlement sites can be identified by scatters of sherds surviving in the plough soil, but much Anglo-Saxon pot was of a friable nature and is not easy to detect.[2] In many regions pottery seems hardly to have been used by the ordinary peasant and to have been virtually restricted to palace- or equally high-ranking sites. Simple earthenware pottery can also be difficult to date. Sunken-floored buildings can sometimes be detected on air photographs, as at Maxey in Cambridgeshire,[3] since the dampness of the below-ground section can affect the strength and colour of growing crops; grain over the damper areas of the house-floors ripens more slowly and shows as darker circles on air photographs at certain seasons. Pagan cemeteries may also be an indicator of lost settlement sites somewhere in the vicinity for 'finds' of skeletons and grave goods have always excited interest and the remains of the dead have sometimes made a greater impression than those of the living.

Where pottery scatters have been intensively studied, as in parts of eastern England and the East Midlands, they confirm that in the earlier centuries of the Anglo-Saxon period the settlement pattern remained largely dispersed, even in regions later characterized by nucleated villages. Thus, small clusters of dwellings were often scattered throughout estates where settlement was later to become nucleated at some focal point, including locations on marginal land or near boundaries. Some parishes have been found to contain as many as nine or ten tiny settlement clusters, although these were not always, or even usually, on the similarly scattered sites of earlier occupation. Chris Taylor notes the examples of Brixworth and Great Doddington in Northamptonshire.[4] Some hamlets were short-lived and 'settlement drift' was as much a feature of this period as of earlier ones. It was to remain a tendency throughout the period in which buildings were impermanent and easily reconstructed. Little is known about the farming methods of those who occupied these scattered hamlets but it is generally believed that they continued to farm the field systems of Roman Britain, only gradually modifying these over a long period.[5]

In spite of the problems of identification, an increasing number of hamlets are being identified. At West Stow in Suffolk the assemblage of buildings of fifth- to seventh-century date appears to represent the same three farmsteads which progressively shifted their position in the course of the two and a half centuries in which they were occupied.[6] Many buildings have been reconstructed at this site, which is open to visitors. Another site at Catholme in the Trent valley of Staffordshire seems to have consisted at any one time of five or six farmsteads (although some have suggested eight) which were continually rebuilt over a period of four hundred years and lasted from just before AD 500 to a little after AD 900, the period when the Danes were attacking the region. Here buildings were grouped into several separate enclosures but the settlement showed no overall regular plan.[7]

It is now possible to recognize a style of Anglo-Saxon building which was as distinctive as the more familiar techniques of later periods.[8] Many early settlements possessed a number of sunken-floored buildings, which were simple constructions of timber and thatch in which a below-ground section was either floored over and used as a cellar or left uncovered. For many occupations ancillary to every-day living these would have been useful workshops and many appear to have been used as weaving sheds, etc. One of the earliest sites excavated, at Mucking beside the Thames, was established during the transition stage between AD 410 and 450 and occupied at least to the beginning of the eighth century. Here, over 200 sunken huts have been identified.[9]

Few excavated settlements of the fifth to eighth centuries, however, were without larger rectangular buildings which provided the main living quarters. At Mucking some 53 post-hole buildings have been identified, most of them in the later contexts as the settlement shifted north-eastwards from its original position.[10] In general, analysis suggests that such buildings increased in number and in size as the period progressed. Built on a variation of a regular plan they often had a door midway along the longer side with subdivisions within, sometimes with an annexe at one or both ends (Figure 36). Hearths would have been centrally placed but much of

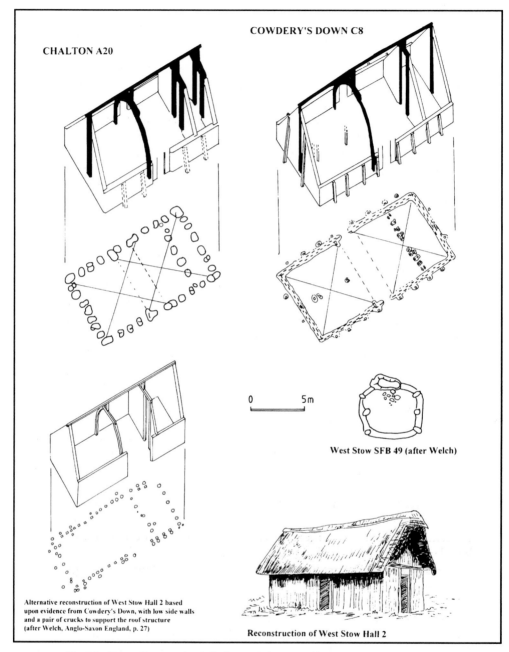

Fig. 36 House plans: timber halls from Chalton, Cowdery's Down and West Stow (after Welch 1992) with an illustration of one of the buildings from the latter village. The plan of one of the West Stow *grubenhäuser* is inserted for comparison (after West 1985). The symmetry of the hall plans follows the analysis of James, *et al.* (1984).

the cooking would have been carried out either outside or in separate kitchens. Outlying huts may have provided more private sleeping quarters for women and children but it is likely that retainers slept in the communal house. From excavation it can be shown that such buildings were constructed in substantial earth-fast foundations and were far from the flimsy constructions once thought to characterize this period.

Some have expressed surprise that the dwellings of these early settlements appear so poverty-stricken, in contrast with the grave goods not infrequently found in early Anglo-Saxon burials. But it must be queried whether archaeology – at least in the climatic conditions prevailing in this country – can generally discover those symbols of wealth which are least likely to have survived. If our present houses had to be reconstructed from ground evidence over 1,000 years later one wonders how faithfully the archaeological ground evidence would express the comforts of modern living. In particular, rugs and textiles would most certainly have disappeared without trace except in very exceptional climatic or environmental conditions. To consider the part such goods play in the domestic life of a so-called 'primitive' society one has only to consider the sumptuous rugs which drape the tents of some Bedouin tribes today, or those of the Afghan yurt, and note the exceptionally fine textiles discovered with very early burials in the South American deserts. The products of Anglo-Saxon weaving looms may not necessarily have been so exotic but, together with cured skins and fleeces, they may have provided much in the way of comfort and decoration.

At a high-ranking site on Cowdery's Down in Hampshire[11] the evidence was sufficiently well preserved to show that timber superstructures were based on deeply founded but low timber walls. One possible reconstruction argues that the roofs had tall gables and a central ridge-piece and were supported largely by the walls with cruck blades less substantial than in later timber-framed buildings. In some, free-standing internal timbers, probably combined with some sort of kingpost, helped to support the central ridge. A settlement at Chalton,[12] also on the Hampshire downland, comprised similar rectangular houses 9 metres by 5 metres more in area (Figure 36), with just a few outlying sunken-floored buildings. These larger buildings were directly derived from neither a Germanic or a Roman tradition, rather, they seem to represent a hybrid technique.[13] Perhaps Germanic immigrants used their own constructional techniques to copy the substantial earlier buildings of Roman Britain but it is also possible that native builders imitated the fashions of their conquerors, just as they appear to have done with pottery styles and jewellery. A favoured building technique seems to have been stave building which employed vertical uprights, possibly linked with a simple tongue and

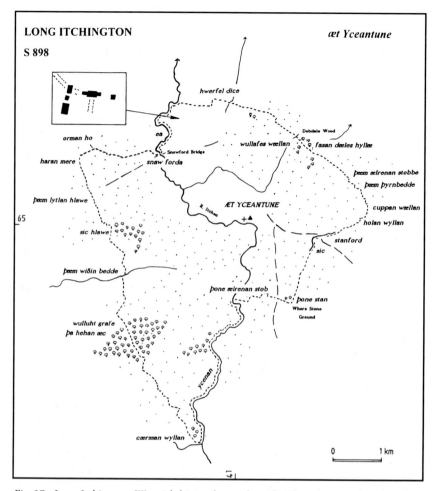

Fig. 37 Long Itchington, Warwickshire: palace and parish. The palace site, known only from crop-mark evidence, bears no relation to present-day patterns of settlement and communications

groove method, or, alternatively, wider spaced vertical supports with horizontal planks set between them (bulwark construction). In both cases the vertical posts were set into the earth. Although oak was the dominant timber used, the life of each individual home would seldom be longer than 15–20 years.[14] Later techniques become more varied with an increasing use of sill beams and a move towards the fuller framed buildings of later periods.

Most early rural settlements that have been identified probably consisted of individual farmsteads, singly or in small clusters, each with its own farmyard. This was also the characteristic type of settlement on the

Continent but in this country the gentler climate meant that sophisticated animal stalls were largely unnecessary. The large byre houses recognized at Feddersen Wierde or Bremerhaven, needed to over-winter stock, are not found here.

Every age has had its superior dwellings and the Anglo-Saxon period was no exception. Long ranges of timbered buildings have been identified from cropmarks and excavated evidence. These seem to have been palaces or large halls. Some were located on royal estates, others seem to have belonged to the Church or the aristocracy. Since they lacked the wall-stone and tiled roofs which characterized many earlier villa systems, only a limited number have yet been discovered but it is likely that many more remain to be found. Any royal estate upon which charters were signed by a visiting king is an obvious candidate for such a building. Many of those that have been located lay in the open countryside rather than in the middle of later villages (Figure 37) but others may well have been lost, like the majority of buildings of this period, beneath the dwellings of later periods. An outstanding example of a royal palace site is Yeavering in Northumbria, first occupied in the time of King Edwin (AD 617–33) when this kingdom was supreme in England. Here a complex of buildings which included a temple or church were associated with a large rectangular hall.[15] A similar complex was excavated at Cheddar, in the West Country, where a bow-shaped long hall was later replaced by a more regular rectangular structure in the tenth century.[16]

It is generally believed that the dispersed settlement pattern found in parts of south-western England may stem from an early date. In parts of Cornwall, for instance, farmsteads bearing names which incorporate Cornish *tre*, 'estate, farmstead', are scattered through the ancient settled regions at a density similar to that of the Roman 'rounds' which preceded them, some of which undoubtedly enclosed hamlets occupied into the sixth century.[17] Where detailed surveys have been possible, however, such as that carried out by the Cornwall Archaeology Unit at Trenithan Bennett, using the evidence of air photographs, discontinuity is apparent between the settlement sites and the field patterns of late Roman and medieval times.[18] In Devon, too, detailed field investigation coupled with site excavation has failed to uncover early material from individual farm or hamlet sites even when these bore a type of place-name recorded in the pre-Conquest period. In other words, the settlement pattern of some western regions may have remained dispersed into medieval times but site continuity has yet to be proved anywhere.

Even where early settlements have been found in appreciable clusters there is little indication of the deliberate planning of roads and house tofts (Figure 38). Perhaps the earliest evidence of a more regular plan comes

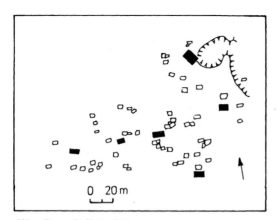

West Stow, Suffolk (C6)

Wicken Bonhunt, Essex

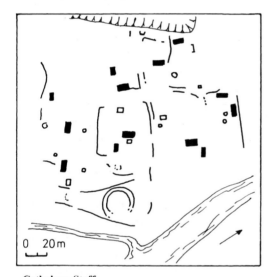

Catholme, Staffs

Fig. 38 Settlement plans; little deliberate settlement orientation is suggested at West Stow or Catholme but elements of planning are suggested at Wicken Bonhunt. (a) West Stow: Phase 2 (after Welch 1992 and West 1985), the sixth-century settlement. *Grubenhäuser* surround a number of timber halls; each hall-based cluster probably represents a farm unit. (b) Catholme: Phase 2 (after Welch 1992) dated to between the seventh and eighth centuries; ditched, hedged and fenced enclosures demarcate farm units of rectangular buildings with a few *grubenhäuser*. (c) Wicken Bonhunt (after Wade 1980). Several phases shown here date from the middle of the seventh century. Buildings are grouped closely together along the western margin of the settlement, the western ditch probably replacing the eastern ditch as the settlement expanded westward.

from two sites in eastern England: North Elmham in Norfolk and Wicken Bonhunt in Essex,[19] which seem to show evidence of deliberate settlement planning by the late sixth or early seventh century. The latter may have been a royal vill[20] and it is possible that planning may have been most readily attained on a royal or high-ranking estate. Evidence of regular subdivision has also been archaeologically attested at West Cotton in Raunds, Northamptonshire. However, it has not yet been tied to individual building plots but to a late Saxon timbered building.[21]

Farming Systems

Throughout the difficult generations following the Anglo-Saxon take-over the land had to be continuously farmed. Although cereal production may have lessened once the Roman towns and the army no longer required provisions, much of the landscape remained open and used for pasture.[22] There is little evidence of any deterioration in the quality of domestic livestock under the Anglo-Saxons and the heavy ploughs used in many areas in Roman times remained available for crop cultivation. The lighter ard plough probably continued in use on some lighter soils but with increasing use being made of the heavier plough on lowland clays – the soils which appear to have continued under the most intensive usage. This type of plough had already been available in Roman Britain and may have been a factor in the perceived increase in the size of fields in some areas.[23]

Fields in general seem to have been enclosed with ditches, banks or hedges but to have been of varying size. In some regions a regular geometric pattern of squarish fields which still underlies the present field pattern seems to date back at least to the Roman period. It shows well in photographs of the Dengie peninsula of Essex and beneath later open-field furlongs in the Vale of the White Horse in Oxfordshire (where it may have been associated with Roman villa estates).[24] Elsewhere the smaller, rectangular 'Celtic' fields of native farming persisted (see Figure 42 and Plate XI on pp. 124, 125). Many on more marginal lands were abandoned and survived as earthworks below pasture, especially upon the English downlands. There are suggestions that one of the oldest fieldscapes surviving today is that of West Penwith, the furthermost peninsula of Cornwall, where the fields associated with Roman farmsteads still form a part of the present pattern. Elsewhere in Cornwall, as in the coastal district of the north coast around Tintagel, field analysis suggests that a pattern of rectilinear fields may have been characteristic in early medieval times, perhaps incorporating the framework of an earlier system.[25]

Plate X Water meadows at Shepreth near Cambridge. Meadows for hay were an essential part of the early medieval agrarian economy. Here the medieval meadows are no longer managed in the traditional way for they are now grazed at all seasons but the willows are once again being pollarded.

Perhaps the greatest change to the landscape of Anglo-Saxon England was that associated with the introduction of open field agriculture. This did not affect all regions but was most influential in the richer crop-growing regions of England. The system infiltrated beyond such regions, however, and is documented in the lightly settled woodland regions of Arden in Warwickshire, for instance, and as far afield as central Cornwall. Systems might vary in character but common ownership is a component of all of them, a cooperative system rather than one based upon individual farms and holdings.

There is little evidence of how land was organized under Roman rule and at least one writer[26] has believed that the changes which took place in early medieval times might have been rooted in a more distant past. Common ownership of land seems to be evident at an early stage, documented in the Laws of Ine in seventh-century Wessex, but common ownership could be based upon kin groups, as in medieval Wales, or upon a whole township or village community. In general, communal land holding frequently gave rise to the fragmentation of holdings, although in some societies this could be limited by regular reallocation of land. In Wales the most intensive form of land allotment amongst a village community seems to have been associated with the more servile tenures of the royal *maerdref* where the community had to support the regular visits of the king and his court.[27] It is interesting that settlement planning, closely associated with the deliberate organization of land holding, seems to be first evident in some royal vills in England.[28] Whatever the origins of the system, the same processes appear to have been taking place on the Continent at a similar date.

This period of reorganization was to completely change the face of English settlement and farming in many regions of England. The way in which open field agriculture, as such a system is called, replaced any earlier system is not documented and, to date, we have not been able to fathom the early origins of the system, but by the late ninth and tenth centuries nucleated settlements at the core of several large open arable fields were gradually replacing earlier scattered farmsteads. The change may have occurred abruptly on some estates, perhaps reflecting deliberate planning; elsewhere there is evidence that outlying farmsteads only decayed over a long period of time. The process was far from complete at the time of the Norman Conquest. In some regions, common ownership was restricted to the inhabitants of individual farm-estates or yokes, as suggested by the evidence from south-eastern England, or to the more restricted kinship holdings of medieval Wales: very different systems are found across the country by the time that the evidence becomes clearer.

One of the oldest features of any open field community appears to be the organization of common pasture on the waste, perhaps a direct inheritance from a past in which this was the traditional way of intercommoning seasonal and wood-pasture regions (see Chapters 3 and 7). The common herd also grazed that part of the arable that was left fallow, thus ensuring its continued fertility. The arable, however, also belonged to the community and only after ploughing did the peasants take over individual responsibility for managing their strips, which were scattered throughout the large open fields of the township. Once the harvest was in, the entire field was once again thrown open for grazing. Meadowland along streams and rivers, valuable for the hay crop needed as winter fodder, was also doled out annually for cutting but grazed communally in the winter season (Plate X).

In the west and other upland regions, in medieval times, we find a simple infield system in which a relatively restricted area of common field was subdivided into strips but kept under permanent cultivation by the generous application of manure. Beyond lay the common grazings but parts of these could be intermittently ploughed and cultivated as the need arose. In parts of eastern England, on the other hand, enormously long strips, often over a kilometre in length, extended from the village core to the boundaries of the township, the individual holdings often laid out in a regular pattern which might reflect the layout of tofts in the village itself. In midland England, however, the pattern of furlongs and parcels of strips seems generally to have been more closely related to the topography and it is in these regions, too, that there is evidence of outlying farms and fields in Anglo-Saxon times, referred to in charter boundary landmarks or known from habitative type field-names, which were only later abandoned, their lands subsequently becoming incorporated into the extended open fields. In marginal zones fields were smaller but more numerous and often less rigorously organized. In general, the open fields appear to have been laid out across land that was already open and cultivated in Roman times and in some valley regions of southern England it seems unlikely that the land which was to remain under cultivation ever went out of use. Even the earliest boundaries in such areas have to zig-zag around pre-existing field systems (see Chapter 4).

As the area of open field in regions of relatively high populations had to be extensive, either at the time of origin or later, so the proportion of land available for common grazing diminished and additional pasture had to be found. It would have become difficult to keep all the land adequately manured with the stock that could be kept on the remaining commons, even if animals were allowed onto the stubble after harvest, and it may have been these factors which led to the introduction of a period of fallow on one of the open fields each year. The importance of population increase in the organization of the open field system has been propounded by Joan Thirsk.[29] In particular, she argues that the acreage under the plough in the more fertile areas seem to have been extended at the expense of common pasture until the latter was in dangerously short supply. To overcome this in medieval times, part of the cultivated land was thrown open after the harvest for grazing, a system which required close cooperation between all members of the community to ensure that harvesting was carried out in a specific period. A system of disordered fields would permit little agreement upon a fallowing system and Thirsk believed that it was this need for cooperation which led to a redistribution of land and the introduction of a system 'in which all tenants shared common rights in all fields'.[30] This theory provides a reason for the reorganization of earlier more irregular, multi-field systems but does not explain the origins of the common field.

While farming techniques such as an increased use of the heavier type plough might influence field size and methods of ploughing, it is unlikely they would lead to the total reorganization of field layout. It seems that more fundamental economic or social reasons must be sought to explain why such changes occurred and we find, indeed, that the process coincided with the major administrative changes that were taking place towards the end of the mid-Anglo-Saxon period, changes which were extended over as long a period as the changes in fields and settlement patterns. It is difficult to avoid the observation that large-scale reorganization went hand in hand, not only with settlement nucleation, but with estate fragmentation, occurring as the newly independent small estates came under firm manorial control and were under pressure to increase both their self-sufficiency and their revenues. Each minor lord was under pressure to increase the estate revenues available to provide for his family and retainers, his taxes and the tithe required by the Church. Farming had often to produce an agricultural surplus that could be sold for profit. Moreover, the old framework of the multiple estate had by now been almost completely dismembered. The loss of pastureland noted by Thirsk may have resulted as much from the loss of distant grazings as from the extension of arable land.[31] Discussing estate subdivision as a factor in agricultural cooperation in early medieval Hampshire, Klingelhöfer comments:

> As the farmers forged new links to create the village community, so earlier links were severed. Villages and their lands were economically independent of the larger territorial unit . . . and of each other. The valley-wide land use of arable, pasture, and woodland was replaced by a land use based on the vill.[32]

It is likely that it was these pressures which contributed to change the face of Anglo-Saxon farming and to extend the notion of a regularly planned field system across the land. Changes in field layout seem to have been accompanied by increasing nucleation of settlement and Higham[33] has argued that farmers were brought into a central settlement in order to achieve greater efficiency and thus to permit the production of a surplus of agricultural commodities. He suggests that the number of plough oxen could be kept to a minimum if farms were located in a central village.

The sharing of land in intermingled strips, apparently common to all systems, might arise from a number of factors: the need for communal ploughing[34] and communal woodland clearance leading to a common system of land ownership;[35] the need for safety in resource management, with equally shared risks within a given area and equal opportunities for procuring a good harvest;[36] the need to have fair and equal access to land manured by the common flock.[37] The reason for this subdivision and fragmentation of holdings is perhaps the most difficult feature of the open

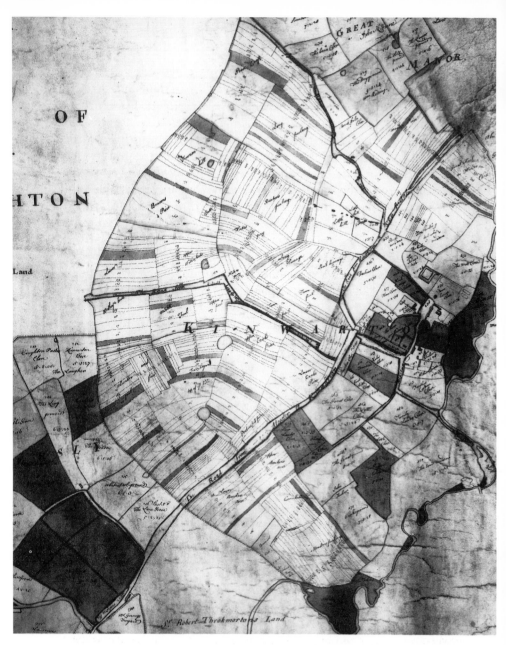

Fig. 39 Medieval open field in midland England: the parish of Kinwarton, Warwickshire, shortly before enclosure on an estate map of 1754. Although the fields immediately around the home farm have been enclosed, most of the arable remained in strips until the mid-eighteenth century. Roads make their way around the open-field furlongs and the deserted site of the medieval moated manor-house, with related fish-ponds, can be seen at the northern end of the village ('A map of the estates belonging to the Rt Hon Earl Brooke in Alcester, Oversley, Great Aln and Kinwarton in 1754', Warwick County Record Office CR 1886 M9).

field system to understand, and one that has interested scholars for many decades, for although the peasants had to cooperate to plough the land, for the period of sowing, weeding and harvesting they were solely responsible for their allocated strips, however separated these were across the township area. While Dahlman and Kerridge[38] rightly stress the importance of fair access to the manured land, one might also query whether fair *time* of access to the prepared land might also have been important. Ploughing was a winter activity but in a relatively large township all the land may not have been ready for sowing at the same time. Given the apparent ratio of plough teams to ploughlands noted in Domesday Book, there must have been enormous pressure upon those ploughing to have had the land ready for sowing, especially in the spring, and if any had to wait until ploughing was complete this would inevitably leave them more vulnerable to inclement weather conditions and a possible late harvest.

The extent of the fields themselves reflected the size of the village or hamlet communities. By medieval times agricultural pursuits were organized through the manorial court. To give some indication of the appearance of open field, Figure 39 shows a small midland township in the mid-eighteenth century prior to enclosure. Some enclosure had already taken place around the home farm and the decayed village but the greater part of the township still lay under open field. The map clearly shows strip holdings, those shaded being the glebe lands of the rector, and access ways between the fields, some of which were to disappear entirely upon enclosure, a process carried out in this particular township – Kinwarton in Warwickshire – by private agreement rather than by parliamentary act.

There is little consensus of debate upon how the system was introduced. While subdivision might arise naturally through a system of partible inheritance, the system as we know it requires considerable community organization. While some feel that the change to the system originated among the peasantry themselves others feel that overlordship must have been an influential agent of change. The system certainly becomes apparent in the documents as territories themselves were being subdivided between minor lords and as concepts of estate ownership evolve. In parts of Central Europe such as the Czech Republic the system was only introduced in medieval times and was well documented. Here, overlordship was unquestionably involved. One has also only to look at events this century to see how rapidly collectivization under a strong central authority can transform both field and settlement patterns. The peasantry themselves may have welcomed a change leading to increased prosperity but it would seem unlikely that they initiated change. The way that landholding in the newly emerging manors necessitated ways of calibrating land has been thoroughly investigated by Dodgshon.[39]

The more organized and extensive systems seem to have involved a greater degree of deliberate planning, and arrangements in the fields in such regions were often linked to the increasing nucleation of settlement. There may have been additional factors involved which speeded up such settlement nucleation: strongly nucleated settlements were not only more easily defended but their lords could more easily wield control over their peasantry. After the Norman Conquest the castle villages of the Welsh Borderland show these considerations at work. Comparison with other types of settlement agglomeration in later periods like, for instance, the fortified town, shows the greater control nucleation gave to a manorial lord, a control less rigidly exercised in many pastoral regions where dispersed settlement patterns persisted.[40] The new church foundations of the tenth and eleventh centuries also provided foci within individual estates which might attract further dwellings near by. It is important to remember, however, that nucleation was not achieved at the same time all over the country, or even completed until well after the Norman Conquest.

Such reorganization, in midland and south-central England, at least, appears to have taken place within the individual township unit, the forerunner of the Domesday manor. This, in itself, indicates that it came into effect with the fragmentation of larger estates which is so clearly evident in pre-Conquest charters. This seems to support the view that the motive behind reorganization might indeed be the wish to improve the efficiency and revenues of the individual manor which depended upon arable cultivation. With the break-up of larger estate units, such self-sufficiency was now enforced within the limitations of the individual manor or township community.

The way that the latter operated as a self-contained unit in the newly emerging attitudes to property and tenure of Anglo-Saxon England is reflected in the pattern of individual estates which attempted to include arable, meadow and pasture within their boundaries. If one or more of these components was insufficient, they might be linked to detached parcels of land elsewhere. In general, such parcels would lie within the boundaries of the larger initial unit and within the holding of the overall lord, as shown in Chapter 4 (see Figure 28 on p. 75). By the tenth and eleventh centuries these smaller units can be seen to become increasingly independent of the capital manor. By the time of the Norman Conquest some estates or manors had become so fragmented that many were little more than individual farms, operating with only the minimum number of labourers. Costen[41] has suggested similar late Saxon dates for estate break-up in Somerset, with new fields and settlements being established together in one period of replanning.

It is noteworthy that the change concerned only major crop-growing regions and did not affect those where farming was of a predominantly pastoral nature to anything like the same degree. Although open field methods operated to a limited extent in some more pastoral regions, they seldom developed into the sophisticated systems of the primarily arable regions and in many areas, like Devon, were already disappearing before detailed documentation.

The Written Documentation

In examining the written sources, the earliest documentary evidence of open field farming appears in the charters of central and southern England. These suggest that the system was becoming widespread in that area by the late ninth century. This coincides with the period of estate fragmentation discussed in Chapter 3.

What did such changes involve? According to the charter evidence, on estates where reorganization had taken place the arable land was communally owned but farmed in the dispersed strip holdings familiar to medievalists. A mid-tenth-century charter relating to Avon in Durnsford, Wiltshire, states that the arable consisted of *singulis iugeribus mixtum in communi rure huc illacque dispersis,* 'single acres dispersed in a mixture here and there in common land',[42] while at Charlton, Berkshire, in AD 982 the five hides granted by King Æthelred to his minister Ælfgar were 'not demarcated on all sides by clear bounds because to left and right lie acres in combination one with another': *Rus namque prætaxatum manifestis undique terminis minus diuiditur, quia iugera altrinsecus copulata adiacent* (as earlier, in AD 956).[43] Meadowland was similarly divided into doles, probably held in proportion to the individual's arable holding. In medieval times this often involved the drawing of lots annually for ownership of the individual doles. Another Berkshire charter of AD 961 for an estate which may have been Ardington in West Ginge notes that the system also included common of pasture: *þas nigon hida licggead on ge mang oþran ge dal lande feld læs gemane 7 mæda ge mane 7 yrþ land gemæne,* 'these nine hides lie intermingled with other lands held in shares: open pasture common, and meadow common, and ploughland common'.[44]

There is ample evidence to show that open field arable was a common component of estate management in central and southern England by the tenth century. Charter evidence is less well preserved for eastern

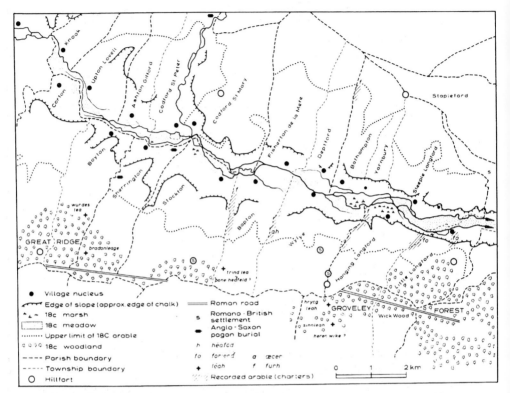

Fig. 40   The Wylye valley to the west of Wilton in Wiltshire showing the bands of differing land use suggested by the pre-Conquest charter evidence. Meadows and marsh occupied part of the flood plain of the river, the lower slopes of the downs were cultivated, and most of the upper slopes formed open pasture land; some woodland regeneration had occurred along the watershed between the Wylye and Nadder valleys.

England but a charter for Newbald in Yorkshire also clearly relates to lands lying in 'every other acre' by this date.[45] The twelfth-century *Liber Eliensis*, using evidence from earlier vernacular documents, suggests that subdivided strips were also present at Brandon in the Breckland of Suffolk.[46]

In Chapter 4 mention was made of the regular pattern of estate subdivision which characterizes some valley areas of southern England, particularly in the chalklands. In the Wylye valley of Wiltshire estate boundaries known to have been demarcated by late Anglo-Saxon times run down from the downland watersheds to north and south as far as the river itself, dividing the valley into a series of parallel estates, each incorporating valley meadowland, arable on the lower slopes and pastureland above (Figure 40). The nature of the land use can be accurately established from the type of landmarks recorded in the boundary clauses

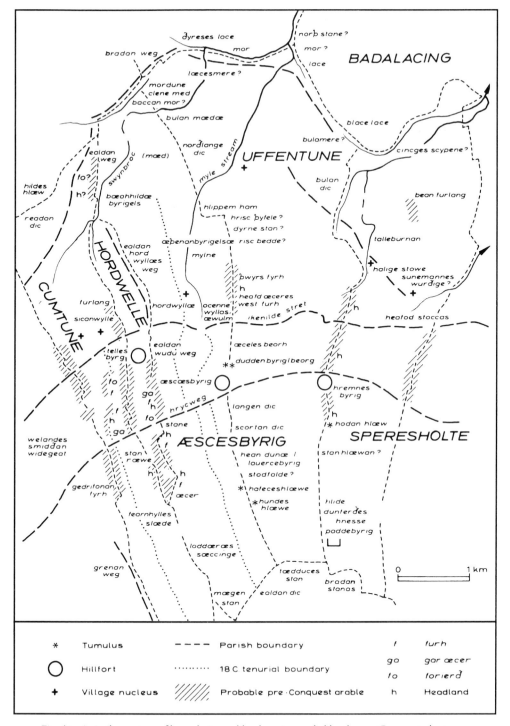

Fig. 41 A similar pattern of boundaries and land use is revealed by the pre-Conquest charter evidence for estates in the Vale of the White Horse (formerly in Berkshire but now in Oxfordshire).

of the region. A similar pattern is represented in the Vale of the White Horse where an extraordinary amount of charter detail is available (Figure 41). It is also quite clear from some of the charters that the land under arable in these regions was being cultivated by open field methods by the tenth century.

A greater area of land in both these valley regions had been cultivated in Roman times but the charter evidence suggests that the upper downland had been abandoned as crop-growing land, the landmarks being either natural features or archaeological remains. This land provided the essential pastureland necessary for domestic stock. Between the Nadder and Wylye there had also been woodland regeneration for the charters refer to *leah* landmarks in the area later known as Great Ridge Wood and the Groveley Forest. Indeed, the field boundaries of Celtic fields, used as late as the fourth century AD, clearly survived until

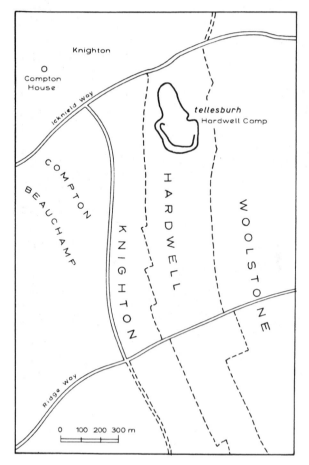

Fig. 42 Key to air photograph in Plate XI (from Hooke 1988).

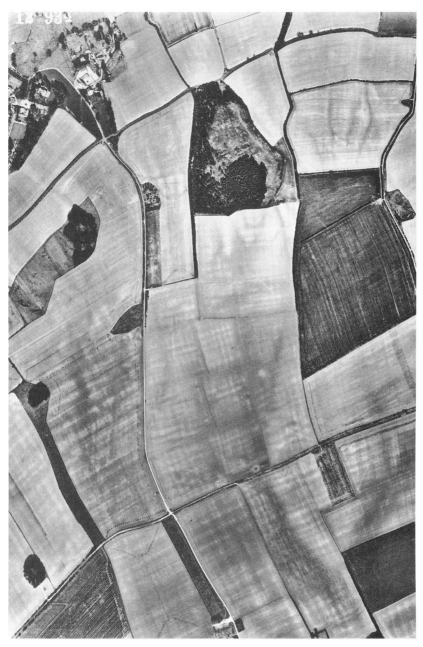

Plate XI   Field systems in the Vale of the White Horse: a system of square-shaped fields is revealed by cropmarks underlying the ridge and furrow of the later medieval open fields. The angular turns of the Hardwell–Compton Beauchamp boundary appear to have been influenced by the earlier layout. © Berkshire Co. Council, Clyde Surveys Ltd.

recent times, untouched by any subsequent ploughing. The (?)Roman fields below, however, were to influence the shape of later open field furlongs and it is unlikely that the land on the lower slopes ever went out of production. The boundaries themselves often make right-angled bends around the pre-existing fields and an air photograph of land near the boundary of Compton Beauchamp in the Vale of White Horse (Figure 42, Plate XI) shows such a boundary making its way around large square fields which certainly pre-dated the open-field furlongs and seem to have been related to a droveway (not visible on the photograph) which bore no relationship to the Anglo-Saxon or later estate boundaries and was also presumably earlier (this type of field has not so far been recognized in the Wylye valley where the smaller rectangular 'Celtic' fields seem to have continued in use to the end of the Roman period). This boundary in AD 903 was described as running to *anne gar æcer on an on hæfde . . . þonone andlanges anre fyrh oð hit cymð to anum byge. þanone of þæm byge forð on ane fyrh oð hit cymð to anre forierðe . . . þon' on icenhilde weg be tellesburh westan*, thus running to a 'gore acre', a 'head (of a plough strip)', a 'furrow', a 'bend', another 'furrow' and a feature called a *forierð*,[47] probably a headland at the end of plough strips, obviously following an irregular course even at this early date.

This example illustrates some of the terms used to denote arable features in charter boundary clauses. The term *æcer* was often used to refer to ploughed land, itself called *earðland*. Its usage seems to indicate strip holdings for these features could have 'heads' and 'ends', and, as such, the term could also be used for doles of meadowland. It obviously implied a notional size but this may not have been standard until a much later date. In late medieval times the acre-strip measured some 22 yards by 220 yards but was based initially on the amount of land one ox-team could plough in a day.[48] The word *furlang* was already in use and was probably both a unit of measurement and a bundle of acre-strips, finally standardized as 220 yards by 220 yards. The *fyrh*, 'furrow', appears to have been produced by the plough as a division within ploughland although it would be difficult at this stage to be sure that it was associated with ridge and furrow methods of ploughing the land.[49] This method of ploughing was commonly used in open fields to cast the soil into long linear ridges separated by furrows which both demarcated strips and assisted drainage. It is still clearly visible in many parts of the country and continued in use in clay regions even after open field farming had ceased. The ploughs were drawn by teams of oxen and there are many references to these animals in the charters. A Worcestershire charter of Himbleton refers to 'the ploughland as the ox turns' [50] and several Somerset charters refer to 'ox fields'.

By the time of these charters the fields were, then, probably organized under an open field system and related to a settlement at the core of each estate unit. In these two valley regions the settlements usually lay at the foot of the downland between the arable and the lower meadows, conveniently placed at or near the point at which springs issued from the chalk. Today they might be represented by a single farm or a hamlet. In one case in the Vale, either two existing hamlets joined or one new settlement was established when an eminent *thegn*, Wulfric, acquired two adjacent holdings within a division earlier known as 'Ashbury', and the resulting village became known as *Olvricestune*, 'Wulfric's *tun*', today Woolstone. The next village to the east, Uffington, lies much further to the north than the other settlements, on the lower land, and is likely to be of much later origin, possibly representing a planned settlement established by Abingdon Abbey. The present size and shapes of the individual villages have been decided by their later fortunes, a number of single large houses like that at Compton Beauchamp probably replacing an earlier hamlet.

Regional Variation

The ultimate degree of planning is that which has been identified in eastern England where long strips were laid out which extended from a central village to the boundaries of individual estates. Sometimes these were over one kilometre in length and occupied the greater part of a township area (Figure 43). At present no precise date can be given for the origin of this system with suggested dates extending from the eighth to the thirteenth centuries.[51] Reorganization of previous regularly planned systems cannot be entirely ruled out nor the fact that this type of organization appears to be most in evidence in regions colonized by the Danes. Some scholars, like David Hall,[52] believe that this most organized pattern of settlement and field furlongs dates from the very origins of the system and is older than the more complex patterns found in midland regions; others see it as a late reorganization which did not spread to more western regions, but only archaeology will one day provide accurate dating.

Settlement nucleation, which seems to have been closely related to the reorganization of agriculture, does not seem to have occurred quickly and may have been an on-going process for several centuries in many areas. In one of the classic 'champion' areas, the Vale of Evesham in Worcester-shire, the villages may have come into being by the tenth century but charter boundary clauses of late Anglo-Saxon date show that outlying farmsteads and hamlets still survived (Figure 44). These had disappeared

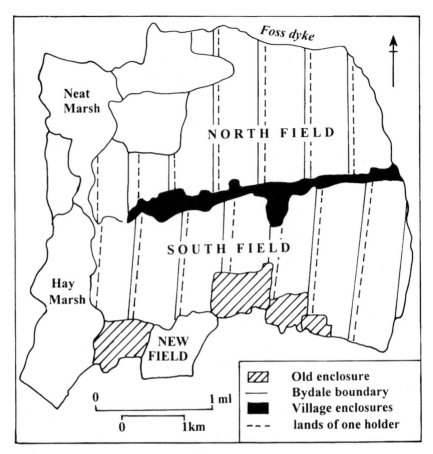

Fig. 43   Long strip cultivation in Holderness, Yorkshire: the field structure of Preston in 1750, showing the approximate location of Chantry lands (after Harvey 1981).

entirely by the medieval period, leaving no trace in the documents or on the ground. An Evesham charter refers to *Poticot*, otherwise known as *Potintun*, near the boundary of Bengeworth, and to *Bunewyrpe* upon the boundary of Church Honeybourne. A farmstead known as *Byrdingcwican* lay upon the boundary of Elmley Castle.[53] Tenth-century charters referring to crofts as landmarks also suggest that some enclosed land lay beyond the open fields in the later Anglo-Saxon period although it was to be incorporated into the latter by medieval times.[54]

Beyond the regions of nucleated villages a dispersed settlement pattern of hamlets and farms characterized much of the rest of the country and was probably the dominant settlement pattern of the period, although it has until recently received rather less attention from archaeologists. Hamlets were often associated with manorial nuclei and small open field

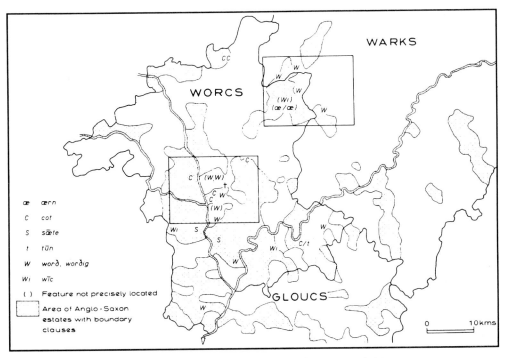

Fig. 44 Outlying settlements near boundaries, Worcestershire, as recorded in pre-Conquest charter boundaries.

systems were to penetrate through Devon into Cornwall and also into the woodland regions of the rest of the country. There were also the isolated farms which will be discussed in the next chapter. The more dispersed settlement pattern seems to have characterized regions where farming was predominantly pastoral, for here settlement nucleation offered few practical advantages; these regions will be discussed in subsequent chapters. Although common fields were present to a limited extent, infield/outfield systems seem to have characterized parts of the South-West. Charter evidence may show the practice of outfield cultivation in Devon in the later Anglo-Saxon period when a tenth-century charter of Ayshford in Burlescombe and Boehill in Sampford Peverill granted by King Eadwig noted that 'here outside the common pasture is [the] street, whence there are many hills which one may plough'.[55] This was a feature, generally, of areas of sparse population and was found throughout Britain in such regions (see, further, Chapter 8).[56]

Beyond the major zones of arable farming, therefore, open fields seldom developed into the sophisticated systems recognized in the medieval Midlands and those fields which did exist were often disappearing before detailed documentation. In general, the differences seem to be initially ones of degree, as the simple model reproduced in Figure 45 indicates, but the changes in farming methods experienced in the later part of the Anglo-Saxon period probably enhanced regional variation in settlement patterns and their related field systems.

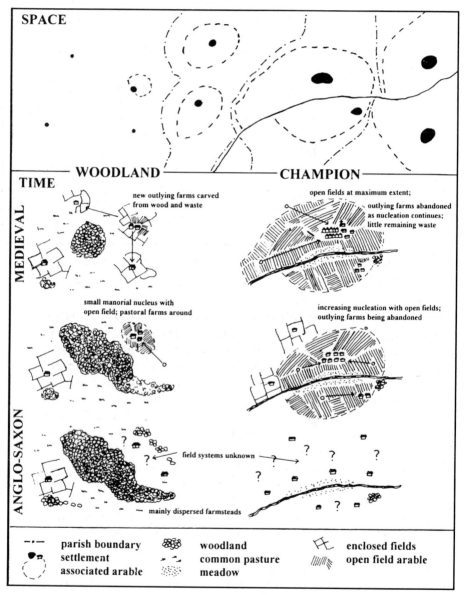

Fig. 45   Simple settlement model in midland England.

Later Anglo-Saxon Settlement Patterns

The evidence of Domesday Book is ambiguous, for an entry under a single name can hide a multitude of individual holdings. Conversely, individual entries cannot be taken as proof of separate settlements but it is likely that separately recorded sub-tenancies were matched by separate settlement nuclei. In Wormleighton, in the Warwickshire Feldon, a classic region of settlement nucleation, Domesday folios record no fewer than six sub-tenants in the period immediately prior to the Norman Conquest where only two medieval village sites are later known to have existed. Higham has suggested that where plough-teams outnumber ploughlands in the Domesday folios these were probably kept on outlying farms. If so, large sections of Warwickshire still maintained a settlement pattern that was far from nucleated in 1086, both within and beyond the regions later characterized by nucleation. In some regions there were special opportunities for settlement to be regrouped and replanned. In the north of England, for instance, William I deliberately harried and destroyed settlements after the Conquest and considerable rebuilding became necessary; many planned villages may date from this period of reorganization.

Many later, medieval, villages seem to follow a definite plan although plan types vary enormously. Some were simple one-row settlements set out along a village street with a back-lane allowing access to the crofts behind the houses. Others followed more complicated patterns and some obviously possessed more than one focal point. These plans can still be identified on the modern map where modern building has not eradicated the lines of the older settlement. When plots are measured it is sometimes possible to detect a regular division which hints at the deliberate laying out of the settlement.[57]

By the end of the Anglo-Saxon period much that one identifies with medieval England had come into being. Even the land under agriculture was in some areas almost identical with that recorded on the earliest maps. The farmer's life, too, was not dissimilar to that of the medieval peasant. Two early estate memoranda dating from the tenth or eleventh century reflect the interests of the farming community, one of them, although more of a literary exercise than a practical guide,[58] describing the type of duties that might befall 'the discriminating reeve' throughout the calendar year:

In May and June and July in summer one may: harrow, carry out manure, procure sheep-hurdles, shear sheep, build, repair, construct in timber, cut wood, weed, make folds, construct a fish-weir and mill; at harvest time reap, in August and September and October: mow, cut wood, gather in many crops, thatch, cover over and clean out folds, make ready cow-sheds and also pig-sties before too severe a winter come to the manor, and in addition diligently promote the well-being of the soil; in winter, plough, and in hard frosts: cleave timber, establish an orchard, and perform many indoor jobs, thresh, chop wood, make cattle stalls and pig-sties, build a stove at the threshing-floor – for an oven and kiln, and many things requisite to the manor – and a hen-roost also; in spring, plough and graft, sow beans, plant out a vineyard, dig ditches, cut a deer-fence, and soon after that, if the weather be fine, plant madder, sow flax, and woad-seed as well, plant out herbs, and many things; I cannot recount all that a good reeve must see to.[59]

The individual farmers owed services to their lord which varied from estate to estate. In general they worked for part of each week for their lord, with additional duties at harvest-time and before Easter. They had, above all, to plough, mow and gather in the harvest. In addition to the farmers who held a normal villein holding were cottagers who held less land but owed lighter labour services. There would also be specialist workers on most estates: beekeepers, swine-, ox- and goatherds, foresters, a hayward in charge of fences and enclosures and someone responsible for making the cheese. There may have been specialist workmen such as the miller, shoe-maker or smith.

Mixed farming seems to have predominated over much of lowland England with most estates carrying cattle, including the plough oxen, and sheep. Some also maintained horse studs. The specialization in crop cultivation suggested by the names of some estates on early multiple estates seems to have been for the most part rejected, although some locations would obviously have favoured particular crops. There are certainly references to 'oatlands' and 'barley lands' in some midland charters. Numerous names such as Barwick or Berwick (like the Domesday vills recorded in Norfolk, Kent, Shropshire, Sussex and elsewhere) refer to the cultivation of barley (OE *bere*), while Whaddon, found in Berkshire, Cambridgeshire, Gloucestershire, Warwickshire and Wiltshire, is 'wheat hill' (OE *hwǣte*). West Midland charters also refer to crops of corn: wheat, barley, rye and oats are named and, in addition, beans and peas. There are many early place-name and charter references to woad, used as a dye for woollens: Waddon in Dorset is 'woad-hill' and Wadborough in Worcestershire 'woad hills' while flax is also often referred to in this way. The cultivation of these and others can be confirmed by environmental studies. These, although biased towards sites in southern and eastern England, support the documentary evidence, confirming that cereal crops comprised bread wheat, hulled barley, oats and rye, with the amount of oats grown increasing in the later Anglo-Saxon period. There seems to have been little selection of particular strains of cereal crops before the end of the Anglo-Saxon period although the pollen evidence from late to early Norman (850–1100/50) levels at Raunds in Northamptonshire suggests that a small amount of a second type of wheat, known as rivet wheat, was also cultivated and would have produced a weak flour suitable for making porridge or gruel.[60] The amount of recoverable data varies enormously between sites, with cereals predominating on all rural sites. Legumes (peas and beans) were probably grown mainly as garden crops (although beanlands are recorded at Bishopton, near Stratford-upon-Avon, in an eleventh-century charter).[61] Flax was processed on many rural sites and plants used for dying (such as elderberries and dyer's rocket) have also been found in close association.[62] The wider range of material available from urban deposits, including those from latrine pits and waterlogged ground at such centres as Winchester, Southampton and Gloucester, reveals the cultivation of hemp and flax, beet, and herbs such as fennel, together with the collection for food of many fruits grown either in gardens or taken from the hedgerows; these include sloe, bullace, plums, cherries, strawberries, blackberries and raspberries.[63]

As increasing attention has been paid in excavations to the study of the bone evidence, the mixed nature of Anglo-Saxon farming has also been confirmed, with stock husbandry maintaining the high standards reached in Roman times. There was no decrease in the size of stock from the Roman to the Anglo-Saxon period[64] and although sheep and goats outnumber other species, cattle were probably the most valuable animals reared, utilized for both meat, dairy produce and hides and as both beasts of burden and plough oxen.[65] Regional differences are becoming apparent across the country in this period with the number of cattle identified forming a higher percentage of all stock in Hampshire than in East Anglia.[66] Few animals appear to have been killed at a young age: mature cattle were present on most sites in high numbers while the more mature sheep may have been kept primarily for their wool. Changing representations of species may denote changing environmental conditions with increasing numbers of pigs, for instance, suggesting the changing availability of access to woodland and pasture, although there is some evidence to suggest that pork may have been a high status dietary item brought in to high-ranking sites such as Wicken Bonhunt.[67] The Southampton evidence also suggests that animals may have been brought in from outlying estates for butchery.

The surveys which were made towards the compilation of Domesday Book, and which survive for south-western and eastern England, show that most manors carried sheep and cattle on their demesne farms. The importance of sheep which could be kept in folds upon the fields to provide manure should not be under-estimated and in the south-west of England they greatly outnumbered cattle on most demesne farms at the time of the Domesday survey. It is likely that their manure helped to maintain the fertility of the 'infield' near a settlement and permitted it to be kept under almost continuous cultivation. Domestic animals, too, are referred to in place-names, especially the all-important plough oxen. Oxcombe in Lincolnshire, Oxendon in Shropshire, Oxenhall in Gloucestershire, all seem to describe the places – a coomb, hill and 'nook' – where the oxen were kept and the better-known Oxford, beside the River Thames, is 'ford of the oxen', apparently Hinksey Ford.[68] Many of the numerous *wic* settlements were dairying establishments and such names are often more frequent in valley locations where rich alluvial water meadows provided both pasture and hay.[69] The many 'Hardwicks', on the other hand, were herding settlements (OE *heord*, 'a herd, flock') and were more commonly found in wooded or grass pasture regions.

The Cotton Tiberius calendar in the British Library[70] shows a sequence of delightful pictures which illustrate the farming year, some of which relate to arable farming and the rearing of domestic stock (Plate XII), although the appropriateness of the placing of some of the pictures has not gone unquestioned.[71] The farming year can be seen starting with the ploughing of the land. Four heavy oxen are illustrated, the ploughboy wielding his goad before and the ploughman steering a simple plough behind, to be followed by the person scattering the seed. This recalls Ælfric's description of the duties of a ploughman:

> I work hard; I go out at day break, driving the oxen to the field, and I yoke them to the plough. Be it never so stark winter I dare not linger at home for fear of my lord; but having yoked my oxen, and fastened share and coulter, every day I must plough a full acre or more. I have a boy driving the oxen with a goad-iron, who is hoarse with cold and shouting.[72]

Although discoveries of parts of ploughs are rare in archaeology, an Anglo-Saxon riddle notes 'the well-sharpened point' of the coulter, and the share which, 'in my head, firm and forward-facing' leaves 'green on one side and black on the other'.[73] Here there is no direct mention of a mouldboard to turn the furrow but the riddle claims that the sods fell to the side and the calendar picture shows that the plough was heavy, requiring at least

Plate XII Scenes from the Cotton Tiberius calendar: *January*: ploughing the fields and sowing; *June*: reaping the harvest; *August*: mowing and haymaking; *December*: threshing.

four oxen to pull it, and wheeled. It is likely that a mouldboard plough was needed to lift and turn the soil in the ridge-and-furrow method of ploughing which seems to be in use by *c.* 1000 at least.[74] It is probable that the lighter ard remained in use for a time in areas of lighter soils.

Other scenes illustrate the mowing of hay (*fileðe*) from the meadows with long straight-handled scythes and the reaping of the corn harvest, high on the stalk, with a short sickle. Later the grain is taken to be threshed and winnowed. The pastoral side of the economy is illustrated by shepherds caring for their flocks. The importance of arable in the economy is stressed by Ælfric's 'Counsellor' who notes how 'the ploughman feeds us all', but the contribution of all types of farming is revealed in the diet of the 'pupil':

> I still enjoy meat, because I am a child living under instruction. . . . I eat vegetables and eggs, fish and cheese, butter and beans and all clean things, with much gratefulness . . . [with] Ale if I have it, or water if I have no ale.[75]

Notes

1. Anglo-Saxon Charms, in *Anglo-Saxon Poetry*, trans. Gordon, p.90.
2. The regional differences in the identification of pottery scatters is exemplified by the work of Hall and Coles, in the Fenland (*Fenland Survey*, pp.122–31), and Foard and Pearson ('The Raunds Project') and Bowman ('Contrasting pays') in the East Midlands who were able to identify Anglo-Saxon settlement sites from such evidence whereas detailed field survey by Shennan (*Experiments*, pp.89–91) in Hampshire produced almost negligible results for the same period.
3. Taylor, *Village and Farmstead*, pp.114–15, Fig. 40.
4. Ibid., pp.113–17.
5. Ibid., p.120.
6. West, *West Stow*.
7. Losco-Bradley and Wheeler, 'Anglo-Saxon settlement in the Trent Valley'.
8. James *et al.*, 'An early medieval building tradition'.
9. Jones and Jones, 'The crop-mark sites at Mucking, Essex'.
10. Hamerow, 'Mucking: the Anglo-Saxon settlement'.
11. Millett, 'Excavations at Cowdery's Down'.
12. Cunliffe, 'Saxon and medieval settlement-pattern'.
13. James *et al.*, 'An early medieval building tradition'.
14. From information given by David Goodburn, Museum of London.
15. Hope-Taylor, *Yeavering*.
16. Rahtz, *The Saxon and Medieval Palaces at Cheddar*.

17. Quinnell, 'Cornwall during the Iron Age and the Roman period'; Miles and Miles, 'Excavations at Trethurgy, St Austell'.
18. Rose and Preston-Jones, 'Changes in the Cornish countryside'.
19. Wade, 'A settlement site at Bonhunt Farm'; Wade-Martins, 'Excavation in North Elmham Park'.
20. Bassett, 'In search of the origins of Anglo-Saxon kingdoms', p.25.
21. *Medieval Settlement Res Rep* 2, p.23; 4, pp.41–3.
22. Murphy, 'The Anglo-Saxon landscape'.
23. Taylor, *Fields in the English Landscape*, pp.52–3.
24. Rackham, *The History of the Countryside*, Plate XIII; Hooke, 'Regional variation'.
25. Rose and Preston Jones, 'Changes in the Cornish countryside'.
26. Reece, 'Town and country'; Seebohm, *The English Village Community*.
27. Jones, 'Post-Roman Wales'.
28. Hooke, 'The mid-late Anglo-Saxon period'.
29. Thirsk, 'The common fields'; Thirsk, 'The origin of common fields'.
30. Thirsk, 'The common fields', p.18.
31. Fox, 'Approaches to the adoption of the Midland system'.
32. Klingelhöfer, *Manor, Vill, and Hundred*, p.114.
33. Higham, 'Settlement, land use and Domesday ploughlands'.
34. Seebohm, *The English Village Community*; Orwin and Orwin, *The Open Fields*.
35. Bishop, 'Assarting and the growth of the open fields'.
36. McCloskey, 'English open fields'.
37. Dahlman, *The Open Field System*; Kerridge, *The Common Fields*, pp.74–86.
38. Ibid.
39. Dodgshon, *The Origin of British Field Systems*.
40. Pesez, 'The emergence of the village in France and in the West'.
41. Costen, 'Some evidence for new settlements'.
42. Sawyer, *Anglo-Saxon Charters*, S 719; Birch, *Cartularium Saxonicum*, B 1120.
43. Sawyer, ibid., S 856, S 634; Kemble, *Codex Diplomaticus Aevi Saxonici*, K 1278; Birch, *Cartularium Saxonicum*, B 925.
44. Sawyer, ibid., S 691; Birch, ibid., B 1079.
45. Sawyer, ibid., S 716; Birch, ibid., B 1113.
46. *Liber Eliensis*, p.111.
47. Hooke, 'Regional variation'; Sawyer, *Anglo-Saxon Charters*, S 369; Birch, *Cartularium Saxonicum*, B 601; Gelling, *The Place-Names of Berkshire, III*, p.684.
48. Ælfric, *Colloquium*.
49. Hooke, 'Open field agriculture'.
50. Sawyer, *Anglo-Saxon Charters*, S 219; Hooke, *Worcestershire Anglo-Saxon Charter-Bounds*, pp.129–34.
51. Harvey, 'The origin of planned field systems'; Harvey, 'Planned field systems'.
52. Hall, 'The Late Saxon countryside'.
53. Hooke, 'Village development'.
54. Ibid.
55. Sawyer, *Anglo-Saxon Charters*, S 653; Finberg, 'Ayshford and Boehill'; Hooke, *Pre-Conquest Charter-Bounds of Devon and Cornwall*, pp.156–60.

56. Baker and Butlin (eds), *Studies of Field Systems (passim)*.
57. Roberts, *The Making of the English Village*.
58. Harvey, '*Rectitudines singularum*'.
59. Liebermann, *Die Gesetze*, pp.444–55; trans. after Swanton, *Anglo-Saxon Prose*, p.26.
60. Campbell, 'The preliminary archaeobotanical results', pp.67–8, 81.
61. Sawyer, *Anglo-Saxon Charters*, S 1388.
62. Murphy, 'The Anglo-Saxon landscape', pp.34–5; Campbell, 'The preliminary archaeobotanical results', pp.75–6.
63. Green, 'Iron Age, Roman and Saxon crops'.
64. Bourdillon, 'Countryside and town'; Albarella and Davis, 'The Saxon and medieval animal bones'.
65. Maltby, 'Iron Age, Romano-British and Anglo-Saxon animal husbandry'.
66. Crabtree, 'The faunal remains'.
67. Crabtree, 'Animal exploitation in East Anglian villages', p.43.
68. Gelling, *The Place-Names of Oxfordshire, I*, pp.xxii-iii, 19.
69. Hooke, 'The Anglo-Saxon landscape', in *Field and Forest*.
70. B.L., Cotton Tiberius BV, part 1.
71. McGurk, 'The labours of the months'.
72. Ælfric, *Colloquium*, pp.19–20; trans. after Scott, *The Saxon Age*, p.86.
73. Anglo-Saxon Riddles, Riddle 32, Baum, *Anglo-Saxon Riddles*, pp.28–9.
74. Langdon, 'Agricultural equipment'; for one source of evidence see Barker and Lawson, 'A pre-Norman field system'.
75. Ælfric, *Colloquium*, p.115; trans. Swanton, *Anglo-Saxon Prose*.

CHAPTER 7

Woodland Resources

The Distribution of Pre-Conquest Woodland

The old idea of a land richly clad in primeval woodland awaiting the incursions of the Anglo-Saxons was rejected long ago but has taken rather longer to dislodge from the popular image. Aerial photography over the last few decades has revealed that enormous areas of prehistoric England were laid out under field systems and boundary divisions which stretched for mile upon mile through open countryside. Agriculture certainly experienced many vicissitudes and might expand and retract under different economic and social pressures but there can have been little 'wilderness' that had not been drawn into the regional economy. Woodland and pasture were valuable assets and, as such, were closely managed.

Woodland and waste did, however, exist in the Anglo-Saxon period and woodland regeneration may have been deliberately encouraged in some regions. There is some evidence to suggest that it survived along many territorial frontiers. Either territorial boundaries had been laid out through sparsely settled regions, often areas of high land or marsh, wood or heath, or development had been restricted in unstable frontier regions. Geography, too, must account for some wasteland frontiers: just as later parishes encircled patches of waste which they subsequently divided between them, so the territory of early kingdoms might extend from a more accessible central region into a more remote borderland/frontier zone. In south-eastern England, for instance, the early kingdoms which were to become fossilized in the counties of Kent and Sussex reached inland from coastal centres into the woodlands of the Weald which was to remain a frontier zone until all these groups were amalgamated into the kingdom of Wessex (Figure 46).

In central England woodland lay thickly along the boundaries of both the Hwiccan and Magonsætan kingdoms, kingdoms which were to become part of Greater Mercia by the end of the seventh century (Figure 47).[1] The Hwiccan kingdom extended over what is now Worcestershire (except its north-western extension), western Warwickshire and all of Gloucestershire except the Forest of Dean. Through areas which were often later to be declared royal forests, its boundary passed in a clockwise

Fig. 46   Anglo-Saxon woodland (after Hill 1981, Fig. 23, based upon Ordnance Survey 1966 and Stenton 1971).

direction through the woodlands of Wyre, Kinver and Arden. Beyond its south-eastern boundary lay Wychwood, 'the wood of the Hwicce', and then the forests of Kemble, Kingswood, Dean and Malvern lay on its southern and western frontiers. Only in its passage through southern Warwickshire did it pass through heavily settled cultivated country. Its western boundary was shared with that of the Magonsæte, whose kingdom extended over what is now Herefordshire and the southern part of Shropshire. The eastern frontier of the Magonsæte was marked, therefore,

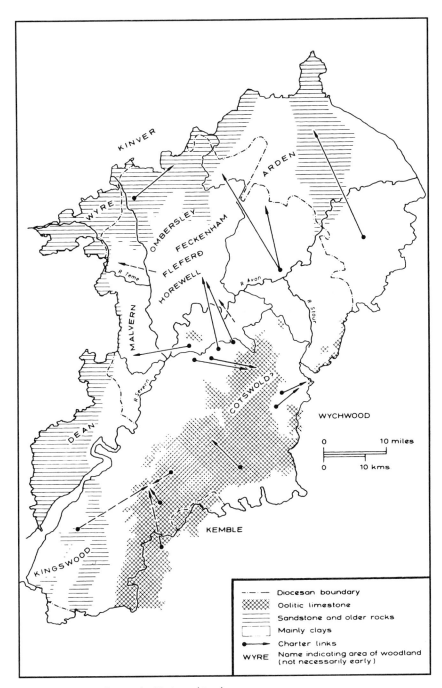

Fig. 47   Frontier forests: the Hwiccan kingdom.

by the woodlands of Malvern and Wyre and, further to, the north, by those of Morfe, while woodland was also thick along its northern frontier with the Wreocensæte in the vicinity of Wenlock Edge. Its western boundary, for the most part, ran through the broken hilly terrain to the west of Offa's Dyke (see Figure 12 on p. 42).

The woodlands of the Chilterns seem to have remained an enclave where British tradition long resisted the Anglo-Saxon advance. The Chiltern range extends from Dorchester on the Thames in the south-west into Bedfordshire and Hertfordshire to the north-east, a portion of the great chalk escarpment of England where this reaches between 600 and 800 feet in height and is covered by deposits of clay-with-flints and drifts, with London clays to the south-east. Like many chalk areas, this was not undeveloped countryside in Roman times but large expanses of woodland apparently survived and formed an effective barrier to Anglo-Saxon incursions. Rutherford Davis notes that 'Throughout the region certain place-names betray the former presence of British people'. with 'unusual frequency'[2] and one is reminded of Gildas' claims that the British took to the densest woods to escape the incoming Anglo-Saxons in the early years of the take-over.[3] Rutherford Davis argues for a continuing British province here based upon the old *civitas* capital of Verulamium lasting until long after the fifth century.

A narrower band of woodland was to play a similarly significant role in hampering the progress of the early Anglo-Saxons westward. Selwood, a wooded region along the borders of what is now Wiltshire and Somerset, stretching into Dorset, marked the divide between the British and the Anglo-Saxons in the late sixth century. The British knew this wood as Coit Maur – the 'great wood' – and although it ceased to be a long-lasting frontier it remained a distinctive barrier. Aldhelm, the bishop established at Sherborne in AD 705, was noted in the Anglo-Saxon Chronicle as the bishop 'to the west of Selwood', his diocese sometimes called 'Selwood-shire',[4] and Stenton notes how the great army levied against the Danes in 893 included men 'from every fortress east of the Parret, both east and west of Selwood'.[5] British traditions remained strong to the west of this frontier, permeating many facets of English culture.

Woodland as Wood Pasture

Woodland was not, however, just an impediment or a refuge: it was a valuable economic asset. Early documentary evidence recognized one of the primary uses of woodland: its value for seasonal pasture. While it is well known that herds of pigs could usefully forage in woodlands in late

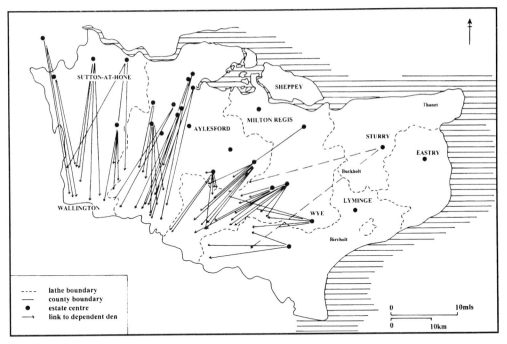

Fig. 48 Wealden links (based upon the identifications of Witney 1976).

summer and autumn, either for acorns or beech-mast, it is more easily
forgotten that woods also provided pasture for cattle and horses and even
sheep. Rights of pasture are clearly documented in the extensive woodlands
of the Weald, for many estates in what was later to be Kent, Sussex and
Surrey held grazing grounds known as 'dens' in the woodland (Figure 48).
Thus it is claimed that in the late eighth century King Offa granted grazing
rights to the abbot of Saints Peter and Paul at Canterbury for pigs and
'animals' (usually cattle, possibly also sheep) and horses in a wood in the
Weald of Kent.[6] Not all the individual dens have been located but certain
areas can be identified and the ancient routeways which linked them to
the home estates can still be followed.

An annal of AD 892 in the Anglo-Saxon Chronicle declares of the
Weald: 'That wood is a hundred and twenty miles long or longer from
east to west, and thirty miles broad.'[7] It extended across a zone of sandstone
and clay formations which lies at the core of an uplifted anticline, reaching
almost as far as the sea in the south-east. Outcrops of chalk and greensand
form a horseshoe of escarpments around the sandstones, with clay vales
separating them. Much of the northern chalk downland is covered by a
deposit of clay-with-flints and this also seems to have been a heavily
wooded region in early medieval times. It was, however, the central Weald
which figured most prominently in the early documented evidence as a
zone of seasonal pasture, a use noted in many of the early charters of the
south-eastern counties.

Originally the dens seem to have been held in common by the men of the different communities, an arrangement which in itself suggests that it pre-dated the changes in forms of ownership which occurred in the early medieval period. An authentic eighth-century charter, for instance, grants swine-pastures in 'the wood of the men of the Lympne district [based on the River Limen] (the *Limenwara*) and in the wood of the men of Wye (the *Weowara*)',[8] referring to the men of the lathes, the administrative districts, of those areas. Other charters relate how the inhabitants of Rochester (the *Cæsterwara*) and of Canterbury (the *Burhwara*) also had common pasture in the Weald.[9] The value of woodland for the pasturing of swine is illustrated in the seventh-century laws of Ine of Wessex where it is noted that a fine of 60 shillings was to be imposed upon those found cutting down a tree that could shelter 30 swine. Fines were also imposed on those found destroying trees in a wood by fire.[10]

In Kent, Alan Everitt[11] has attempted to explore the way in which seasonal shielings gave way in a woodland zone to permanent settlement (see Chapter 10). He suggests that the Wealden dens were pastured by the old primary communities of the Foothills and Holmesdale in the seventh and eighth centuries, with swineherds spending the pannage season in forest lodges. Only gradually did these become permanent farms, but some had become established by the time of the Norman Conquest; others took longer. He examines the evidence of dependent settlements and the date of church foundation to back up the dates he suggests. Similar processes probably occurred earlier in many other localities. Many of the features Everitt notes in Kent can be recognized in other woodland regions but few have yet received such close analysis.

The Recognition of Wooded Areas

How can woodland regions in Anglo-Saxon England be recognized? First it must be noted that all attempts to map early woodland are conjectural (Figure 46 on p. 140 is based upon David Hill's map showing interpretations of the distribution of early medieval woodland by Stenton and the Ordnance Survey)[12] and debate still continues about both the survival of even earlier woodland and the date of woodland regeneration. For there is certainly evidence to show that many areas of early farming passed out of arable cultivation in the Anglo-Saxon period. The higher slopes of the chalk escarpments had been intensively cultivated under Roman rule, usually by a method of native farming which entailed the use of so-called 'Celtic' fields – smallish, rectangular fields whose boundary lynchets often survived into the present century. The removal of pressures to maintain both the Roman army and the towns that the Romans had established may partially account for this but it is likely that the thin chalk soils had already been over-cultivated under these conditions and were marginal enough to become neglected when such pressures were withdrawn. This would not, however, necessarily lead to woodland regeneration and the evidence of Anglo-Saxon charters in such regions as the Vale of the White Horse (now in Oxfordshire) suggests that such land usually reverted to pasture, its predominant use throughout the later historical period.[13]

It now seems likely that woodland regeneration was not necessarily an immediate result of the Roman withdrawal apart from in some marginal zones. This may have been the case in parts of northern England[14] but in many areas regeneration occurred at a rather later date as land use changed. To judge the extent of this change one must carefully review the types of evidence available for the presence of woodland. The most unambiguous, environmental evidence, including such methods as pollen and snail analysis, is still limited but will provide valuable information as it accrues. It is the evidence from pollen analysis that suggests that parts of the North were reverting to woodland and waste in the Anglo-Saxon period as the more intensive use of the land characteristic of Iron Age and Romano-British times diminished. Pollen diagrams from sites in Northumberland, County Durham, Yorkshire and the Lake District have provided evidence for such reversion although a few sites in more favoured areas provided evidence of continued cultivation.[15] Conversely, studies in the region of Shotover Forest, Oxfordshire, showed little woodland regeneration until late Saxon or even early Norman times.[16] A possible reason for this will be discussed below.

Contemporary narrative sources are almost entirely silent upon different regional geographies, as noted earlier, and it is place-names which provide the framework for a discussion of early medieval land use. A suggested chronology of place-names, now regarded with greater caution than was previously the case, is of less relevance here although it appears that certain terms were in use earlier than others.[17] The woodland term *leah* is included within those terms used most frequently between AD 400 and 730 but is one which continued in use after that date. Ultimately derived from the same root as Old High German *loh*, 'grove; bush-grown clearing, under-growth',[18] this Old English term has always implied open woodland and it is not surprising to find it occurring most often upon the edges of thickly wooded regions although it sometimes continued in use in the names of individual woods. It was, indeed, in the form *Andredesleage* used as an alternative name for the Kentish Weald, otherwise known as *Andredesweald*. This is the type of woodland which was of most use as wood-pasture, a use which helped to maintain its character of stands of woodland interspersed

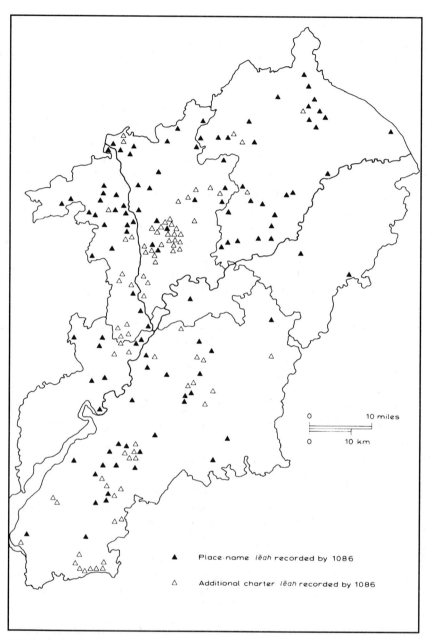

Fig. 49a   The distribution of the *leah* term in the West Midlands: early recordings clearly show pre-Conquest woodland well represented across most of Worcestershire, north-west Warwickshire and along the Cotswold scarp in Gloucestershire. Gaps in the evidence indicate most extensively cleared areas or, paradoxically, the most heavily wooded regions in which there was little settlement (e.g. the Forest of Dean in west Gloucestershire).

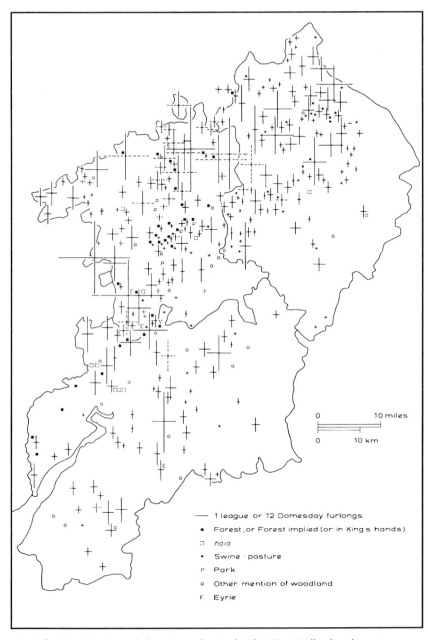

Fig. 49b Woodland recorded in Domesday Book. The West Midland evidence is reproduced so that this may be compared with the place-name evidence shown in Fig. 49a.

Plate XIII Ancient woodland: Clowes Wood, Tanworth-in-Arden, Warwickshire. While individual trees are not old, the site has never been cultivated.

with open glades and pastures set with scattered trees (Plate XIII). The term may even have conveyed a meaning associated with a direct economic usage to the Anglo-Saxons: perhaps, indeed, 'wood-pasture'.

When the incidence of the *leah* term recorded in pre-Conquest place-names is plotted, regions characterized by this type of open woodland become quite clear (Figure 49a). It must be remembered that the place-names which are being plotted are almost always those associated with settlement and presumably relate to the nature of the countryside in the surrounding area when the names were first formed. In such areas settlement was often of a dispersed nature and the named settlement may have been but one of many within any estate. The term continued in use throughout the early medieval period and in itself gives no confirmation of antiquity but few place-names were coined at the time they were written down and are usually older than their recorded date. It is likely, however, that the pre-Conquest names genuinely indicate the nature of land use in the later Anglo-Saxon period when their literate meanings were still understood. Areas in which the term fails to occur might be heavily cultivated and without wood-pasture or, conversely, areas of little settlement, perhaps even of rather dense woodland.[19]

To the *leah* term, today reflected in many place-names ending in '-ley', may be added a large number of other Old English wood names, many of them with precise meanings. The terms *wald* and *wudu* probably indicated extensive woodland while the terms *graf*, 'a grove, a copse', *bearu*, 'a wood, a grove', and *holt*, 'a wood, a thicket', implied woods of smaller dimensions, the latter perhaps one dominated by a particular species; *sceaga* is 'a shaw, a small wood'. *Hyrst* seems to have been used in most regions to describe 'a wooded hillock' or 'an upland wood' while the term *hangra*, 'hanger', is still used to describe 'a wood on a steep hillside'. A term *fyrhð* also seems to have implied 'wooded countryside' (many 'Thrift' woods survive today) but one term was most commonly used on woodland margins: *feld*, which originally meant 'open land' but came to mean 'field', seems to have described open land which lay in direct contrast to adjacent woodland.

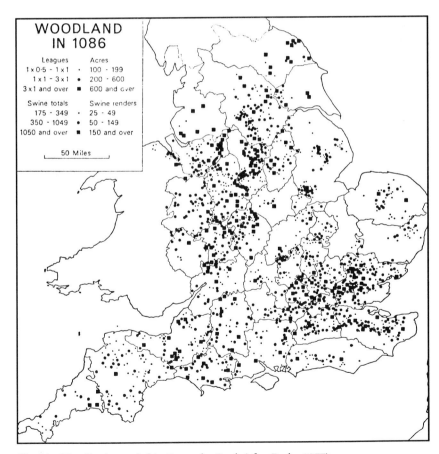

Fig. 50 Woodland recorded in Domesday Book (after Darby 1977).

Pre-Conquest charters have been shown to contain many references to land use especially in the minor names of boundary markers. These references can be used to supplement the place-name evidence and to provide greater and finer detail in those regions well covered by such charter evidence. The terms used are the same as those found in major place-names but the locations of the features they describe can often be pinpointed with considerable accuracy.

Finally, Domesday Book records the amount of woodland present on a manor and this can be compared with the earlier evidence (Figures 49b, 50). This survey aimed at recording all the manorial assets of the king's tenants in 1086 and in effect, summarized the situation at the very end of the early medieval period. In many regions amounts of woodland recorded on any one manor were added to provide a formal assessment which was then expressed as 'wood so many leagues, furlongs or perches in length by so many leagues, furlongs or perches in width'. The Domesday league appears to have been one and half miles long although this is not undisputed. For some parts of the country, woodland was given in acres. In eastern England, woodland was measured by the number of swine it could support while in the South-East it was expressed as the amount of rent that was payable in return for the right of pannage (so much for so many pigs).[20] Although the amounts sound enormous, Oliver Rackham has suggested a formula which reduces these assessments to definite acreages. This, too, is a subjective analysis not accepted by all authorities but it does provide a rule of thumb which allows Domesday woodland to be compared to that existing today. Rackham assumes that a Domesday acre is 1.2 times a modern acre and that the area of woodland given by linear measurement can be calculated by multiplying them, and then multiplying the sum by 0.7. He makes no attempt to suggest precise figures for woodland calculated in relation to the swine it supported.[21]

Two grave problems arise, however, in the use of the Domesday evidence. First, the woods were not recorded individually and might be listed under the name of a capital manor many miles distant from where they actually lay. Thus the woodlands of Brailes, an estate in the Feldon of Warwickshire very close to the southern boundary of the county, are known to have lain in Tanworth-in-Arden over 25 miles to the north-west, for Tanworth was a dependent manor of Brailes. It is likely that most of the woodland recorded in south-east Warwickshire in 1086 actually lay within Arden and not on the manors on which it was recorded. The picture is similarly distorted in south-eastern England where woodland in the central Weald is recorded on the valley and coastal manors to which it belonged. Second, not all woodland was necessarily recorded in Domesday Book. Often woodland is noted as having been 'put outside the manor' or having passed into 'the king's hands'. This usually implied that it had become part of royal forest and was no longer available to the manorial lord or his tenants. As such, its mention was incidental in a survey aimed at noting the assets of the king's tenants and it might remain entirely without mention. Land placed under forest law was not necessarily wooded but in most lowland parts of the country, at least, it usually comprised regions which were more marginal for agriculture and contained a degree of woodland and heath. Domesday Book cannot thus, for the reasons given above, be always accepted as a reliable record of all the woodland existing at the time of the Norman Conquest. However, Rackham's estimates clearly indicate the well-wooded areas of the West Midlands and the Weald.[22]

He reckons that England was about 15 per cent woodland in 1086, but both his map and that of Darby[23] (Figure 50) strongly support the concentration of wood in the Weald, Chilterns and Essex in south-eastern England. The woodland belt which extended from Dorset northwards to the Peak and into Yorkshire is more prominent on the maps produced from Domesday statistics (Rackham notes that Worcestershire was about 40 per cent woodland in 1086). The largely cleared belt extending from east Gloucestershire through south-eastern Warwickshire, western Northamptonshire and eastern Leicestershire into Lincolnshire, on the other hand, is more noticeable. It is likely that regeneration along the Welsh Border, even if localized, is poorly represented on these maps for, as Darby notes, wasted vills in Herefordshire and elsewhere were overgrown with wood and being used for hunting by the Marcher lords.[24]

No single source of evidence gives a true indication of the extent of woodland in the early medieval period and studies within several counties in southern and central England will illustrate the sources of evidence most readily available and some of the problems involved in their use.

Berkshire is not an easy county to study. It is not one in which woodland is suggested on any large scale by early recorded *leah* names but in the eastern section of the county woodland was possessed by all settlements at the time of the Domesday survey.[25] It is one of the counties for which woodland was recorded as swine render and the distribution of manors paying such renders shows a marked concentration across the south of the county. This was an area underlain by successive bands of strata less favourable to farming than the northern limey Corallian beds or the chalklands which cross the middle of the county. The more southerly chalklands are overlain by clay-with-flints deposits and finally give way to varied Eocene deposits in the Kennet–Loddon Vales. These contain bands of sands and clays, many of which remain infertile today. While both the charter and Domesday evidence suggest that woodland increased on the southern downlands, it was the more southerly region which paid the highest swine rents in 1086. Domesday Book also refers incidentally to two main areas of royal forest: Cookham, Windsor and Winkfield all lay within the area of Windsor Forest in the eastern sector of the county; further to the west forest law had been imposed in Bucklebury and Kintbury, the warden of the forest of Kintbury already mentioned before the Norman Conquest during Edward's reign.[26]

There is no obvious direct link between the areas shown to be wooded in 1086 and the early recorded *leah* names (Figure 51). Although not numerous in Berkshire these occur in the north-eastern projection of the county (now taken into Oxfordshire) which formed the hundred of Hormer (Bessels Leigh and *Earmundesle*); in the southern downlands in the heart of the county (including Chieveley, East and West Ilsley, Streatley near the county boundary); in the Thames valley to the north-west of Reading (Purley); and on the fringes of Windsor Forest (Earley and Hartley in Shinfield to the west and Hurley to the north). In fact, several of the *leah* areas in the south of the country lay upon the fringe of relatively 'empty' areas of woodland or heathland. The Forest of Windsor appears from the Domesday evidence to have been well wooded and later-recorded

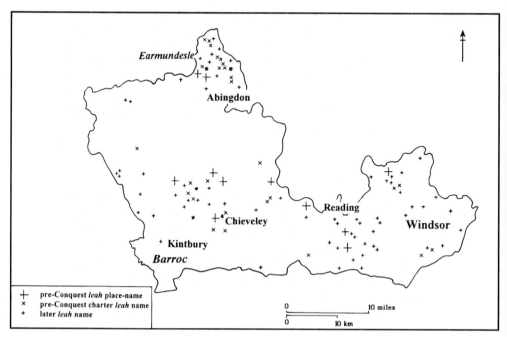

Fig. 51   Berkshire woodland in the early medieval period. Place-name evidence may be compared with the woodland entries in Domesday Book (after Campbell 1971).

leah names crowd further into its recesses.[27] A place-name blank in the south-west of the county appears to represent the ancient woodland of Barroc which lay 'on the clay lands between and including Enborne and Hungerford'[28] and was centred upon Kintbury, later also to be royal forest. The Kennet valley is still heavily wooded today. *Feld* names (indicating open land on the margins of wooded areas) lay thickly upon the fringes of the Windsor Forest woods and two are also recorded to the north of the Barroc woods.

Further to the north, a little more detail is available for the clay-covered central downlands because charter boundary clauses are available for this region. Here, apart from the *leah* names of Ilsley and Chieveley, many of the estate names are of a habitative or topographical nature, but the charter boundary clauses reveal many other *leah* features lying along estate boundaries. Since the boundary clauses tell us nothing of conditions within the boundaries it is not possible to know how representative these were of the general countryside but late recorded *leah* names also lie in similar locations. If the *leah* features represented pockets of wood-pasture then this seems to have been largely pushed back in this region to estate margins, representing an intermediate stage in woodland cover.

The same situation may be suggested in the north-east of the county, in Hormer Hundred. Several early *leah* place-names occur and one of them refers to a region once widely referred to as *Æaromundeslee* or *Earmundeslea*, an area where clay soils are widespread. Bessels Leigh, *Leie* in Domesday Book, is the only estate name recorded by 1086 although Wootton, 'farm in or near a wood', also occurs. The pre-Conquest charters show that woodland was certainly present before 1086, and later maps show that it was present in later periods, yet this is one of the areas where it failed to get into the Domesday record. It is difficult to explain this apparent anomaly and this discrepancy implies omission in the Domesday survey. Later recorded *leah* names continue to reflect the presence of a degree of woodland. Today the woodlands of Wytham Hill are preserved as a valuable area of ancient woodland and they must incorporate the *yrdyrleage, wadleahe,* 'woad *leah*', and *plumleage,* 'plum-tree *leah*', of Anglo-Saxon times. Further to the south, woodland lies on the slopes of Boar's Hill. This was earlier known as *abbedun* and was the hill which gave its name to the monastery of Abingdon, founded a few miles to the south in the valley of the upper Thames. This woodland, too, is represented by *leah* names in the charters.

The Berkshire evidence echoes that for Worcestershire, examined in the author's previous books. The areas in which *leah* survived for one or two central estate names in early medieval times, but was mostly recorded along parish boundaries, as in central Berkshire, echo the situation found in central Worcestershire on the claylands of the Central Worcestershire Plain. The 'empty' areas of Berkshire, characterized by woodland and heath, match the border regions near the western boundary of Worcestershire where, like Kintbury and Windsor, they were to become incorporated into the Norman forests of Malvern and Wyre. The most fertile areas of Berkshire lay to the south of the Upper Thames near Sutton Courtenay and Long Wittenham and although these are not discussed in the present chapter, they too are matched by Worcestershire's Vale of Evesham. While geological factors and soil quality seem to be basic factors influencing such regional variation, consideration must also be paid to the geography of territory and the influence of core regions and tribal frontiers.

Woodland Regeneration and Wood for Hunting

The previous paragraphs have appeared to presuppose the antiquity of woodland but this is not necessarily the case. Across northern Hampshire is a zone which by medieval times was almost entirely royal forest and which later maps show well provided with woodland cover. Archaeological evidence, however, reveals wide areas of 'Celtic' fields accompanied by Iron Age and Romano-British farmsteads. It is in zones such as this that woodland regeneration seems to have been taking place in the later Anglo-Saxon period. The underlying rock is chalk, although overlain by patches of clay-with-flints. Much of the land was in royal hands and at a manorial site excavated in Faccombe the number of fallow deer hunted increased dramatically under the Norman kings,[29] suggesting that a change of land use was taking place by the medieval period.

Charter evidence, however, suggests that the change may have preceded the official afforestation of the area. As in southern Berkshire, a boundary feature which recurs in charter boundary clauses is *haga*, the term used for some kind of strong fence, often around woodland. In Berkshire *haga* fences running for long distances have been noted along parish boundaries to the north of Roman Silchester, and in Hampshire these seem to have run along boundaries for several kilometres in the region to the north-east of Andover (Figures 52a, 52b, 53, Plate XIV).[30] This was a marginal zone in Anglo-Saxon times and much of it was to be granted into ecclesiastical hands, *leah* place-names suggesting that woodland was then already present. Two of the *haga* fences ran along boundaries which were later those of the medieval forests of Finkley and Dygherlye in Andover parish; another ran along the boundary of Crux Easton parish which was held by a huntsman in 1086. Strangely, very little wood was held by

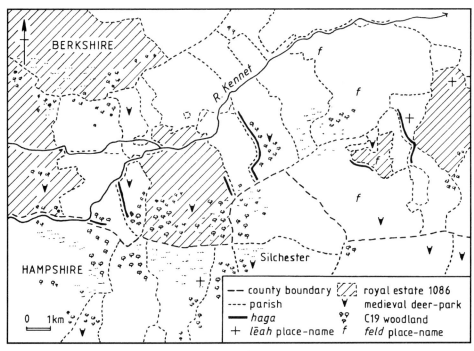

Fig. 52a *Haga* features in southern Berkshire.

Legend (Fig. 52a):
- — — county boundary
- - - - parish
- ▬▬ *haga*
- + *lēah* place-name
- ▨ royal estate 1086
- ∨ medieval deer-park
- ᵠᵠ C19 woodland
- *f* *feld* place-name

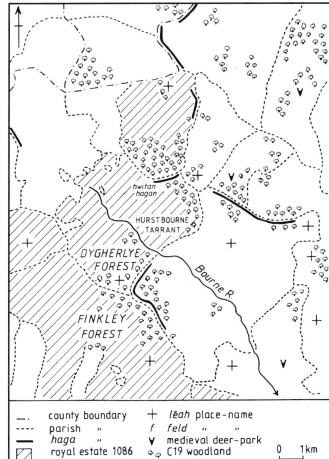

Fig. 52b *Haga* features in northern Hampshire.

Legend (Fig. 52b):
- —.— county boundary
- - - - parish "
- ▬▬ *haga* "
- ▨ royal estate 1086
- + *lēah* place-name
- *f* *feld* " "
- ∨ medieval deer-park
- ᵠᵠ C19 woodland
- 0 1km

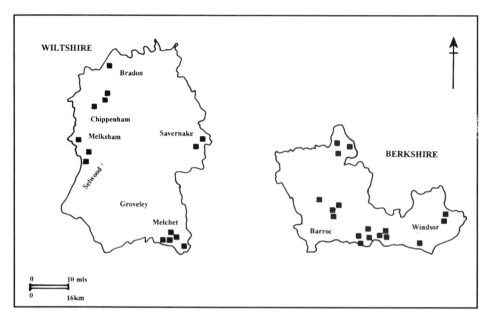

Fig. 53   The distribution of *haga* features in Wiltshire and Berkshire.

Plate XIV   A wood-bank on the site of one of the Berkshire *haga* boundaries. Such features are difficult to date but obviously marked the boundary of a wood.

manorial lords in this region in the Domesday survey but this may be because it had already been incorporated into the Forest of Chute, the bulk of which lay in Wiltshire.

It seems likely that the *haga* features recorded in the charters were some kind of pale, perhaps an earthen bank with a timber palisade or hedge above. The hedge may have consisted of dead hawthorn branches laid on top of each other which would soon form an impenetrable barrier, for the term *haga* is also used for the haw of the hawthorn. If the hedges were first made in open countryside it is possible that they were indeed living hedges, but a barrier of thorns, soon overgrown with other undergrowth, seems more likely in thickening woodland. In places where such features are recorded in the charter bounds of Berkshire and Hampshire abraded earthen banks may be seen today. The 'white *haga*' of Faccombe is a fine example, the presence of flints explaining its nomenclature. The fences were almost certainly intended for the control of deer and the term was in fact used for a deer-park at Ongar in Essex in the eleventh century and for another deer-park at a later date in Gloucestershire.[31]

Hunting was a right occasionally mentioned in charter grants, only recorded in appropriate regions. A charter grant of Grimley in west Worcestershire, for instance, notes among other appurtenances of the estate *siluis uenationibus*, 'woods for hunting',[32] while certain royal estates probably possessed hunting lodges: a grant of AD 904 which refers to 'that hunting vill which is called by the Saxons Bickleigh'[33] probably refers to Bickleigh in Devon. Although formal afforestation did not take place until after the Norman Conquest, forests were being demarcated in the Frankish kingdoms by the seventh century and it is unlikely that Anglo-Saxon kings would be slow to take heed of Continental practices. Even if official deer-parks and forests were of late creation, the *haga* boundaries almost certainly demarcated areas set aside for hunting. Established in areas where the intensity of farming was often already lessening, this change of use may have encouraged woodland regeneration in late Anglo-Saxon times.

The importance of hunting in Anglo-Saxon England has often been under-estimated but Anglo-Saxon law specified that every man was free to hunt on his own land and many animals would have been captured: literary sources name wild fowl, deer, wild boar and hares. Contemporary writings also provide some details about the way hunting was carried out. The monk Ælfric, writing in the later tenth century when he was in charge of a monastic school at Cerne Abbas in Dorset, composed his Colloquy to incorporate sentences in both Old English and Latin in order to educate his scholars. He describes how dogs were used in the dangerous practice of hunting the wild boar:

Fig. 54 (a) Wild boars in a fourteenth-century manuscript *The Hunting Book*, by Gaston Phœbus. These are more realistic than the mythological creatures decorating one of the Sutton Hoo shoulder-clasps (b), dated to the seventh century. The boar was associated with the northern god and goddess Frey and Freya but also plays a part in many ancient cults.

Hundas bedrifon hyne to me, and ic þær, togeanes standende, færlice ofstikode hyne.

the dogs drove it towards me, and I stuck it quickly, standing there in its path.[34]

The boar had formidable tusks and the same method of capture is illustrated in the fourteenth-century French manuscript of Gaston Phœbus (Figure 54).[35] Dogs were also used in the capture of stags, roe-buck, does and, sometimes, hares. Wolves, foxes, beavers, otters, hares, wildcats and martens were all taken, some for their coats and some because they preyed upon domestic stock, but the deer was hunted later both for sport and food.

It is unlikely that deer-hunting had acquired the enormous ritual with which the sport was associated in medieval times and Ælfric explains

ic brede me max, and sette hig on stowe gehæppre, and getihte hundas mine, þæt wildeor hig ehton, oþ þæt þe hig cuman to þam nettan unforsceawodlice, þæt hig swa beon begrynode, and ic ofsleah hig on þam maxum.

I weave myself nets and set them in a suitable place, and urge on my dogs so that they chase the wild animals until they come into the nets unawares and are thus ensnared; and I kill them in the nets.[36]

That the 'wild animals' meant or included deer is shown by further remarks: *Heortas ic gefenge on nettum*, 'I take the stags in nets'.[37] Later evidence shows that the nets could be spread across a gap in a hedge where archers might be hidden.

To turn once more to the evidence of south-central England, *haga* features in Wiltshire charters are found to occur in three localities (see Figure 53 on p. 156). In the east of the county three of the features lay in the area of clay soils on the southern margins of the later Forest of Savernake. A further four lay in the valley of the Avon in the west of the county in an area later to be included within the Forests of Melksham, Chippenham and Selwood. The greatest concentration, however, lay upon the boundaries of estates later in the Forest of Melchet, a region territorially linked with the royal vill of Wilton to the north-west. Here, as in Berkshire, early and late recorded *leah* names lay on the fringe of the wooded area to the north. The area is again one where chalk deposits overlain with clay-with-flints give way southwards to the infertile Eocene beds. Although entries for woodland in Domesday Book do not show significant amounts, much of the wood here may have been contained within the abnormally concentrated assessment for the royal vill of Amesbury[38] although 'pasture for 80 swine, 80 cartloads of wood, and wood for the repair of houses and fences' recorded for the manors of South Newton and Washern show the territorial links to the Wilton region.[39] Melchet may, indeed, have been a region of intercommoning.

Boundaries in Wooded Countryside

Many marginal zones of summer pasture seem only gradually to have been subdivided by fixed boundaries, earlier intercommoned by lowland communities. In the Warwickshire Arden, specific townships are often found to have been linked to others in the south of the county, the links perpetuated in manorial dependencies (like that between Brailes and Tanworth-in-Arden or Bushwood and Stratford-upon-Avon) or dependent chapelries upon mother churches (like Baddesley Clinton upon Hampton-in-Arden or Packwood upon Wasperton). But surviving field-names may betray other links between Arden and Feldon which involved smaller pockets of land and hint at an arrangement earlier than parish formation. In Oldberrow, Kineton Field and the adjacent Kington Coppice in the north of the parish may represent early links with the manor of Kineton in the Feldon while a Billesley Meadow, again adjacent to a patch of ancient woodland in the adjacent parish of Ullenhall, may similarly indicate a link with Billesley Trussel in the Avon valley. Both lie alongside parallel roads running in the north-west/south-east direction which characterizes the routes between the two regions and may have had its origins in an early pattern of droveways (Figure 55). The same orientation is expressed in the parish boundaries which were eventually to subdivide the region (see Figure 15 on p. 48). Brian Roberts, too, believed that parish formation was late in Arden, as in many other wooded regions. It is possible, of course, that medieval colonists from the Avon valley and the south of the county brought such names to Arden in the twelfth and thirteenth centuries when movement of peoples into this under-developed zone was encouraged by some manorial lords. The Charlecotes of Tanworth-in-Arden, their family name that of the parish they had left, offer one such example.[40]

Such tracts of wooded countryside were only subdivided between parish or township estates as the Anglo-Saxon period progressed; in some areas partition was not complete until as late as the twelfth century. Some of the complex boundary patterns which arose are discussed more fully in Chapter 10. Some parishes show long thin tongues of land stretching into

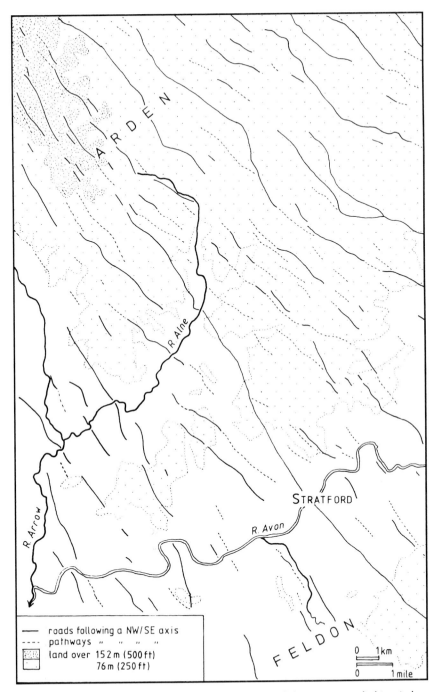

Fig. 55 Possible droveways in Warwickshire. The Warwickshire routeways linking Arden and Feldon are not as securely identified as droveways as those of Kent (Fig. 69) but one of them was certainly known as 'the way to the shire wood' in a charter of AD 963 (S 1307).

the woodlands (as discussed and illustrated in Chapter 4) while a typical feature is a pattern of interlocking boundaries as a wood became partitioned between parishes. Taking an example from near Elham in the northern downland of Kent, Everitt illustrates the boundaries separating the parishes of Upper Hardres, Barham, Elham and Stelling which show this particular shape, an area still well wooded today but with farms now established where there was formerly woodland (see Figure 30 on p. 78).[41]

The Nature of Pre-Conquest Woodland

The probable open character of much pre-Conquest woodland has already been suggested. This type of cover would have been of much greater use to medieval man than any impenetrable wood. In it, deer and domestic stock could graze the open pastures between the trees. Few have made more detailed studies of the character of ancient woodland than Oliver Rackham who discusses the apparent conflict between tree and animal and the balance that had to be achieved in the case of wood-pasture: 'The more trees there are, the less abundant and the worse will be the pasture; and the more animals there are, the less likely saplings or coppice shoots are to survive to produce a new generation of trees.'[42] (The effects of overgrazing are only too well manifested in many parts of the world today.) Because of this, the woods used as wood-pasture had different kinds of trees and plants to those that were not pastured. In Domesday Book the former are often referred to as *silva pastilis* and probably constituted the greater part of the Domesday woodland.

Few such areas survive but an impression of what the countryside may have looked like can be gained from a visit to Epping Forest in Essex, Bradgate Park in Leicestershire or Sutton Park near Birmingham. In the latter the woods were protected by wood banks in medieval times and there are still clumps of trees and bushes scattered across open grassland. At Bradgate, deer still wander the more open parkland. Trees may show a distinct browse-line where animals eat the leaves that they can reach. The height of the line reflects the type of animal browsing – whereas the roe-deer can only reach to about 4 feet (1.2 metres), the red deer can reach 5 feet (1.5 metres). Probably most people are more familiar with the browse-line produced by cattle.[43] Most animals have preferred tastes: deer enjoy ash, elm, hazel and hawthorn and the first three remain uncommon in wood-pasture where oak, beech, hornbeam and aspen are either left uneaten or rapidly recover.[44] For this reason the oak, scattered as isolated trees, has become one of the most characteristic landscape features of English parkland. The effects of grazing on woodland regeneration have

Plate XV Woodland scenes from the Cotton Tiberius calendar: *March*: digging and clearing land; *July*: woodcutting; *September*: swine in the wildwood; *November*: smithing, warming and torching poles.

also been studied by Watkins who has noted how the woodland cover might fluctuate according to the extent to which it was grazed.[45] Such fluctuation may account for some of the *leah* names noted in Worcestershire charters, where 'the thorny *leah*' and 'the *leah* of young saplings' appear to suggest that changes in the woodland cover were taking place.[46] Grazing was often seasonal. In many areas domestic stock were driven away from the arable lands and hay meadows in late spring while in late summer and early autumn acorns and beech-mast were foraged by pigs, as shown by the Anglo-Saxon charter evidence. In later times, in some areas like Exmoor, stock were brought down from the open moorlands as winter approached and moved into the lowland woods for the winter season.[47] There are few detailed records of how early medieval man managed the woodland and the evidence of palaeobotany will in time be of immense value.

Although the Cotton Tiberius calendar was probably based upon Classical exemplars, and the illustrations it uses are not set into their exact seasonal location, it is likely that the scenes it depicts are true to English practices – indeed, they may have been altered slightly for this purpose.[48] The month of July is headed by an illustration of workers cutting wood (Plate XV). It clearly shows pollards and one is reminded of the *coppendan ac*, 'the copped oak-tree', mentioned in a charter boundary clause of Stoke by Hurstbourne in Hampshire, this adjective meaning 'polled, without a top', a term which also occurs in place-names.[49] By this method suitable wood could be obtained that was out of the reach of grazing animals (see Plate X on p. 114). Direct references to coppicing, in which wood is cut back to the stump on a regular cycle and then allowed to regrow, appear to be later, but both methods were widely used in medieval times to ensure a supply of the required type of timber from managed woodland and appear to be indicated by the timbers found in archaeological excavations. A later, November, illustration shows the ends of lengths of timber being charred in a fire to prevent them from decay while other workers take the opportunity to warm themselves at the fire. Again, place-names incorporating such terms as *proc*, 'support', indicate one of the uses for the timber. Only the September illustration shows anything approaching the wildwood for here what may be swineherds are perhaps taking pigs into the woods to forage for acorns. This picture is ambiguous, however, for the men appear to carry a hunting horn and a spear and are accompanied by two dogs: this may actually be a hunting scene and the pigs could be wild boar. While woodland in some regions was being allowed to regenerate, probably due to the exclusion of domestic stock and the cessation of agriculture as certain regions were set aside for hunting, others were subject to increased clearance or assarting: the ploughman was described in literature as *harholtes feond*, 'the gray enemy of the wood',[50] and the March calendar illustration shows labourers breaking up rough ground for cultivation.

Anglo-Saxon law recognized the pressure upon woodland and timber trees were protected. Already by the seventh century the Laws of Ine in Wessex instituted penalties for their destruction:

> *Đonne mon beam on wuda forbærne, 7 weorðe yppe on þone ðe hit dyde, gielde he fulwite: geselle LX scill., forþampe fyr bið þeof.*
>
> *Gif mon afelle on wuda wel monega treowa, 7 wyrð eft undierne, forgielde III treowu ælc mid XXX scill.; ne ðearf he hiora ma geldan, wære hiora swa fela swa hiora wære; forþon sio æsc bið melda, nalles ðeof.*
>
> *[Be wudu andfenge.]*
>
> *Gif mon þonne aceorfe an treow, þæt mæge XXX swina under-gestandan, 7 wyrð undierne, geselle LX scill.*

If anyone destroys a tree in a wood by fire, and it becomes known who did it, he shall pay a full fine. He shall pay 60 shillings, because fire is a thief.

If anyone fells a large number of trees in a wood, and it afterwards becomes known, he shall pay 30 shillings for each of three trees. He need not pay for more, however many there may be, as the axe is an informer and not a thief.

If, however, anyone cuts down a tree that can shelter thirty swine, and it becomes known, he shall pay 60 shillings.[51]

For lord and peasant, one of the main uses of woodland was for building and domestic usage, such as the 'five wainloads of good brushwood, one oak annually and other timber necessary for building, firewood sufficient for his needs and other rights in woodland' allowed to the grantee of an estate at Seckley in Wolverley, Worcestershire, in AD 866.[52] Timber was a requirement for most domestic building, required in considerable quantities, and carpentry techniques appear to have been sophisticated, employing a wide range of tools. Excavation, mainly of three ninth- and tenth-century sites in Durham, Cambridgeshire and Yorkshire, has produced evidence of hammers, adzes, boring-bits, a gouge, a plane, a draw-knife, saws and a wedge, but the axe was the basic tool for felling the trees and lopping the trunks and for forming the wedges used to split the trunk.[53] Knowledge of Anglo-Saxon building techniques is increasing and oak appears to have been the most valued building material. While

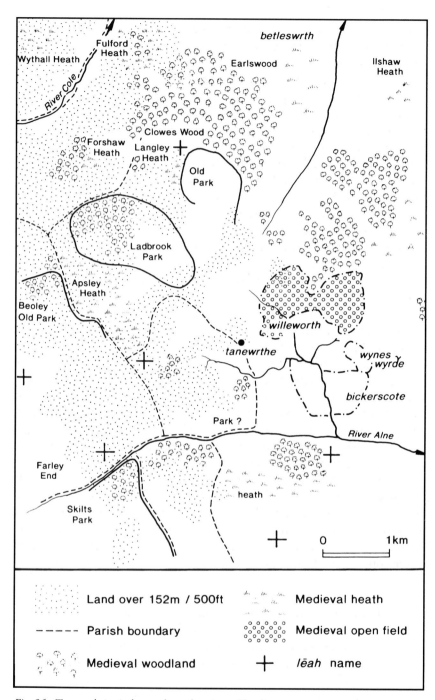

Fig. 56 Tanworth-in-Arden: early settlement and land use.

some of the stave buildings used timber from trees of considerable girth, use was also made of smaller timbers which were probably obtained from coppice woodland with standards, woodland which was less intensively managed than in medieval and later times.[54]

Woodlands also supplied timber for industrial usage. In the West Midlands this often meant supplies of wood for the salt industry of Droitwich. Domesday Book reveals manors possessing salt rights in exchange for which they appear originally to have had to send fuel for the 'ovens' in Droitwich where the salt was obtained by evaporation (Chapter 9).[55] Similarly in Kent, a ninth-century charter of Lenham notes that the wood of Blean provided cartloads of wood for the manufacture of salt along the coastal marshes.[56] The Wealden woods undoubtedly provided timber for the iron industry in the Anglo-Saxon period and a bloomery at Millbrook, on Ashdown Forest, has been radiocarbon dated to the ninth century.[57]

Settlements in woodland regions usually remained dispersed and only rarely congregated into sizeable villages. In part this may be due to the fact that the predominant type of farming in such regions was more concerned with rearing animals than growing crops and that arable fields usually needed to be enclosed to protect them from foraging animals. There would be little to gain from moving all farmers into a central village location. Although open field farming did penetrate into woodland zones, the open fields often remained small and scattered and many were subjected to early enclosure. The age of the hamlets and farms which characterized large regions of medieval England has rarely been discovered but their dispersal echoes the characteristic pattern of settlement in woodland and pasatoral regions in early medieval times.

Traditionally, woodland regions have been seen as areas where medieval colonization was a decisive factor in defining settlement patterns but the work of Tom Williamson in Essex and East Anglia shows how much earlier patterns of settlement and land use could survive to influence the later landscape. He has shown how in many well-wooded regions of this part of the country the landscape

results not from the slow and piecemeal expansion of cultivation at the expense of forest and waste, but from centuries of piecemeal alterations to landscapes that were originally planned, often on a very large scale, in the Romano-British or prehistoric periods . . . early medieval settlement did not develop within the context of a *tabula rasa*.[58]

Part of this region will be discussed further in Chapter 10.

Within or on the fringe of many woodland zones, settlements bearing *worth* names are particularly common, and the term seems to have been used for a farmstead within an enclosing fence. Michael Coston, working in Somerset, feels that many of the *worth* settlements may go back to an origin in the seventh and eighth centuries.[59] Some, he suggests, were survivals of an agricultural arrangement which was older than the open field system.[60] Similarly in Tanworth, in the Warwickshire 'Forest of Arden', several *worth* settlements, plus an additional *cot* and a *wic* settlement, seem to have been established in the parish, three of the *worths* on the better soils near the manorial centre (Figure 56). Only the latter, one of those bearing a *worth* name, had associated open field; this seems actually to have spread over the site of one of the other *worth* features, as if introduced at a later date. However, recent excavations of a *worth* settlement at Roadford in Devon[61] have failed to find any evidence earlier than the twelfth century. This may be a warning against presupposing the antiquity of many dispersed settlements but also perhaps a reminder of the ease with which such settlements could shift across the countryside.

Notes

1. Hooke, *The Anglo-Saxon Landscape*, Fig. 20; Hooke, *Anglo-Saxon Territorial Organization*.
2. Rutherford Davis, *Britons and Saxons*, p.42.
3. Gildas, *The Ruin of Britain*, 25.1, p.28.
4. *Anglo-Saxon Chronicle*, 709, ed. Swanton, p.41.
5. Stenton, *Anglo-Saxon England*, p.65; Campbell, 'The lost centuries', p.21.
6. Sawyer, *Anglo-Saxon Charters*, S 140, Kelly notes that this is a 'fabrication based on a genuine charter'.
7. *Anglo-Saxon Chronicle*, 893 [892], ed. Swanton, p.84; Wickham, 'European forests', p.502.
8. Sawyer, *Anglo-Saxon Charters*, S 1180,
9. Ibid., S 30, S 157; Birch, *Cartularium Saxonicum*, B 175, B 303; Campbell, Charters, no.16.
10. Attenborough, *The Laws*, pp.50–1, Ine c.43, 44.
11. Everitt, *Continuity and Colonization*.
12. Hill, *An Atlas of Anglo-Saxon England*.
13. Hooke, 'Regional variation'.
14. Higham, *Rome, Britain and the Anglo-Saxons*, p.78.
15. Turner, 'The vegetation'.
16. Day, 'Reconstructing the environment'.
17. Cox, 'The place-names of the earliest English records'.
18. Johansson, *Old English Place-Names*, pp.8–10.
19. Gelling, 'Some notes on Warwickshire place-names', pp.68–9.
20. Darby, *Domesday England*, pp.171–88.

21. Rackham, *Ancient Woodland*, pp.113–15, cited by Watkins, *Woodland Management*, pp.47–8.
22. Rackham, *The History of the Countryside*, p.77, Fig. 5.4.
23. Ibid.; Darby, *Domesday England*, p.193.
24. Ibid., p.202.
25. Rackham, *The History of the Countryside*, pp.76–8, Fig. 5.3.
26. Morgan (ed.), *Domesday Book 5, Berkshire*, 31,4 (D. Bk. fo.61c).
27. Gelling, *The Place-Names of Berkshire, III*, map 3.
28. Peake, *Trans Newbury & District Field Club*.
29. Fairbrother, 'Faccombe Netherton'.
30. Hooke, 'Pre-Conquest woodland'.
31. Hooke, *Anglo-Saxon Landscapes of the West Midlands*, pp.236, 245.
32. Sawyer, *Anglo-Saxon Charters*, S 1370; Birch, *Cartularium axonicum*, B 1139.
33. Sawyer, ibid., S 372; Birch, ibid., B 613.
34. Ælfric, *Colloquium*, p.22, trans. Swanton, *Anglo-Saxon Prose*, p.110.
35. Phœbus, *The Hunting Book*, pp.74–5.
36. Ælfric, *Colloquium*, p.21; trans. Swanton, *Anglo-Saxon Prose*, p.109.
37. Ælfric, *Colloquium*, p.22, trans. Swanton, *Anglo-Saxon Prose*, p.109.
38. Bentley Wood in Melchet later belonged to Amesbury Abbey, *VCH Wiltshire, III*, p.244.
39. Thorn and Thorn (eds), *Domesday Book 6, Wiltshire*, 13,10; 13,18.
40. Roberts, 'Settlement, population and land use'; Hooke, 'Names and settlement'.
41. Everitt, *Continuity and Colonization*, pp.282–3, map. 14.
42. Rackham, *The History of the Countryside*, p.120.
43. Watkins, *Woodland Management*, p.122.
44. Rackham, *The History of the Countryside*, p.140.
45. Watkins, *Woodland Management*, pp.116–17.
46. Hooke, 'Anglo-Saxon landscapes of the West Midlands' (EPNSJ).
47. Watkins, *Woodland Management*, pp.116–17.
48. McGurk, 'The labours of the months', pp.40–3.
49. Sawyer, *Anglo-Saxon Charters*, S 359; Birch, *Cartularium Saxonicum*, B 594.
50. Riddle 21, trans. Mackie, *The Exeter Book*, II, pp.110–11.
51. Attenborough, *The Laws*, pp.50–1; Ine, c.43.
52. Sawyer, *Anglo-Saxon Charters*, S 212, Birch, *Cartularium Saxonicum*, B 513.
53. Wilson, 'Craft and industry'.
54. Rackham, *Ancient Woodland*; Goodburn, 'Fragments of a 10th-century timber arcade'; Coles and Goodburn (eds), *Wet Site Excavation and Survey*, pp.51–3.
55. Hooke, 'The Droitwich salt industry'.
56. Sawyer, *Anglo-Saxon Charters*, S 324, Birch, *Cartularium Saxonicum*, B 854.
57. Tebbutt, 'A Middle Saxon iron-smelting site'.
58. Williamson, 'Settlement chronology'.
59. Costen, *The Origins of Somerset*, pp.93–4.
60. Ibid., p.125; 'Huish and worth'.
61. From information given by P. J. Weddell and C. G. Henderson (Exeter Museums Archaeology Unit); brief notes in *Medieval Archaeology* 36 (1992), pp. 217–19.

CHAPTER 8

Marshland, Wetland and Moorland
The Use of the Margins

> *There is in Britain a fen of immense size, which begins from
> the River Granta not far from the city of the same name, called
> Grantchester. There are immense swamps, sometimes dark
> stagnant water, sometimes foul rivulets running; and also many
> islands and reeds and tummocks and thickets. And it extends to
> the North Sea with numerous wide and lengthy meanderings.*[1]

Grantchester was Cambridge, set amidst the eastern fenland which was
perhaps the most extensive area of wetland existing in early medieval
England. Here, according to a saint's life copied in the eleventh century,[2]
the saintly Guthlac had sought obscurity in the remote marshlands to
contemplate God.

In prehistoric times the area of fen and saltmarsh covered some million
acres of what now lies within the counties of Cambridge, Lincoln, Norfolk
and Suffolk, crossed by the rivers Witham, Welland, Nene and Ouse. The
whole region lay at little more than two metres above sea level and had
been subjected to a rising water table since the last Ice Age. Iron Age
communities exploited fenland margins, fishing, fowling and making use
of seasonal pasture. Salt-making was an important activity. The fenland
environment was seldom static as freshwater, marine and brackish
conditions developed, matured and generally shifted in relation to
settlements. Recent survey has identified many more Iron Age settlement
sites than were previously known but most were located along the fenland
margin and on islands in the southern peatlands for at that time wetland
was at a maximum.[3]

Under the Romans, colonization took advantage of falling water tables
and for the first time 'there was appreciable modification of the landscape
by large-scale engineering works, as well as the establishment of
settlements'.[4] Roads and dykes have been identified and rural settlement
sites lay thick along the peat/siltland margin and on the southern islands,
with urban sites generally restricted to the fenland edge. In Lincolnshire,
especially, aerial photography has revealed a complex and dense pattern

of settlement with fields defined by man-made drains and canals. The fen edge on the landward side was so massively developed in the second century that its management as an imperial estate concentrating on salt production and on the production of meat, leather and wool has been suggested. However, the absence of villas may alternatively suggest a simpler farming economy.[5] Much of the peat fen, however, probably continued to provide summer grazing. Changing sea-levels caused parts of the seaward silt fen to emerge as dry land and there was extensive settlement for stock rearing, the ground water probably remaining too brackish for corn cultivation: cropmarks reveal droves and square-shaped enclosures which appear to have been used for the management of domestic stock. A widespread saltern industry flourished and turbaries have been identified that supplied turf for both domestic fuel and the salterns.[6] Settlements tended to congregate along the banks of streams which were tidal in character. In Norfolk, near Welney, a string of Roman sites follows the old dry course or 'roddon' of the Great Ouse. These silted-up former estuaries began to rise as underlying peats were increasingly compressed, providing dry ridge-top sites through the marshes between the intermittently available pastureland. The Roman period is the earliest phase during which settlement became widespread on the silt fen but increased flooding occurred between the fourth and fifth centuries AD.

Settlement continued to be unstable in Anglo-Saxon times as the fenland followed its changing natural pattern, subject to sea flood and river flood and with a gradually increasing water table leading to further peat formation and true fen conditions in many regions. Many Roman sites were covered by the encroaching peat, especially in regions behind the seaward silt fen. Recent work in The Netherlands has illustrated how peat lands, once raised well above sea-level, will become depressed when the land has been drained for agriculture.[7] This allows the further oxidization of the peat which had been repressed under water-logged conditions. Thus the high levels of Roman farming may have contributed to the sinking of the peatlands.

Early Saxon settlements continued in much the same areas as their Roman predecessors but with far fewer sites known (Figure 57); later, increasing wetness may have caused widespread devastation but settlement desertion, especially along the fen edge, was also probably associated with the general trend towards nucleation common elsewhere in this period. Some areas, like the empty fenland to the south of Spalding, indeed, appear to have been abandoned: Guthlac's hermitage (later to be the site of Crowland Abbey) was founded there upon an island amidst a 'hideous fen of a huge bigness'. Here fresh water had become impounded as the mouth of the River Welland had become progressively impeded by

Fig. 57   The eastern Fens (based upon the work of Hall and Coles).

developing marshes.[8] Freshwater fen also appears to have been advancing across the western siltlands in Lincolnshire. Towards the end of the Anglo-Saxon period, perhaps in the ninth or tenth century, a massive flood defence, the Sea Bank, was constructed all round the Wash to protect

Plate XVI   Marshland reed-bed, Cambridgeshire.

settlement and agriculture on the siltlands.[9] In general, large areas of the peatlands became and remained empty areas not extensively reclaimed until the seventeenth century.

The utilization of resources in the fenlands gave rise to characteristic patterns of settlement and estate formation: the northern marshlands of Norfolk appear to have been used initially as summer pastures by communities established on the high siltlands engaged in stock rearing and salt production and the marshland itself provided peat for fuel, thatching materials, fish and fowl (Plate XVI). Such communities also grazed the coastal saltmarsh. Eventually settlement was to polarize in a restricted number of more permanent locations but subsequently sent fingers of colonization along drove roads into the fen (Figure 58). Parishes related to these settlements were characteristically long and narrow. In Lincolnshire the fenland also provided pasture for stock during the summer months with intercommoning in the Anglo-Saxon period preceding later manorial organization.[10]

A number of monastic sites were founded on islands in the fens, including Crowland and Thorney abbeys. Ely, to the north-east of Cambridge, was one of the great fenland abbeys refounded during the monastic revival in the second half of the tenth century on an earlier

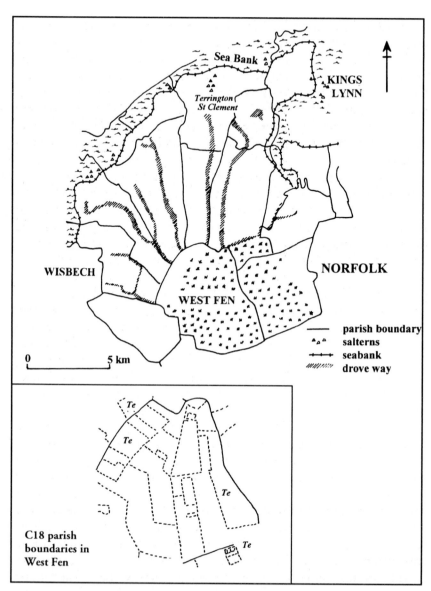

Fig. 58   Fenland parishes in Norfolk (after Silvester 1988 and Darby 1977) showing how a group of Norfolk parishes near Kings Lynn intercommoned on West Fen which was subsequently divided between them. To illustrate the holdings of one parish the inset map shows the outlying detached parcels of Terrington St Clement.

monastic site (see Figure 57). Its name may mean 'eel-district', incorporating Old English *ge*, 'district', and the abbey buildings rise strikingly out of the flat surrounding lowland which was once very much more marshy. Gelling[11] notes the concentration of *eg* names in the Ely region: Manea, Coveney, Stuntney in Ely and Barway in Soham, perhaps 'island of common pasture', 'Cofa's island' or 'island in the bay', 'Stunta's isle' and 'hill-island', names discussed by Reaney who notes Atkyns's description of the latter place as a 'myerie island . . . and is environed with fens on each side'.[12]

In Cambridgeshire the whole region came under monastic ownership. The resources of the fens continued to be exploited, like the shallow but wide stretch of freshwater known as *witlesmere*, Whittlesea Mere near Peterborough, where Peterborough, Ramsey and Thorney Abbeys held rights to fish and fowl (see Figure 57). Throughout the later Anglo-Saxon and medieval period there were attempts to improve the economic potential: the massive earthwork known as the Sea Bank, noted above, protected arable fields on the siltlands; another, the Fen Bank, kept out winter floods from the fen. Flood-gates and sluices removed surface water. A complex system of canals linked the monastic sites on their islands in the peatlands and a new cut for the Nene drained land around Wisbech. To the north, Crowland Abbey also sought to improve the surrounding marshland. Today the landscape is far removed from the 'obscure island' chosen by Guthlac in 'the loneliness of the broad wilderness' with its 'swampy thickets'.[13]

Rackham notes that the best remaining areas of fenland include the little-altered Dersingham–Wolferton Fen in a remote corner north of King's Lynn in Norfolk, where copious springs of acid water feed into an area rich with mosses, bog-asphodel, cranberry, sundew and other species of raised bogland, including patches of birch. The best relict of the medieval silt fens he finds in the Ouse Washes between the Old and New Bedford Rivers, 'which survive because they are still used as a flood reservoir every winter'.[14] In summer they dry out and are used for cattle grazing, and even some common rights remain. The fact that they are grazed prevents them from becoming overgrown by woodland and many kinds of fen vegetation are found. The Washes are alive with migrating birds in season. One rather better-known remnant of East Anglia's great fens is Wicken Fen in Cambridgeshire, now partly managed by the National Trust (Figure 59). A complicated pattern of ownership prevented the enclosure of its 600 acres and it was divided into strips like a dole meadow; the ridge and furrow of former ploughing and the signs of peat-digging reflect centuries of continued use, but neglect led to an over-growth of woodland after 1920. The raised fen still supports

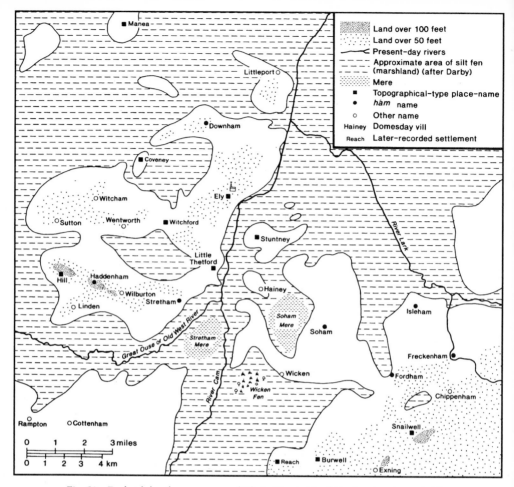

Fig. 59 Fenland detail: estates around Ely in Cambridgeshire showing the probable extent of marshland at the end of the Anglo-Saxon period.

a wide variety of flora and birdlife but now has to be artificially prevented from drying out.

Similar reclamation of marshland appears to have been carried out in Romney Marsh. The marshes were still in the process of formation in late Roman times as shingle was carried eastwards towards the mouth of a large estuary fed by the rivers Brede, Tillingham and Rother. A cuspate headland gradually formed, curved at right angles to the main beach. Salt extraction again gave rise to settlements within the marshland. Movement of shingle eastwards allowed the sea eventually to break through the barrier and flood the lowlying marshes in the west of the area, some rivers being diverted southwards directly to the sea, and increased silting occurred in the old estuary.[15] The area continued to be drained by two arms of the River Rother, both referred to as the Limen in pre-Conquest charters.

The coastline had not acquired its present-day form even by medieval times but the charters show that the marshland was being reclaimed in the eighth and ninth centuries, divided and apportioned between various landholders. One of the earliest grants concerns pasture in the marsh granted by King Wihtred of Kent to St Mary's church, Lyminge, in AD 697 or 700.[16] The produce from such marshland pastures is described in a charter of AD 858: when Æthelberht of Kent granted one estate in exchange for another, the marshes attached to Wassingwell (probably Westwell in the upper Stour valley) yielded 40 weys of cheese, 20 lambs and (?)10 fleeces from the sheep pastured there.[17]

There were other areas in coastal and riverine situations where marshland was found in significant quantities. The Vale of York and areas along the Lancashire coast are two such regions but more is known about the Anglo-Saxon situation in the Somerset Levels because, again, contemporary evidence exists in the form of charters. Between the

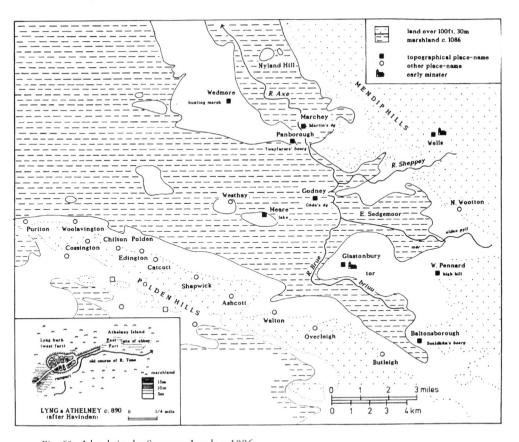

Fig. 60   Islands in the Somerset Levels *c.* 1086.

Mendips and the Quantocks, where a low clay ridge impedes drainage seawards, stretches the low flat land which until the eighteenth and nineteenth centuries was regularly subject to inundations from both freshwater rivers and high tidal floods, especially in the winter months. Asser's *Life of Alfred* describes how Alfred had to make his way 'in difficulties through the woods and fen-fastnesses' to Athelney, *æpelingas ieg* (the West Saxon form of *eg*, i.e. 'the island of the princes'), an island only twelve metres high near the southern margin of the southern Levels 'which is surrounded on all sides by very great swampy and impassable marshes, so that no one can approach it by any means except in punts'.[18] After his victory against the Danes at *Ethandun* (*c*. 878) Alfred founded a monastery there and this was connected to the dry land by a bridge giving access to the fortified burh of Lyng (Figure 60, inset, south of the area shown on the main map).[19] A monastery at Muchelney, some ten kilometres to the south-east, had been established on an island in the River Parrett earlier (possibly before the end of the seventh century). On the northern side of the main section of the Levels, Glastonbury had reputedly long been a sacred site, its tor once rising up as an island above the marsh, to become one of the earliest British monasteries established in Somerset.

The Levels had provided summer pasture for stock since prehistoric times and their continued use in this way may be reflected in the name of Somerton, the royal estate at the head of King's Sedgemoor. This means 'the summer *tun*', the place visited in summer.[20] This may indicate a place of summer pasture, probably for cattle, and is incorporated in the name of the county of Somerset: *Sumorsæte*, 'the people dependent on Somerton'. Much of the marshland was to be granted to the Church: early grants to Glastonbury, their originals now lost, appear to have concerned islands of dry land in the marshes. These include two small islands in the marshland of *Ferramere* (Meare) at Westhay and Godney ('Goda's island'), given with fisheries and woods (the charter mentions *paludibis*, 'marshes', and *pascuis apium*, 'green meadows') in AD 670, and others at Beckery, Marchey and Nyland.[21] An estate at West Pennard, to the east of Glastonbury, was allegedly granted to the monastery as early as AD 681.[22] It is accompanied by a later boundary clause [23] which takes the western boundary from woods to the old course of the River Brue in the south-western corner of the land unit (*eobbanlege* and *totalege*; another version[24] names these as *obanleighe* and *cantanleighe*) northwards into Sedgemoor 'along the marsh out to the Brue' across then eastwards along the *aldan pyll*, 'old brook or creek' (see Figure 60).[25] The badly drained marshland is referred to by the Old English term *mor*. However, dykes, probably used for drainage, begin to appear in the late Anglo-Saxon boundary clauses.

The monasteries at Glastonbury and Muchelney also had fisheries in the rivers Parrett and Axe. What may appear as an interesting reference to monastic initiative is also found in the Somerset Levels, for the church of Glastonbury maintained a vineyard at Panborough in AD 956.[26] This vineyard was not alone in the county for a second is noted on a estate of Watchet in AD 962,[27] on the north coast of the county overlooking the Bristol Channel, an estate then being granted to Abingdon Abbey in Berkshire.

If the pasturing of cattle in summer was a prime type of land use in the Levels, the importance of fishing and fowling should not be overlooked. Ælfric in his Colloquy notes the fisherman stating

> I board my boat and cast my net into the river; and throw in a hook and bait and baskets; and whatever they catch I take. . . . Eels and pike, minnows and turbot, trout and lampreys and whatever swims in the water. Small fish.[28]

Weirs were also constructed across rivers and a survey of Tidenham in Gloucestershire[29] describes *cytweras*, 'basket weirs', and *hæcweras*, 'hackle weirs', which were used in the estuaries of the Severn and Wye. The former appear to have been rows of tapering baskets of the sort still in use in the late nineteenth century to catch salmon; the latter were barriers of fence or wattle set across the current to produce an eddy in which fish could be caught from a boat.[30] Another term used in pre-Conquest charters and place-names is *hæc(c)*, 'a hatch, a sluice' and also a kind of fish-trap.

Ælfric's fowler states: 'I trap birds in many ways; sometimes with nets, sometimes with snares, sometimes with lime, by whistling, with a hawk or with a trap.'[31] Young hawks were collected in autumn to be trained and the sites of eyries in the woods were well known.

Sum sceal wildne fugel   wloncne atemian
heafoc on honda   oþþæt seo heoroswealwe
wynsum weorþeð   deþ he wyrplas on
fedeþ swa on feterum   fiþrum dealne
lepeþ lyftswiftne   lytlum gieflum
oþþæt se wælisca   wædum ond dædum
his ætgiefan   eaðmod weorpeð
ond to hagostealdes   honda gelæred

Another shall tame the proud wild bird,
the hawk on his hand, until that fierce swallow
becomes gentle; he puts foot-rings upon it,

and so feeds the fettered bird, proud of its plumage,
weakens the swift flyer with small pieces of food,
until the Welsh falcon in its garb and deeds
becomes humble towards its feeder
and trained to the young man's hand.

> (The Fates of Men (fo.88b),
> *The Exeter Book*, ed. Mackie, pp.30–1)

Native hawks included the peregrine falcon, the sparrowhawk and the goshawk. The former was much prized for falconry in historical times and could capture sizeable prey. Although its preferred habitat is sea-cliffs and hill crags, it has been known to nest in wooded lowlands and returns year after year to the same eyrie. Today it is chiefly restricted to Scotland. The goshawk used to breed regularly in parts of Britain but is now scarce. The sparrowhawk is the commonest native hawk found in England today and was much used for hawking although regarded as rather inferior (in a fourteenth-century tale regarded as 'an hawke for a preste'), for its prey is restricted to small birds, especially blackbirds, thrushes and sometimes larks, and its appetite is small. Small birds did, however, form a substantial part of a luxury diet in the Middle Ages (as in parts of southern Europe to this day) and the goshawk and the sparrowhawk, although both birds of unpredictable behaviour, were regarded as 'hawks of the fist' in the fourteenth century. At that date the larger birds were regarded as 'hawks of the tower'.

The fourteenth-century *Boke of St Albans*[32] attempted to show how different species of birds were suited to different ranks of the nobility, although the listing cannot have been factual. Thus the 'egle, bawtere and melowne' were regarded as the birds of 'an Emprowre', the 'gerfawken' the bird of a king, the 'Fawken gentill' the bird of a prince. Ranking continued down to the 'Goshawke' of the yeoman, the sparrowhawk of the priest noted above and the 'Muskyte' of the 'holiwater clerke'.

The Anglo-Saxon Cotton Tiberius calendar[33] for October (Plate XVII) shows falconers with hawks and several Mercian charters specifically mention this method of hunting. One of these was a grant of 844 by King Berhtwulf to Æthelwulf, *dux*, which freed an estate at Pangbourne, Berkshire, 'from the entertainment of ealdorman and from that burden which we call in Saxon *fæstingmen*; neither are to be sent there men who bear hawks or falcons, or lead dogs or horses'.[34] A more questionable charter of King Berhtwulf, allegedly of 845,[35] grants similar privileges to the monastery of *Ufera Stretford*, at Stratford-upon-Avon in Warwickshire, and a further authentic charter issued by Burgred, King of Mercia, in 855, exempted the minster at Blockley in Gloucestershire from dues which

Plate XVII   Scenes from the Cotton Tiberius calendar: *May:* shepherds and sheep; *October:* falconry and fowling.

included 'the feeding and maintenance of all hawks and falcons in the land of the Mercians, and of all huntsmen of the king or ealdorman except only those who are in the province of the Hwicce'.[36]

Obviously hawking could be carried out over any kind of open terrain but the Blockley charter is a reminder that the Bishop of Worcester's manor there overlooked the marshlands which lay around the headwater streams of the Knee Brook, a tributary of the River Stour, and those of the Evenlode. The valleys are underlain by Lower Lias clays but with extensive overlying deposits of glacial boulder clay and patches of sands and gravels, and the two river systems are separated only by a narrow watershed of glacial moraine. The area was long frequented by fishermen and fowlers but in the thirteenth century the Abbot of Winchester established the new centre of Moreton-in-Marsh on an island of glacial sand and gravel and this was to flourish as a market for the corn crops of the valley region and the wool trade of the Cotswolds.

The ridge and furrow technique of ploughing arable land in medieval England must have helped to drain the land and this technique is likely to have been in widespread use in early medieval England. Although it provided raised ridges on which crops could be grown, the intervening

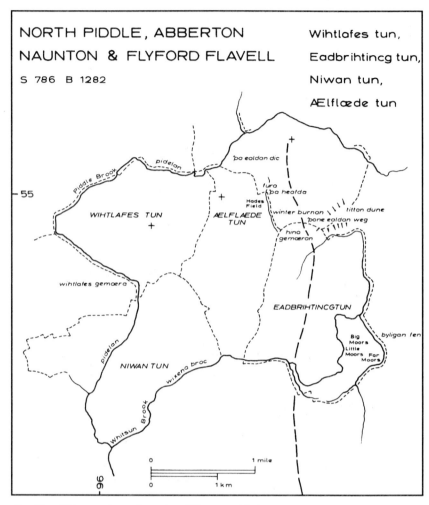

NORTH PIDDLE, ABBERTON   Wihtlafes tun,

NAUNTON & FLYFORD FLAVELL   Eadbrihtincg tun,

S 786 B 1282   Niwan tun,

ÆLflæde tun

Fig. 61a   Abberton charter boundary (Worcestershire).

furrows also facilitated run-off and the technique was used into the modern period even within enclosed fields in many parts of England. Land drains only came into general use in the seventeenth century and even today many people are unaware of the complicated patterns of drainage pipes which underlie modern fields.

In early medieval England areas of poor drainage must have been common and charter boundaries frequently help to build up a picture of such land. The commonest term used to refer to this type of land in the southern and midland England and in the eastern fenlands is *mor*, although the original meaning of the word may have been 'barren waste-

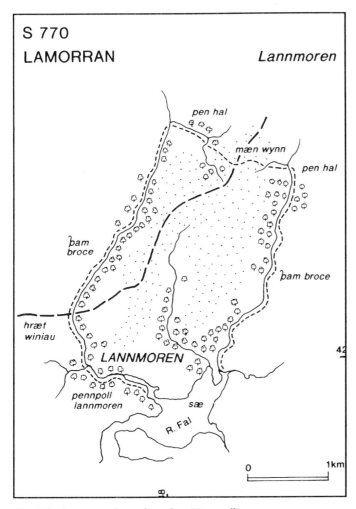

Fig. 61b   Lamorran charter boundary (Cornwall).

land'. *Mersc*, 'watery land, a marsh', is also common and regions settled by Scandinavians have an old Norse word *mos*, meaning 'a bog, swamp', which is found largely in the north and north-west midlands. 'Fen' to describe 'a fen, a marsh, marshland' can be derived from either Old Norse *fen* or Old English *fenn* (East Saxon *fænn*) while *sloh* is an Old English word for 'a slough, a mire'. Some streamlet names, too, seem to have been used more commonly in marshy areas, with Old English *lad* giving rise to the modern dialect term 'lode', which is used commonly for a fenland drainage channel, and Old English **læc*, 'a stream, a bog', giving rise to the northern term 'lache, letch', a term which is used to describe a stream flowing through boggy land. The old English term *lacu* also seems to have been used for the type of slow-moving stream which characterized areas of poor drainage.

Sometimes these features figure prominently in particular charter boundaries or along parts of a boundary. One such instance occurs in central Worcestershire, on a flat part of the Central Worcestershire Plain, where *byligan fen*, perhaps 'the bag-shaped fen', described an area of poor drainage which lay along headwater streams of the Whitsun Brook (Figure 61a). Later field-names 'Big', 'Little' and 'Far Moors' used another marsh term to describe the same area.[37] Today the area has been drained and forms unimpressive cropland but *ðeornan mor*, 'the thorny marsh', on the boundary of Martin Hussingtree, is still a waterlogged area.[38] This strongly suggests that pressure on the land in this region was insufficient to take development right to township or parish margins if the land there was difficult or of a marginal character.

Much the same situation appears to have existed in many regions. In Cornwall several charter boundary clauses refer to marshy areas along creeks and streams. Here the landmarks are often given in Cornish so that the boundary of Trethewey in St Martin-in-Meneage in the Lizard peninsula commences at *pennhal meglar*, 'the head of the marsh' (here perhaps compounded with a saint's name).[39] Landmarks along the boundary of Lamorran, a parish to the east of Truro, include *pen hal*, also 'head of the marsh', and *oðrum pen hal*, 'the other head of the marsh', showing how marshland lay at the head of the streams which defined both the western and eastern boundaries of the parish (Figure 61b) and the boundary of Trenowth in Probus also ran *adune to pen hal*, 'down to the head of the marsh', as it approached the River Fal.[40]

Man's use of the wetlands throughout prehistory and later times has now been sufficiently investigated to show how valuable they were as a resource. Hunting and fowling provided valuable additions to the food supply, a feature much appreciated in many parts of Europe to the present day. Indeed, in parts of France, like the *étang* areas of the Dombes Plateau to the north-east of Lyons or the Brenne region of central France, stretches of water have been artificially created since at least the twelfth century to fulfil this need and are actually being extended today. Peat-cutting has been a source of fuel in such areas for generations and had also provided materials for the construction of warm, weatherproof houses in such places as Dartmoor and Exmoor, and especially in regions where timber was in short supply. The lowland marshes provided invaluable summer pasture for the communities that surrounded them, and were often to become subdivided, like pockets of woodland, between parishes when rights were eventually restricted to individual manors.

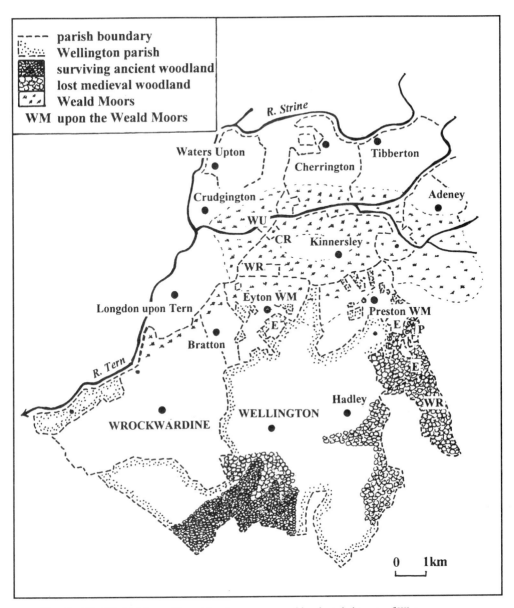

Fig. 62 The Weald Moors, Shropshire, intercommoned by the inhabitants of Waters Upton (WU), Cherrington, Tibberton, Adeney, Kinnersley, Crudgington (CR), Wrockwardine (WR), Eyton upon the Weald Moors (E), Preston upon the Weald Moors (P), and Wellington. Wrockwardine and Wellington were capital manors of which most of the other vills were dependencies.

Another example of such partition is seen in the case of the Weald Moors in Shropshire, 'by far the largest spread of peat in the vicinity of the Wrekin'[41] (Figure 62). This area was referred to as *le Wildmore* or *Wyldmore* in medieval times from Old English *wilde-mor*, 'waste moor', (a rare element in place-names)[42] and this area of low marshland was used as an area of summer pasture before being drained and enclosed after the sixteenth century, the final stages of enclosure only being completed in the 1830s. Manors which were in the hands of the king or powerful noblemen in 1086, like those of Wrockwardine and Wellington, held berewicks upon the fringes of the Moors and a series of villages grew up encircling the moor, like Eyton upon the Weald Moors and Preston upon the Weald Moors on the southern side, and Crudgington, Cherrington and Tibberton to the north. Kinnersley, on raised ground in the heart of the Moors is 'Cyneheard's island' (incorporating Old English *eg*) but with alternative forms which contain Old English *(ge)hæg*, 'an enclosure in woodland'.[43] Although mentioned already in 1086, the well-defined plans of some of these settlements strongly suggest medieval planning, for Kynnersley and Preston cluster around a well-defined, if small, village green while Cherrington and Longdon-upon-Tern have linear plans.[44] These settlements probably intercommoned at first but detached portions of parishes show how the moor was finally subdivided between them. Today the area is criss-crossed with drainage ditches to render it suitable for farmland but seventeenth-century documents still refer to the men of the surrounding villages taking their cattle 'unto the Wildmoor'.[45]

Transhumance and Moorland Regions

Exploitation of fenland marshes or such localized patches of marshland such as the Weald Moors could be used by the inhabitants of the surrounding settlements but already a number of cases have been presented of pastures being used on a seasonal basis by more distant communities. Two typical regions in which transhumance may have been practised at some early stage are Kent and the Warwickshire Arden, both regions of woodland pasture (see Figure 48 on p. 143). The practice was, however, widespread across much of England, Wales and southern Scotland and also involved the movement of stock on to upland moorland. This is still common in many areas of Alpine Europe and Scandinavia today. In northern England, where the upper moorlands of the Pennines and other hilly districts still preserve something of their inhospitable nature, it is not difficult to envisage a preference for seasonal use of the land for summer shielings. In reality, the necessity to move stock away from the lowland arable and hay meadows is also an important factor in the development of such a system. Shielings have only occasionally left traces which have been archaeologically investigated but were often flimsy impermanent structures. Ælfric notes the shepherd's daily duties in his Colloquy:

> In the early morning I drive my sheep to their pasture, and in the heat and in cold, stand over them with dogs, lest wolves devour them; and I lead them back to their folds and milk them twice a day, and move their folds; and in addition I make cheese and butter.[46]

The Cotton Tiberius calendar also shows shepherds under the month of May (Plate XVII). Here the shepherd, with his characteristic cloak and crook, is being offered a lamb while other sheep, one of them being suckled by a lamb, graze on a nearby hill. There are also rams in the foreground, the sheep apparently white and long-tailed.[47]

The actual movement of stock between the lower and upper pastures is clearly evidenced in Lancashire where Mary Atkin[48] has noted stock tracks extending for miles along township boundaries linking the two. The tracks of different communities often ran parallel before funnelling out onto the moorland, like those linking Croston in Leland Hundred with its upper pastures at Chorley on the flanks of the Pennines. Interestingly, she also identifies a distinctive settlement pattern in this area based upon a series of 'double ovals', with a small 'arable' oval lying very close to a second larger 'pasture' oval. She finds these in both lowland and upland terrain (Chapter 10). At Roystone Grange in Derbyshire Martin Wildgoose and Richard Hodges[49] identified a similar system as Roman in origin, associated with a Romano-British farmstead, but the pattern does not yet seem to have been observed in other more southerly regions. It may have been an early land use pattern which managed to survive in the north of England because population densities remained relatively low in the early medieval period and even longer in upland regions.[50]

Scandinavian names clearly perpetuated the arrangement of transhumance in those parts of northern England settled by the Danes and Norwegians. In the Lake District, names containing 'scale' are derived from West Scandinavian *skali*, 'shed', while Old Norse *sæter* and *erg* referred to the actual summer pasture ground, the latter used for lowland moorland. A concentration of shieling names (shieling itself is a Middle English word *scele* meaning 'a temporary building, a shepherd's summer hut') also suggests that transhumance was practised along the eastern flanks of the Pennines in medieval times. In north Cumberland and Northumberland the practice survived into the seventeenth century with stock being driven a distance of 10 to 20 miles, as between Askerton North Moor and the seven baronies of Gilsland barony in Cumberland.[51]

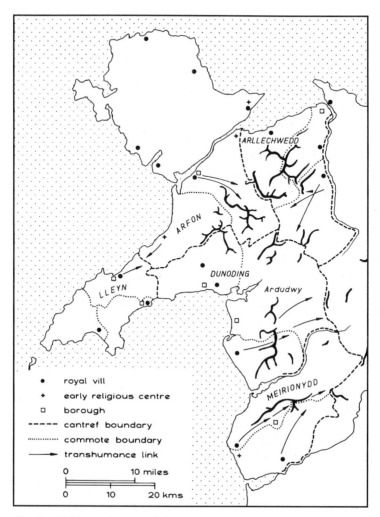

Fig. 63   Welsh transhumance links.

The system was so deeply entrenched by early medieval times in both Anglo-Saxon, British and Scandinavian areas that it was to have a marked influence upon territorial organization and the demarcation of boundaries. Barrow[52] showed how closely ecclesiastical organization mirrored early arrangements in south Scotland and in Wales Glanville Jones[53] shows how estate linkages between lowland and upland were fundamental in the development of the commotal system. Medieval extents made in Wales after its conquest by Edward I show places in the Conwy valley utilizing the valleys below Snowdon for their summer pastures with Prince Edward maintaining studs of horses in these fastnesses (Figure 63). Further to the south, pastures around Trawsfynnyd ('across the mountains'), beyond the Rhinog mountain range, were similarly used by royal estates on the coastlands of Merioneth. The royal *maerdref* of Ystumgwern, for instance, in Ardudwy, was linked to pastures at Bryn Coch, Prysor and Y Feidiog on the inland moors.[54] It would be stretching the evidence to suggest that this type of regional transhumance necessarily stemmed from a Celtic or pre-Roman past but Higham[55] has recently noted the allusion to transhumance in the works of Gildas, compiled in sixth-century Britain.

Although the early evidence for the woodlands of the Warwickshire Arden and the Kentish Weald suggests use by distant communities, in both Wales and northern England rights to the use of the upland pastures seem to have been vested in the royal overlord. Jolliffe[56] showed how cattle dues still payable to an overlord in medieval times represented the manner in which the peasantry paid for the right to pasture on the shire moorlands. Ownership by individual manorial lords is, however, likely to be a later development in the tenurial structure. By medieval times the upland moorlands of the Lake District were regarded as the lord's demesne hunting reserves with the peasant farmers having to purchase rights to make use of demesne land.

The parcelling up of regions of marginal pastureland is illustrated by the evolving parish system. As in wooded zones, the estates often remained dependent manors and chapelries of more major units located in more favourable areas.

The Roystone land unit mentioned above lies on the limestone heartland of the White Peak at the southern end of the Pennine spine. Here the thin soils and exposed nature of the land have rarely been easy, at least under present-day climatic conditions, for crop cultivation, apart from the few valleys draining towards the River Dove. The climate was similar in the Anglo-Saxon period and, despite the incidence of many pagan burials in older tumuli in the surrounding region (burials attributed to the *Pecsæte*, the 'Peak-dwellers'), an Anglo-Saxon presence at Roystone has not been detected between the fourth and tenth centuries.[57] The Roman farm seems to have abandoned yet the region remained important enough to form part of a five-hide estate granted by King Edgar to a certain Æthelfrith in AD 963.[58] The estate, however, remained a subsidiary estate of Bradbourne, a few kilometres away to the south. This area of dry pasture, therefore, provides the same evidence of estate parcellation as that noted over most of the rest of England. Such linked vills are a characteristic feature of those northern counties recorded in Domesday Book. The Roystone study emphasized the importance of such marginal zones as important pastoral regions.

Plate XVIII   Dartmoor moorland. View across central Dartmoor from Bennett's Cross near Soussons Down. Soussons Down is named from a landmark on the Anglo-Saxon boundary of *Peadingtun* (S 1547, Hooke 1994, pp. 218–19). The boundary clause runs to *sufonstanas*, 'seven stones', a name now found in the west of Manaton parish.

In Devon, Harold Fox[59] is researching the links which existed between lowland manors and holdings on the moorlands of Dartmoor (Plate XVIII). Here, transhumance gave way to a system of the guardage of stock, whereby the tenants of the lowland manors paid the officials of the moor to care for their stock during the summer season. The heart of Dartmoor was a royal forest in medieval times and this may have led to the formal arrangements and rents recorded for pasturage. Cattle were still being summered on Dartmoor in the early fifteenth century. Earlier, Domesday Book reveals linkages between manors on the western side of the Exe estuary and on the Devon coast with Dartmoor (Figure 64): the Dartmoor manor of 'Dewdon', probably Jordan in Widecombe in the Moor, is recorded as a dependent member of the manor of Cockington on Tor Bay.[60] Jordan is situated in the valley of the West Webburn and the links were maintained into the seventeenth and eighteenth centuries. Today the settlement of this name lies near the junction of the cultivated and open land on the eastern side of the moor. Similarly, Kenton in the Exe valley was linked to Chagford on the south Teign.[61]

Another link identified by Fox is that between the bishop's estates on Tor Bay, centred upon Paignton, and the stretch of moorland, including

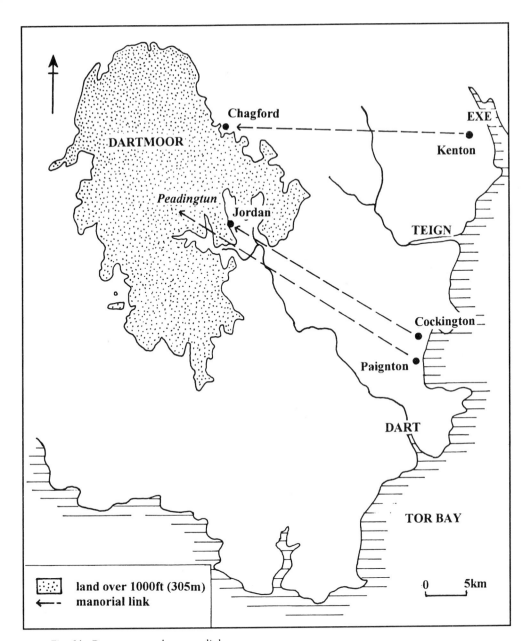

Fig. 64   Dartmoor transhumance links.

most of the parish of Widecombe in the Moor, called *Peadingtun* in the pre-Conquest period.[62] The latter land unit can be identified from its boundary clause and the bishop continued to hold these estates at a later period. *Peadingtun* seems to have been 'the estate or farmstead of . . .' compounded with a name resembling 'Peat' or 'Pead' but a corruption of either name might allow for an association between this name and *Peinton* (Paignton), 'Pæga's farmstead/estate'. Undoubtedly, the moorland provided summer pasture for the lowland manors just as it does for the farmers around the moor today. In time, many of the summer shielings gave way to permanent settlement but upon the higher land many of these medieval hamlets were not to prove long lasting. On Hound Tor in Manaton, two hamlets appear to have replaced summer shieling settlements, and were permanently occupied in the thirteenth and fourteenth centuries, but both were abandoned after this date, perhaps due to climatic deterioration.[63]

In Cornwall, too, place-names clearly attest to the previous practice of transhumance between more fertile lowland and upland pasture. Names containing Cornish *haf*, 'summer', **havek*, 'summer-land', *havos*, 'shieling', and *havar*, 'land left fallow in summer', all indicate their previous use as summer shielings. Most of them are located upon marginal land, in contrast to the **hendre*, 'winter homestead, home farm', the latter one of the commonest Cornish farm-names.[64] The largest number of *hendre* names cluster around Bodmin Moor but the name is found all over the county. In a study of the Davidstow region,[65] it has been noted that the *hendre* names are themselves on the periphery of the settled parts of the parish and this suggests that they may represent components of a later phase of transhumance when common grazing by the entire community was perhaps being appropriated to particular farms and hamlets.

In west Wales, where transhumance continued to be practised into relatively modern times, exploitation of the uplands by township communities also seems to have been replaced later by separate *hafodydd* based upon individual farms, themselves often bearing *hendre* names like their Cornish equivalents. The remains of the earlier house sites lie abandoned on the *friddoedd* beneath the fields of what were probably Tudor enclosure, or beyond the mountain wall which demarcated this period of enclosure from that carried out under parliamentary act in the eighteenth and nineteenth centuries.[66] Although the permanent farmstead, the *hendre* or 'old settlement', sometimes lay only a few hundred feet below, the transfer of stock was not only a system traditionally established in the local culture but remained a worthwhile way of exploiting the more difficult terrain into the sixteenth century at least.

Vaccaries and permanent farmsteads must have replaced seasonal use in many of the transhumance zones at an early stage, especially in lowland England, but there is ample evidence of common grazing surviving in later times. Mary Atkin[67] examined the way that the moorlands of Leyland Hundred were organized in medieval times. Large areas were taken into royal forest after the Norman Conquest, whether they were woodland or moorland, but communities still enjoyed rights of common pasture. In

Leyland Hundred she was able to identify lowland 'moors' which were probably intercommoned by township communities and 'greens' which seem to have been the property of individual townships, the latter including parts of the linear stock tracks to the upland grazings. The woods of the Hundred, too, could be held in common or by severalty and the former were particularly important as a source of mast for pigs. The upper moors carried large numbers of stock in medieval times, although these are rarely detailed in the medieval records. Such was the surplus production of Lancashire in medieval times that in 1210 it was possible to contribute 200 salted pigs for the king's army in Ireland and 400 pigs, 100 cows and over 150 horses in 1211 for the campaign in Wales.[68] A thirteenth-century grant of grazing rights in Withnell by the lord of one of the hamlets of Gunnilfmoors mentions 300 animals with their young and similar grants indicate the high stock-rearing capacity of the upland townships.

Continued development gradually changed the landscape until only vestigial relics of the early system survived. Some of these have been noted above, including, on the ground, evidence of a road pattern which may incorporate earlier droves or long stock tracks to seasonal pastures and settlement patterns of considerable antiquity; administratively, territorial links (recorded but rarely functioning today); and, above all, the evidence of place-names. Although moorland and marshland may have been marginal land in the Anglo-Saxon period, such land undoubtedly played an essential role in the economy of the tenurial units of early medieval England and was to have a profound effect upon later economic and administrative arrangements.

Few areas of Britain were, however, without a mosaic of permanent early settlement and mention must be made again of the hamlets and their associated field systems which were found in the less intensively developed parts of Anglo-Saxon England. In some areas an early underlying pattern of regular enclosed fields has been detected, in others more irregular enclosures appear to have survived from prehistoric times, but by the early medieval period the infield-outfield system was present and is attested by pre-Conquest charter evidence in the south-west of England (see Chapter 6). The infield was a relatively restricted area of arable which was kept under permanent cultivation, usually by the liberal application of manure to at least one-third of it each year. This system was a feature of sparsely populated regions and was present across England, wherever pastoralism predominated and there was abundant land for pasture, with suitable localities that could be used for occasional ploughing (outfield) as required. In discussing this system in comparison with the more sophisticated two-field or three-field system of open fields, which involved leaving part of the land fallow each year, Dodgshon concludes that 'they were systems to be arranged along the same line of development or continuum rather than historically discrete systems born out of separate cultures', with the latter starting to replace the infield–outfield during the early medieval period.[69]

Notes

1 Swanton, *Anglo-Saxon Prose*, p.44: 'The Life of St Guthlac'.
2. B.L., MS. Cotton Vespasian, D.xxi, fos 18–40.
3. Hall and Coles, *Fenland Survey*, pp.92–4.
4. Ibid., p.105.
5. Ibid., p.121, citing Stukeley.
6. Ibid., pp.11–19; Hall, 'The changing landscape'.
7. de Bont, 'Reclamation patterns of peat areas'; see, too, for later periods, Taylor, *The Cambridgeshire Landscape*, pp.198–200.
8. Hayes, 'Roman to Saxon'.
9. Hall and Coles, *Fenland Survey*, p.127.
10. Hoskins and Dudley Stamp, *The Common Lands*, pp.10–12.
11. Gelling, *Place-Names in the Landscape*, p.37.
12. Reaney, *The Place-Names of Cambridgeshire and the Isle of Ely*; Atkyns, *Notes on the Fens*.
13. Swanton, *Anglo-Saxon Prose*, p.44, 'The Life of St Guthlac'.
14. Rackham, *The History of the Countryside*, pp.391–3, especially 392.
15. Cunliffe, 'The evolution of Romney Marsh'.
16. Brooks, 'Romney Marsh', p.93; Sawyer, *Anglo-Saxon Charters*, S 21.
17. Sawyer, ibid., S 328; Birch, *Cartularium Saxonicum*, B 496.
18. Whitelock, *English Historical Documents*, I.273.
19. Havinden, *The Somerset Landscape*, pp.93–5.
20. Ekwall, *The Concise Oxford Dictionary*, pp.430–1.
21. Finberg, *The Early Charters of Wessex*, p.109.
22. Sawyer, *Anglo-Saxon Charters*, S 236.
23. Birch, *Cartularium Saxonicum*, B 61 (Marquess of Bath Muniments).
24. Kemble, *Codex Diplomaticus Aevi Saxonici*, K VI.225 (MS. Bodl. Wood).
25. Havinden, *The Somerset Landscape*, p.87, Fig.6;
26. Sawyer, *Anglo-Saxon Charters*, S 626; Hooke, 'A note on the evidence for vineyards'.
27. Sawyer, ibid., S 701.
28. Ælfric, *Colloquium*, p.23, trans. Swanton, *Anglo-Saxon Prose*, p.110.
29. Sawyer, *Anglo-Saxon Charters*, S 1555; Robertson, *Anglo-Saxon Charters*, pp.204–7.
30. Seebohm, *The English Village Community*, pp.150–3.
31. Ælfric, *Colloquium*, p.25, trans. Swanton, *Anglo-Saxon Prose*, p.111.
32. *Boke of St Albans*.
33. B.L., MS. Cotton Tiberius BV, part 1.
34. Sawyer, *Anglo-Saxon Charters*, S 1271.
35. Ibid., S 198.

36. Ibid., S 207.
37. Hooke, *Worcestershire Anglo-Saxon Charter-Bounds*, pp.190–3.
38. Ibid., pp.196–8.
39. Hooke, *The Pre-Conquest Charter-Boundaries of Devon and Cornwall*; Sawyer, *Anglo-Saxon Charters*, S 832, S 1027.
40. Hooke, ibid.; Hooke, 'Saxon conquest and settlement'; Sawyer, ibid., S 770.
41. Jones, 'Continuity despite calamity', p.25.
42. Ekwall, *The Concise Oxford Dictionary*, pp.172, 374, 519.
43. Gelling, *The Place-Names of Shropshire, I*, p.167.
44. Rowley, *The Shropshire Landscape*, p.74.
45. Trinder, *A History of Shropshire*; Eyton, *Antiquities of Shropshire*, pp.18–19.
46. Ælfric, *Colloquium*, p.20, trans. Swanton, *Anglo-Saxon Prose*, p.109.
47. Hill, *The Turning Year*.
48. Atkin, 'Stock tracks along township boundaries'.
49. Hodges, *Wall-to-Wall History*.
50. Darby, *Domesday England*, Figs 35, 36, pp.91, 93.
51. Winchester, *Landscape and Society*, p.92.
52. Barrow, *The Kingdom of the Scots*.
53. Jones, 'Post-Roman Wales'.
54. Extent of Merioneth, 1284.
55. Higham, 'Old light'.
56. Jolliffe, 'Northumbrian institutions'.
57. Hodges, *Wall-to-Wall History*, p.94.
58. Brooks *et al.*, 'A new charter'.
59. Fox, 'Peasant farmers', pp.61–3; Fox, 'The bounds of Paignton'.
60. Thorn and Thorn (eds), *Domesday Book, 9, Devon*, 20, 10.
61. Ibid., n.16, 61–2.
62. Sawyer, *Anglo-Saxon Charters*, S 1547; Hooke, *The Pre-Conquest Charter-Bounds of Devon and Cornwall*, pp.217–24.
63. Austin, 'Dartmoor and the upland village'.
64. Padel, *Cornish Place-Name Elements*, pp.124, 127, 129.
65. Preston-Jones and Rose, 'Medieval Cornwall', p.144.
66. Hooke, 'Llanaber'.
67. Atkin, 'Early territorial organisation', Chapter 7, pp.147–85.
68. Ibid., citing Slade (ed.), *Pipe Roll Soc.* 26 (1949), p.63; Stenton (ed.), 28 (1951–52), p.149.
69. Dodgshon, *The Origin of British Field Systems,* especially Chapter 1 and Fig. 6.

PART IV

Towards the Future:
The Anglo-Saxon Achievement

CHAPTER 9

Urban Development and Trade

Markets and Urban Centres

One type of settlement emerged in the early medieval period which was to meet with rather more lasting success than in any earlier period: the town. Whenever a society became sufficiently sophisticated and sufficiently productive to maintain groupings of people not directly employed on the land, 'proto-urban' centres began to develop. In late Iron Age times such centres were represented by the larger hillforts and the defended lowland oppida. Defence was a prime characteristic but within these enclosures could be found specialized craftsmen. Marketing often focused on such centres and many became engaged in commerce and trade. The towns of Roman Britain had also become the centres of new cultural aspirations, with their great markets, townhalls and bath-houses. Most were, however, failing miserably in later Roman times.

The newly emerging aristocracy of the sixth and seventh centuries may have felt that the old Roman towns were the right and proper place for their minsters and centres of government but by that date the decaying centres were no longer of an urban character, although their massive walls often remained standing.[1] Some were probably still occupied by a semi-rural populace, and at Gloucester the Abbey of St Peter, founded by King Osric in about 679, was squeezed into a corner of the old Roman town as if little room was available elsewhere,[2] but almost invariably the lines of Roman property divisions and even street lines were irrelevant to later layouts, a situation now clearly seen at Lincoln, Winchester and elsewhere. Sometimes an entirely new site developed in the same focal region as the Roman town: this seems to have been the case at Nottingham, Derby, Anglo-Saxon Southampton (*Hamwih*) and even London.

But these new towns did not develop straight away. Coastal or riverine trading centres were among the first to be established: *Hamwih* in Wessex; Fordwich, Sandwich and Dover in Kent; Ipswich in East Anglia; York (*Eoforwicceaster*) in Northumbria; London (*Lundunuuic* or Aldwich) on the Thames, all were recognizable centres by the eighth century, apparently serving other settlement centres inland (*Hamwih* the outlet for Winchester, the Kentish ports for Canterbury, for example). In these cases the *wic* place-name almost certainly indicates 'place of trade' (a nomenclature also found in the names attached to the great inland salt-producing centre of Droitwich in Worcestershire). As Welch notes, 'They are usually seen as royal foundations created to provide a secure and controllable market place on the margins of a kingdom.'[3] From the seventh century, the larger Anglo-Saxon kingdoms established their own independent trade agreements with the Frankish kings, the English ports matched by others across the Channel and on important river routes.

Many inland settlements were high status centres which only slowly became towns. Canterbury was an early trading centre in its own right, a royal centre with a palace, cathedral and churches, a market and mint by the ninth century,[4] but Winchester cannot be regarded as an urban community until the tenth century, if a relatively dense population and intensive trading or industrial activity are seen as the criteria defining a town.[5] Between the seventh and ninth centuries, *Lundenburh*, the successor to Roman London, appears to have functioned more as an ecclesiastical centre around the present St Paul's Cathedral with nearby royal palaces in the Cripplegate area of the City and with rural farming settlements strung out along the Thames valley.[6] It was at Aldwych, 'the old *wic*', that a river market developed to lay the foundations of the *emporium* of *Lundenwic* referred to by Bede and only later were the inhabitants to move back within the old Roman walls.[7]

Just as defended hillforts had become growth centres in the Iron Age, so did defence become an important factor in the urban development of Anglo-Saxon England. It is now known that the Mercian Borderland centre of Hereford was already fortified by the ninth century,[8] presumably in the face of Welsh attacks, but it was the threat of Viking attacks which gave impetus to town building across southern and midland England. It seems that the system of fortified burhs which were established across Wessex (Figure 65) and subsequently across Mercia in the late ninth century incorporated deliberate urban planning. The majority of these centres were successful enough to remain important regional centres in medieval times. Their sites were chosen with defence in mind; some, like Winchester and Exeter, were re-used Roman walled towns; others, like Wilton and Cricklade, were new towns on open sites; a number were re-used Iron Age or Roman forts which were not necessarily meant to become permanent. Those that were meant to last show signs of deliberate urban layouts in their burgage plots and grid pattern of streets (with an intra-mural wall-street), the whole defended by a surviving Roman wall or by a newly built earthen rampart, both with an outer ditch.

Fig. 65   The Anglo-Saxon burhs of southern England (after Hill 1981).

The layout can still be seen in a number of towns which were planned as ninth-century burhs. In Winchester the late Anglo-Saxon road pattern is still dominant in the town centre today. The burh was located within the walls of Roman *Venta Belgarum,*[9] and the shortest route between the two opposing gates became the High Street but the Anglo-Saxon road diverges from the course of the Roman street, showing that there was little continuity of property boundaries.[10] Indeed, the intermural area was relatively empty in the eighth century, despite the presence of a royal residence and a minster, but by the late ninth century Winchester had become a notable administrative and market centre, its growth necessitating a major realignment of the existing roads. Markets were held in High Street, then *ceap stræt*. Side roads running southwards from the road now called North Walls were part of the Anglo-Saxon grid pattern, with St George's Street part of the back lane behind the properties abutting on to the High Street. The ecclesiastical centre lay in the south-eastern corner of the town where the New Minster, Old Minster and Nunaminster gave way to the cathedral begun in 1079 and its associated buildings (Plate XIX, Figure 66). There are a number of Anglo-Saxon charters which refer to plots of land within the town and the boundaries can still be identified today. At Wareham, in Dorset (possibly the port for Dorchester), the ramparts which enclosed the burh on three sides can still be seen and the

Plate XIX   Winchester cathedral from St Catherine's Hill.

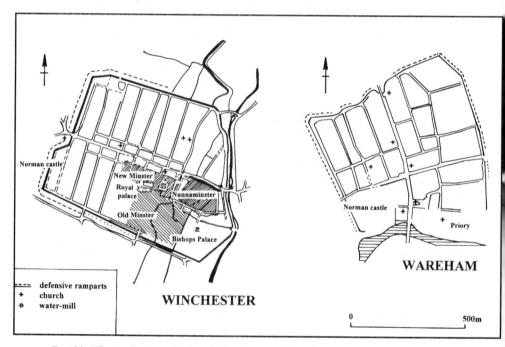

Fig. 66   The Anglo-Saxon burhs of Winchester and Wareham.

River Frome formed a natural boundary on the southern side. The grid pattern of the streets is also well preserved (Figure 66).[11]

The burhs were originally seen as defended centres which were kept garrisoned and were supported by appendant territories; many gained importance as the foci of the administrative units they served, becoming county towns. In Wessex the shires had probably come into existence by the late eighth or ninth century and may be older, while some of the south-eastern counties represent the early Anglo-Saxon kingdoms of that region. In the Midlands, however, the shires seem to have come into being after 900. Here it was said that the shire system was 'impressed on the face of the land without regard to the ancient distribution of the peoples, or the divisions of the dioceses'.[12] Thus Warwick, fortified in AD 914, was transformed from a border market town upon the boundary of the Hwiccan kingdom and Greater Mercia into the nodal centre of the new county of Warwickshire. Once established, the counties became the basic units of local government for the next thousand years.

Viking culture, too, was based upon trading centres which rapidly became true towns. Anglian *Eoforwic* became Viking York and recent archaeological work at such places as Coppergate has revealed the far-flung trading connections which brought prosperity to the town and maintained its many and varied industries. In Coppergate alone these included glass manufacture, metalworking in gold, silver, lead-alloy and iron, the making of jewellery in amber and jet, the lathe-turning of wooded bowls and cups, leatherworking and perhaps the minting of coin, none but the latter actually mentioned or alluded to in Domesday Book. Goods were imported from as far away as 'the North Cape of Norway in the north to the Red Sea/Gulf of Aden in the south, and from Ireland in the west to Samarkand in the east'.[13] In the East Midlands, the 'Five Boroughs' of Leicester, Derby, Nottingham, Stamford and Lincoln were the centres of Viking control by the mid-tenth century, serving as prominent regional centres within that part of the 'Danelaw', the area over which Danish rule was firmly established and which differed markedly in its legal administration.

Much of the impetus for urban growth undoubtedly came from those in political power. A wholly rural population can probably manage to exchange goods without urban centres and even craftsmen could be supported within rural communities. Royal palaces could be, and indeed were, often located in the open countryside. Why, then, should towns develop? Some of the answers to this question have been suggested above: for defence and for trade but, above all, there had to be some authoritative body which would benefit from urban growth and in the ever-increasing sophistication of early medieval England this role was filled by both secular leaders and the Church. While the Wessex burhs were established under royal leadership, urban markets deriving their profits from trade and tolls were being established by both local administrators and churchmen in later Anglo-Saxon England. Many a minster encouraged the development of a small town at its gates, a move which was frequently repeated in later times and especially in the twelfth century, when new plots and street layouts were to characterize the planned extensions of often earlier centres.

Discussing the role of the Church in promoting urban growth, John Blair notes that 'the four extant sets of pre-Conquest gild statutes all come from minster towns (Cambridge, Exeter, Bedwyn and Abbotsbury)'.[14] These provided masses for the dead. As at Winchester, Exeter grew up within the walls of the Roman town but had a different road pattern by the eleventh century. The early minster lay not far distant from the present cathedral and, as in many late Anglo-Saxon towns, numerous churches had been established by the time of the Norman Conquest, the majority standing along the four main streets of High Street, Fore Street, North Street and South Street: St Olave's church, the only parish church of Exeter to be mentioned in Domesday Book, already occupied a plot fronting on to the upper part of Fore Street by the mid-eleventh century.[15] The mints established within these towns attest to their growing importance as market centres. While the mainstay of the local economy was undoubtedly the produce of the surrounding region Ælfric's merchant speaks of the goods brought in by luxury trade: 'Purple cloth and silks, precious jewels and gold, unusual clothes and spices, wine and oil, ivory and bronze, copper and tin, sulphur and glass and many similar things.'[16]

Industrial Resources

Before leaving Anglo-Saxon England it remains to examine what other resources were contributing to the increasing wealth of the nation. Some of these are brought to our attention by the Normans, themselves enquiring about the wealth of their newly conquered lands.

Throughout these chapters have appeared references to the salt industry of Droitwich. Here we see Old English *wic* used in the sense of 'building or place associated with a trade'. The salt welled up naturally from beds in the Mercia Mudstone and most of the activity seems to have been concentrated in Droitwich itself, for 'Upwich', 'Middlewich' and 'Netherwich' all lay within the town.[17] Salt was traded both in and beyond the confines of the Hwiccan kingdom but by 1086 this was not the only centre. In Cheshire salt was being drawn from an area surrounding the three 'wiches' of Northwich, Middlewich and Nantwich, the first and the last some 15 miles apart (Figure 67).[18] Domesday Book also notes the

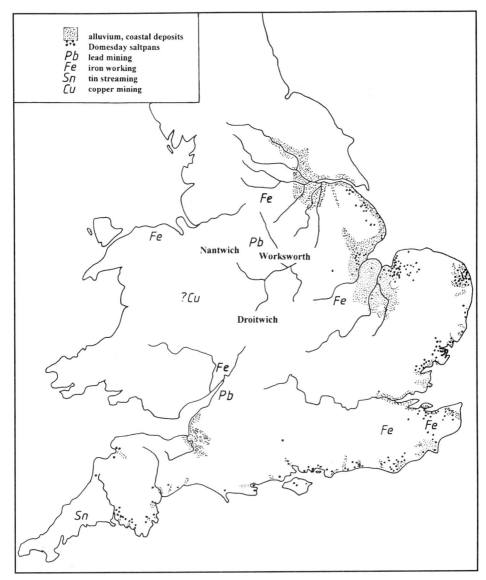

Fig. 67 Salt works and mineral resources of Anglo-Saxon and Domesday England.

saltpans along the coasts of southern and eastern England, extending from the Lincolnshire coast to the western boundary of Devon (with one just across the boundary in north Cornwall) but clustering in eastern England around the Wash, Norfolk Broadland and the estuaries of Suffolk and Essex, and in southern England around Romney Marsh and the Pevensey Levels and, further west, along the river estuaries of south-western Devon. The charter evidence reveals a great deal about the processes involved in salt evaporation at Droitwich and again Ælfric speaks of the salter:

What man enjoys pleasant foods to the full without the flavour of salt? Who fills his pantry or storeroom without my craft? Indeed you will lose all butter and cheese-curd unless I am present with you as a preservative; you couldn't even use your herbs without me.[19]

Mineral extraction, especially of iron, was widespread but it is recorded in Domesday Book that the Forest of Dean was supplying iron for the king's ships. Iron was still being obtained from the Weald and iron workers are recorded elsewhere in Domesday Book, as in the West Riding of Yorkshire and near Corby in Northamptonshire; smiths and forges are mentioned in many places, but not with any consistency. After wood, iron was probably the most important element in the material culture of the Anglo-Saxons for it was used in weapons, tools and domestic equipment.[20] Some of it was obtained by open-cast working and some from mines and the smith had played a special role in heroic literature since pagan times. Techniques for applying silver, bronze or copper to the surface of the iron were well-known and even a hard steel edge could be welded to an iron body to manufacture the most revered weapon – the sword.

Lead was being worked in Derbyshire, obtained from the metalliferous veins of the Carboniferous limestone, and several mines were associated with the manor of Worksworth; a render in kind from the three royal manors of Bakewell, Ashford and Hope in 1066 was replaced by a money render by 1086. This was traded throughout the country and it seems likely that the abbey of Ely in Cambridgeshire may have had its supply of lead for roofing from Derbyshire.[21] Lead for the Droitwich salt vats seems to have come from deposits beside the Severn estuary for a lead digging occurs as a landmark on the boundary of Stoke Bishop in a charter of AD 883 [22] and the vats were being manufactured on the Bishop of Worcester's manor of Northwick, near Worcester, in 1086. The documentary evidence for tin-working in the South-West Peninsula is slight but it is likely that the region's prosperity in part reflected this activity while copper was obtained in Shropshire.

Copper and tin are alloyed to produce bronze, and crucibles for melting bronze have been found on many Anglo-Saxon settlement sites. Metal-working probably depended very much upon imports for its source of precious and semi-precious metals, brought in as coins, plate or ingots, while garnets were the most common inlay used in the fine brooches found in rich Kentish graves of the seventh century. Ælfric talks of the craftsmen who worked on monastic holdings in the late Anglo-Saxon period and numbered among the blacksmiths, carpenters and 'workers in many different crafts', the goldsmith, silversmith and coppersmith.

The excavations at Coppergate, York, have shown considerable evidence of metalworking in an urban context but the production of textiles was probably more of a rural industry throughout much of the period, although evidenced on late Anglo-Saxon sites in London.[23] Nearly every Anglo-Saxon house would have possessed a loom. England was famous in medieval times for its embroidery and several relics of Anglo-Saxon date also survive. A 'chasuble' at Maaseik in Belgium contains some Anglo-Saxon embroideries from southern England which were preserved in the convent of Saints Harlindis and Relindis at Aldeneik until the sixteenth century. These depict birds and animals accompanied by interlace and scroll-work and the silken threads were dyed cherry red, beige, green, yellow, light and dark blue while the gold thread was strips of pure gold foil wound around a core of horse hair and flattened. The panels were exhibited at the British Museum in 'The Making of England' exhibition in 1991. Other embroideries from England have been found in the great Viking Age ship-burial at Oseberg in Norway. Best known is the stole and maniple made probably at Winchester between 909 and 916 which were later placed in the coffin reliquary of St Cuthbert (and which is still visible in Durham cathedral today), which were carried out in silk and gold threads in a variety of stitches.[24]

England as Part of Continental Europe

The discovery of luxury church items on the Continent is a reminder that England has never in history stood alone. To the Romans, it was a distant but important province of the great Roman Empire and there are indications that it was still viewed in this way by the Franks of Merovingian Europe. It was they and the pope who sent clerics and bishops like Augustine and Theodore to convert and then to organize the Anglo-Saxon Church and saw to it that England remained safely within the control of the Roman rather than the British Church. In turn, England would send out missionaries like Boniface and Willibrord to preach to pagan peoples beyond the Rhine; later Alcuin of York joined the entourage of Charlemagne as a teacher and advisor and made a direct contribution to continental scholarship.

Anglo-Saxon legal arrangements also owed much to continental practices. Augustine appears to have been involved in the discussions which led to the issue of Æthelberht's laws in Kent after his conversion, perhaps in AD 602–3, although he was not necessarily involved in their final content. The models for these early law codes, however, were continental parallels, including genealogical claims to a descent from legendary gods and heroes. Some of the earliest legal tracts survive in the *Textus Roffensis*, a twelfth-century compilation which was produced in the scriptorium of Rochester in Kent and preserved in the cathedral library. It contains the only surviving copy of the Laws of King Æthelberht I of Kent, 'the oldest known document in English'.[25] The charters which were drawn up by the Church as a formal record of their title to land granted them were also based upon both Frankish and Italian custom; although it must be remembered that Latin parallels also gave rise to a lesser known group of early British texts.[26] While no continental country possesses a comprehensive survey on the scale of Domesday Book, primarily a land register recording ownership, Roman census documents were to influence subsequent estate inventories which referred more directly to dues and services. Professor R. Davis believed that there was sufficient evidence to suggest that Charlemagne contemplated the idea of having the whole of his kingdom surveyed in the early ninth century. Charlemagne's kingdom was vast, covering a large part of continental Europe from France eastwards to Thuringia and Bavaria, and the idea was never executed, but in the following centuries surveys of considerable variety of form and content did appear and were similarly produced in some of the reformed monasteries of tenth-century England.

England, too, was not remote from the Carolingian renaissance which characterized Charlemagne's empire in the early ninth century, a resurgence of Classical values and their manifestation. It is reflected in the English Church in the plans of church buildings, and especially in the freestanding tomb which gave rise to the crypt at Repton, excavated by Martin Biddle, a detached structure similar to a Roman mausoleum.[27] Associated with mortuary rite and the public display of relics, this is but one instance of the Mercian connection with the Carolingian empire, expressed elsewhere in church plans and sculptured friezes, like that at Breedon-on-the-Hill, which 'blend indigenous and Carolingian motifs in a distinctive hybrid' (Figure 68).[28] Some of the Church's illuminated books of the period were also inspired by Carolingian workmanship while coinage and jewellery from Offa's reign betray the same connection.

In Alfred's reign, English scholarship was deliberately encouraged by royal initiative and in spite of the need to look to the defence of a country under Danish threat, his success was to unify that part of England which was Anglo-Saxon. The Scandinavians brought their own stimuli to trade and the economy in the form of urban markets and trade and perhaps, too, in agricultural reorganization. One aspect of the political propaganda of the earlier Carolingians has never dated. To quote Richard Hodges, 'Essentially, this taught that it was important for the community to appreciate its past, its traditions and its sense of ethnicity'.[29] In England,

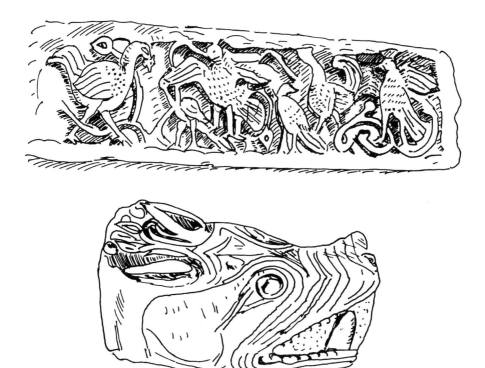

Fig. 68   Sculptured frieze from the church at Breedon-on-the-Hill (Leicestershire), and an animal's head from Deerhurst church, Gloucestershire (*c.* AD 804).

this meant a rich amalgam of many peoples and influences: The Anglo-Saxons were themselves drawn from a variety of different races: Angles, Jutes, Frisians, Saxons and others; they eventually merged with the native British and in turn incorporated the Vikings – Norwegians and Danes. Influences continued to be absorbed from continental Europe throughout the period and on the eve of the Norman Conquest one finds a prosperous country with a flourishing economy reflected in its rural countryside and growing towns, a Church renewed in strength and vigour by tenth-century reform and an administrative system which was to last to the present day. This was the Anglo-Saxon achievement.

The very claimants to the throne at the death of King Edward in 1066 illustrate the strength of continental links. Harold Hardaada of Norway, 'the last great warrior-hero of the Viking age'[30] represented the interest of the Scandinavian throne, and Harold Godwinesson, Earl of East Anglia, Essex, Cambridgeshire and Huntingdonshire, the 'Saxon' claim (in reality that of a rival family). But it was another Northman from the Norman lands in what is now France that was ultimately successful. Having been reared in the French court with a Norman mother Edward had employed many Normans in powerful positions and William of Normandy may well have had his blessing as his future heir. Although the influence of the Norman French was perhaps to be rather more limited in the everyday world of rural England, the new overlordship by this group of Norman nobility did serve to hold England fast together and to give it time for its peoples to be truly welded together as 'the English'.

Notes

1. Vince, 'Saxon urban economies', pp.108–11.
2. Heighway, *Ancient Gloucester*.
3. Welch, *Anglo-Saxon England*, p.119.
4. Tatton-Brown, 'The towns of Kent'.
5. Biddle, 'Towns'.
6. Rackham, 'Economy and environment'.
7. Vince, *Saxon London*.
8. Shoesmith, *Hereford City Excavations, II*, pp.74–7.
9. Rivet and Smith, *The Place-Names of Roman Britain*, p.492.
10. Biddle, 'Towns'; Biddle, 'The study of Winchester', pp.125–6.
11. Keen, 'The towns of Dorset'.
12. Finberg, *Gloucestershire Studies*, p.26.
13. Hall, 'The making of Domesday York', p.241.
14. Blair, 'Secular minster churches', p.141.
15. Allen, *et al.* 'Saxon Exeter'.
16. Ælfric, *Colloquium*, p.27, trans. Swanton, *Anglo-Saxon Prose*, p.112.
17. Hooke, 'The Droitwich salt industry'.
18. Darby, *Domesday England*, pp.261–3.
19. Ælfric, *Colloquium*, p.28, trans. Swanton, *Anglo-Saxon Prose*, p.112.
20. Wilson, 'Craft and industry', p.261.
21. Darby, *Domesday England*, p.269.
22. Sawyer, *Anglo-Saxon Charters*, S 218, Birch *Cartularium Saxonicum*, B 551.
23. Pritchard, 'Late Saxon textiles from the City of London'.
24. Webster, 'Metalwork, ivory and textiles'.
25. Prescott, 'Manuscripts', p.41.
26. Davis, 'Domesday Book'; for a recent study of this subject see Campbell, 'The late Anglo-Saxon state'.
27. Biddle, 'Archaeology', p.22, n.31. For a fuller discussion of continental parallels, see Campbell, 'Observations on English government'.
28. Hodges, *The Anglo-Saxon Achievement*, p.129.
29. Ibid., p.144.
30. Humble, *The Saxon Kings*, p.193.

CHAPTER 10

Towards the Future
Landscape Regions

So far in these chapters we have moved away from the heartland regions towards the margins. We have seen how regional landscapes had already acquired their special identities by the end of the Anglo-Saxon period. Since the underlying geology and soils were often dominant factors influencing regional resources it is not perhaps surprising that many regional characteristics should prevail throughout the centuries. The Carboniferous limestones of the Peak District, for instance, have supported short turfland pasture for stock and provided the characteristic white stone which has been used for field wall and cottage alike, and influenced other features of historical land use which give this region a personality of its own. In contrast, the dark moorland grits often produce an entirely different heather-covered terrain. But, as Paul Vidal de la Blache pointed out over 70 years ago,

> Une individualité géographique ne résulte pas de simples considérations de géologie et de climat. Ce n'est pas une chose donnée d'avance par la nature. Il faut partir de cette idée qu'une contrée est un réservoir ou dorment des énergies dont la nature a déposé le germe, mais dont l'emploi dépend de l'homme. C'est lui qui, en la pliant a son usage, met en lumière son individulalité.[1]

Nature merely sets the scene and it is man's activities which ultimately produce the individual characteristics which identify the regions today.

Indeed, if we were able to reconstruct the Roman or even the prehistoric landscape, we should probably be able to recognize the same basic regional divisions. But regional differences can be more or less apparent at different periods of history. Fox[2] notes how, in the South-West of England, the twelfth and thirteenth centuries was a period of 'convergence' in land use between region and region. Pressure of population stimulated the conversion to arable of some of the most unsuitable soils. On the fringes of Dartmoor and Bodmin Moor summer shielings often became permanently occupied settlements, with crops of rye and oats being coaxed even from these thin, hungry, stony soils. In Wales at this time cultivation was carried out on the hills of Penmachno in North Wales at heights of over 300 metres (1000 feet).[3] In lowland England, too, the differences in land use between regions was muted, as noted by Dyer[4] commenting upon the distinction between the 'woodland' Arden and the 'champion' Feldon. It is likely that the Roman period, too, had been one of convergence, marked by attempts to colonize and cultivate marginal lands.

In contrast, the early and later medieval periods were ones when regional differences became more marked as a 'divergence' in the characteristics of regions took place, reflecting both climatic and economic conditions. A period of climatic deterioration can be dated to the mid-sixth century[5] from the evidence of tree ring analysis and peat formation but other factors undoubtedly led to an abandonment (however slow) of marginal land: removal of the requirement to feed the Roman army and urban populations; soil deterioration; a greater concentration upon livestock rearing and other less intensive types of land use. Under the latter regime, marginal lands may have been much more valuable as pastureland than as relatively poor arable land, while it has been argued in Chapter 7 that woodland regeneration was deliberately encouraged in some areas as a byproduct of a growing interest in hunting. What is certain is that by the time of the Norman Conquest regional differences were clearly apparent and can be traced through the evidence of Domesday Book.

There can be little doubt that the early medieval period was one of the most formative periods in English history. While the amount of land under arable diminished in some marginal zones, giving way to pasture and woodland, considerable change also occurred in the more intensively cultivated regions. It was during this period that the open field farming methods discussed in Chapter 6 developed to such a marked degree. The same developments can be identified in continental Europe. With the reorganization of farming, settlement patterns also began to achieve their medieval form: by the end of the early medieval period, village clusters were becoming characteristic of many of our richest farming regions. These were not patterns brought in by the conquering Anglo-Saxons – or patterns determined by a particular set of natural conditions – but forms which evolved again in response to changing economic and cultural conditions. The response varied from region to region but in predominantly arable areas gave rise to a type of countryside long recognized as *plain* or *champagne* countryside, our 'champion' crop-growing lands.

No longer is it possible to draw a hard line between the early medieval (here the period from the fifth century to 1086) and the medieval periods. Although the nucleated village was beginning to dominate the settlement pattern in some regions many, if not most, villages are in fact the product of changes which continued well into the medieval period. Not only were many replanned as time went by but outlying farmsteads were only slowly abandoned and in some cases gave rise to those of later periods. The open field systems themselves did not reach their greatest extent until the twelfth or thirteenth centuries and the complexity of arrangements recorded in the transactions of medieval court rolls, or depicted on even later maps, undoubtedly reflects development and compromise over many centuries. In many regions, both pasture and woodland were considerably diminished by the medieval period. In such regions most of the land by then lay under arable and while the large open fields might be hedged, the individual strips at this stage were not. In general, this is the zone of Rackham's 'Planned Countryside',[6] really referring to the planning of the eighteenth- and nineteenth-century surveyors.

Few open field systems escaped the massive replanning period of enclosure by private or parliamentary Act after the mid-seventeenth century. Laxton in Nottinghamshire offers an almost unique survival of an organized common field system but the surviving part of Braunton open field in Devon, five miles north-west of Barnstaple, or the open field above Boscastle in Cornwall are probably more visually arresting despite some consolidation of the strips. Parliamentary enclosure frequently entailed new straight field boundaries which ignored the sinuous curves of the open field furlongs (produced by the route followed by the plough oxen) or the corrugations of medieval ridge and furrow but the earlier picture is better preserved where enclosure took place at an earlier date under a piecemeal process. Sometimes the medieval strips have been fossilized in enclosure boundaries to produce a striking pattern of narrow hedged or walled fields. This has been offered as an explanation of the pattern observed at Chelmorton in the White Peak district of Derbyshire (the closes bounded by limestone walling) and at Deeping St James in Lincolnshire (hedgerows), both admirably portrayed in Beresford and St Joseph's *Medieval England: An Aerial Survey.*[7] There is at present no knowledge, however, of how far these late surviving patterns incorporate the field systems of early medieval England.

The other main type of region recognized in lowland England was that of the 'woodland' landscape, more frequently found in Rackham's zone of 'Ancient Countryside'. Such regions were often ones where seasonal pastures gave way in time to more settled pastoral farming.[8] In general, settlement remained largely dispersed and open field systems were of limited extent, associated with hamlet settlements. Trackways linked the hamlets and farmsteads to give rise to a largely irregular road pattern, although sometimes a prevailing orientation of routeways may suggest a pattern of ancient droveways. Some woodland regions continued to evolve in a different way to the champion crop-growing lands as open field was enclosed at a relatively early date and new farms established within their own holdings, thus perpetuating the pattern of scattered farmsteads. Smallholders and landless labourers clustered around patches of waste, their cottages and hamlets intensifying the dispersed pattern of settlement, although many such settlements were of an ephemeral and shifting nature. Fields, often arising as woodland assarts, tended to remain small and were also bounded in many areas by hedgerows set with woodland type trees: there are countless permutations of these 'enclosed' or *bocage* countrysides – far more than can be investigated here. In other regions, woodland survived longer, and late enclosure produced the familiar pattern of larger, more geometric fields associated with enclosure of eighteenth-century or later date, little different to that of the open field country enclosed only a few decades before. Upland and wetland regions developed their own particular patterns of settlement, some of which will be briefly mentioned below.

The regional types noted above are obviously superficial and general and would have been expressed in many different ways in different parts of the country. They may, however, be recognized again and again in many parts of lowland England. Figure 45 (see p. 130) is a simple way of suggesting some of the variations in settlement patterns that existed and changes that took place. It is not possible to give an exact scenario for any one English county, although the survival of Anglo-Saxon pottery in parts of the East Midlands and East Anglia brings us closer to such an achievement for that particular area. The right-hand part of Figure 45 illustrates a region of widespread cultivation, probably supporting relatively high population levels. In such an area settlement agglomeration seems to have been taking place in the later Anglo-Saxon period, probably related to the reorganization of farming under a regular open field system. Each nucleated settlement was perhaps served by two great arable fields with domestic stock pastured on the fallow and remaining waste. Workers in Northamptonshire[9] feel that such a pattern was emerging in some regions by the ninth century, replacing a more dispersed pattern of farmsteads and tiny hamlet clusters. Once nucleation occurred, or was encouraged to take place, it appears to have led to the elimination of most outlying farms.

At the other end of the scale, dispersed hamlets and farmsteads seem to have been characteristic of areas that were primarily associated with pastoral farming (the left-hand side of Figure 45). Many of the hamlets were to possess their own tiny common field systems, perhaps superimposed upon an earlier pattern of holdings associated with single farmsteads. New waves of settlement served, however, to perpetuate the characteristically dispersed pattern as new farmsteads were established, both on 'green-field' sites (often assarts) or around the margins of waste. The gradual changes to the early pattern are expressed in the right-hand diagrams.

The visible difference between 'woodland' and 'champion' regions probably reached its most intense expression in the later medieval period as zones of dispersed farmsteads scattered through a countryside and linked by an irregular system of roads and tracks formed a sharp contrast with the large villages of arable areas. Land-use patterns intensified the image, for the great expanses of arable were often almost treeless and internal hedges were few while the pastoral zones, usually established in regions which were less favourable to crop cultivation, still supported ancient hedgerows and patches of often tree-covered waste.

In the west and north of England more realistic divisions can be made between 'upland' and 'lowland' landscapes. Almost invariably, the latter were the areas of early settlement and there are hints that settlement patterns in several areas still incorporate ancient elements. This is not to say that change has been absent, for the pressures which brought change to the rest of Britain were influential here, too. In general, hamlet-type settlement predominated, in association with limited development of the open field. Village nucleations were limited to such foci as royal or monastic centres. Areas of permanently cropped infield, heavily manured, can sometimes be identified, especially in the South-West, around the settlement cores, with intermittently cropped outfield beyond. Place-name and archaeological evidence suggests that the uplands were much less intensively settled in the early medieval period,[10] despite their importance for prehistoric farming. Many seem to have been regions of seasonal grazing. As in woodland regions, however, permanent settlement on the fringe of most marginal areas was often to replace earlier seasonal shielings as the limit of settlement and farming fluctuated with changing climatic, social and economic conditions.

Although this can serve as a very basic model, every region has its own special characteristics. Studies from different regions may suggest a very approximate chronology in settlement development. Evidence from Anglo-Saxon Kent perhaps illustrates one of the earliest scenarios.

The Weald of Kent seems to have been a well-wooded region which was still used as seasonal wood-pasture in the early Anglo-Saxon period. Alan Everitt's[11] study of Kent argues that permanent settlement in the Wealden core was very much a feature of the later parts of the period and was still only taking place in some parts of the region after the Norman Conquest, having been achieved earlier on the chalk downland. Drove roads leading into the Weald mark the routes followed by the commoners of the surrounding lowland and valley estates as they accompanied their

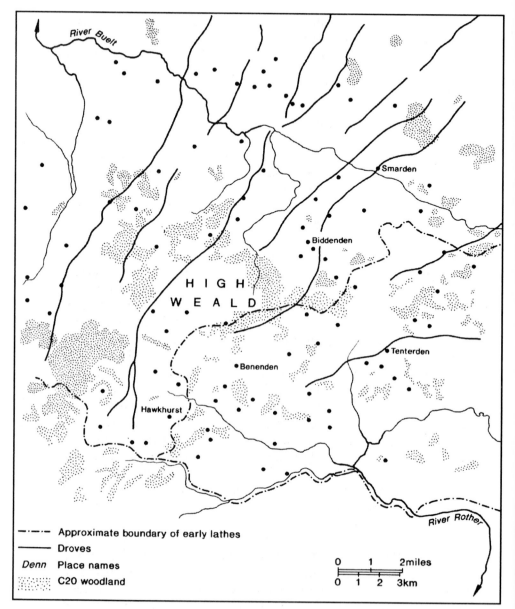

Fig. 69   A portion of the Kentish Weald: dens and drove-ways.

herds of cattle and pigs into the woods to forage in the summer and autumn. These woodland pastures were known as 'dens', a suffix still common in the village and farm names of the area today. The droves have given rise to a system of parallel routeways (Figure 69).

Everitt argues for late subdivision of the core region and occasionally the bounds of five or six parishes can be seen to be either interlocking or converging where they subdivided an area of old common woodland (see Chapter 5). The parishes themselves were of late formation, with churches being founded in the outlying territories of the minster or mother churches of the lowland vales and coastlands only at a much later date. This he sets against the wider estate structure:

> In their foundation, in fact, what we are really witnessing is the gradual break-up of the old river-estates, with the conversion of their outlying *wald* and marshland, little by little, into permanent farms, and the establishment of settled farmsteads or 'manor houses' in place of seasonal shielings.[12]

Most Wealdan churches are recorded as being in existence by *c.* 1100, suggesting that 'the parochial structure . . . seems to have been almost complete by the thirteenth century', but 'In wooded or heathy districts . . . the practice of intercommoning at times precluded precise lines of demarcation between them [the churches], and in some areas intercommoning survived until after the end of the Middle Ages.'[13]

Figure 69 shows an area of the Weald that provided woodland pasture for the *Weowara* or 'men of Wye' and for the *Limenwara*, 'the men of the Lympne district', later parts of the lathes of Wye and Lyminge. The frequency with which the den name survives on the modern map clearly illustrates the partitioning of the woodlands and the incidence of dependent blocks of land used for seasonal pasture. Many of these have been identified as the early medieval dens noted in pre-Conquest charters or recorded at a later date. Part of the lathe of Wye, for instance, was held by Battle Abbey in the thirteenth century when dens in the outer area of the wood remained liberties of the manor but when twelve dens within Hawkhurst and adjoining parishes were subject to an agreement concerning timber rights. The first group included Bethersden, Plurenden in Woodchurch, Washenden in Biddenden and Romden, probably in Smarden, although not all the named dens bore the place-name suffix; the twelve dens within the forest included Delmonden and Fissenden in Hawkhurst and Chittenden and Wichenden with *Omynden*, now Homerden, in Cranbrook, Markden or Marden. The ancient droves running first northwards and then north-eastwards can be identified in the modern road pattern, a major one running through Smarden and a more southerly route in the eastern part of the region through High Halden, with numerous other parallel lines.[14]

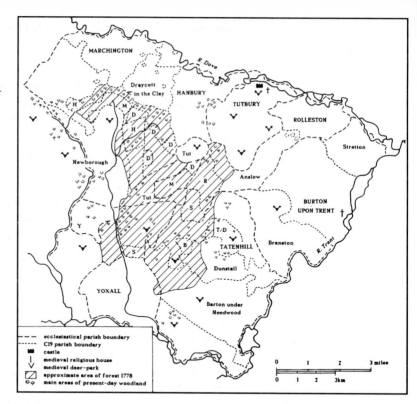

Fig. 70a, b
Parish patterns
in the forests of
Needwood and
Charnwood.

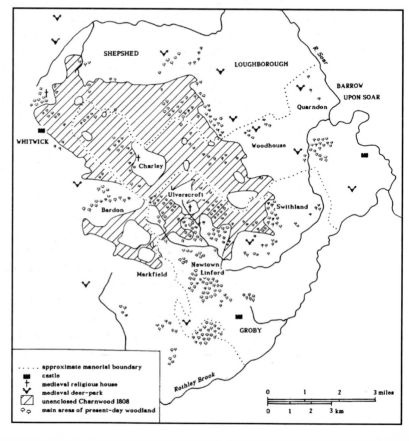

The Warwickshire Arden in the early medieval period perhaps represented a further step in the development of woodland regions. There are similar hints of roughly parallel droveways leading into the region from the surrounding lowlands and the region seems to have been intercommoned by communities located to the north, east and south-east, themselves part of larger folk-groups (see Figures 15 and 55 on pp. 48 and 161).[15] By the time of the Norman Conquest the area was permanently settled but links between the Arden woodland and the cultivated Feldon to the south-east survive through the system of manorial and ecclesiastical dependencies. At this date the region remained well wooded and was to remain so until a period of active colonization in the twelfth and thirteenth centuries. Small open field systems associated with hamlet cores are clearly attested in medieval documentation (as at Tanworth, discussed in Chapter 7) but enclosure took place at a relatively early date. Many subsidiary farmsteads, often established in the period of twelfth- and thirteenth-century colonization and often moated, were able to group their lands around them very quickly and enclosed irregular fields were characteristic of the region throughout medieval times.[16]

The Forest of Needwood in Staffordshire also provided woodland pasture in the Anglo-Saxon period for the settlements which lay around it (Figure 70a). The boundaries of the ecclesiastical parishes show how these pushed into the forest to claim this resource which, with the subsequent subdivision of these larger units, gave rise to a complicated pattern of detached portions of parishes within the woodland core.[17] Similarly, the woodlands of Charnwood in Leicestershire were subdivided between the three great manors which lay upon their fringes – the manors of Barrow-upon-Soar, Groby and Whitwick – and only at a much later date were civil parishes carved out within the woodlands themselves as subdivisions of these earlier units (Figure 70b). Barrow lies on the east bank of the Soar to the north-east of Charnwood and the manor belonged to Earl Harold before his death at the hands of William I at Hastings. From this great manor were carved within Charnwood the units of Charley and Woodhouse. Groby, to the south, was itself ecclesiastically dependent upon Ratby but was a separate manor before the Norman Conquest. Its waste lay within Charnwood and the manor initially included Swithland, Ulverscroft and Newtown Linford. Whitwick lay to the west and its lands included Bardon and Markfield. In Domesday Book the woods of these great manors are recorded under the manorial name but there is little doubt that they represented Charnwood Forest itself. Islands of open land developed in Charnwood in medieval times, largely around religious foundations in the forest, but most of the area remained common pasture and woodland until nineteenth-century enclosure, unlike the situation

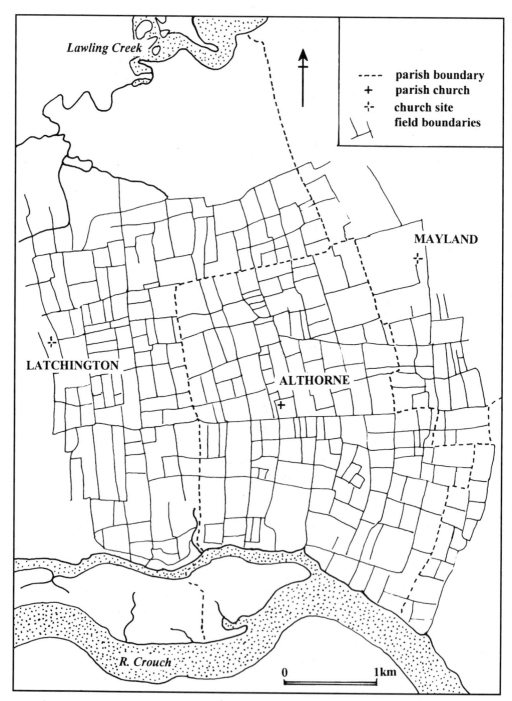

Fig. 71   Field patterns on the Dengie Peninsula, Essex.

found in such wooded areas as the Warwickshire Arden or the Forest of Neroche in Somerset.

Not all woodland regions were, however, necessarily ones of sparse population at the time of the Norman Conquest. Some wooded regions in eastern England supported relatively dense populations throughout the Anglo-Saxon period, reaching some 15–20 recorded people per square mile at the time of the Norman Conquest. The work of Warner and Williamson and others illustrates for the early medieval period a stage in the developing settlement pattern which was only reached in the twelfth and thirteenth centuries and even later in the Warwickshire Arden.

On the boulder-clay-covered plateau around Great Chesterford, population densities remained high in the Anglo-Saxon period and the characteristic pattern was one of scattered farmsteads dependent upon the larger nucleations of the major valleys. Earlier field patterns, perhaps even pre-Roman in origin – regular rectangular fields between approximately parallel roads – managed sometimes to survive, especially on the less dissected parts of the plateau in north Suffolk and south Norfolk. It is likely that continued grazing here kept woodland in check. Irregular open fields developed around the main settlements, presumably as land was converted to arable as population expanded, but only rarely were the fields of entire vills reorganized in the manner of the 'champion' landscapes. The regular co-axial field patterns are similar to those in the Dengie Peninsula of Essex, illustrated by Rackham (Figure 71).[18]

In the north-east of this area there was also the beginning of the drift to certain greens and commons which intensified in subsequent centuries, a move which Williamson believes may reflect 'the increasing importance of the residual areas of grazing as arable intensified on the clays'.[19] In Suffolk, Peter Warner[20] has noted the same drift to the commons and believes that it began early enough for some of the common-side settlements and important churches to have established well before Domesday. He does not argue for continuity of settlement from Roman to Anglo-Saxon times and notes that woodland often regenerated over areas of early Roman occupation, to be continuously used as wood-pasture, especially for swine. Although they formed areas of 'secondary settlement' – secondary, that is, to the scattered farms on the valley gravels of the region – permanently occupied hamlets grew up on the fringes of the commons at an early date and were to acquire churches of their own before the Norman Conquest, becoming regrouped into 'secondary parishes'. Adjacent to some of these, Warner also notes 'hall' estates which also seem to have been secondary settlements in regions of wood-pasture (Figure 72). They represent manorial demesnes already established by late Saxon times, their curving ring-fence boundaries

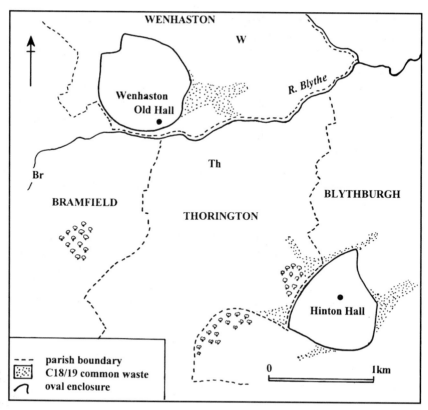

Fig. 72   Anglo-Saxon field patterns in Suffolk.

fossilized in present-day field patterns. This oval pattern also resembles the hall estate noted by Roberts at Cockfield in County Durham which he believed to date from before 1100.[21]

A further case study is taken from the south-west of the country. In much of what is popularly referred to as the 'West Country', villages were so small in medieval times that they were hardly more than hamlets. Surrounded by a dense pattern of tiny fields, towering hedgerows and sunken ways, they give an impression of an ancient countryside almost devoid of change (Plate XX). But this is far from true for many, if not most, areas. Certainly, the documents suggest that parts of the region supported a relatively dense settlement pattern of small village/hamlet/ farmsteads but many of these possessed tiny open field systems which were only enclosed in medieval times. The nature of settlement at the time of Domesday Book cannot yet be understood. The numerous small vills of parts of Devon, for instance, were often assessed at as low as half a virgate but still contained a number of villein holdings, not to mention a few smallholders. These people may have occupied separate farmsteads, the forerunners of those we see today, or they may have lived together in small hamlet communities. In Cornwall, the place-name *tre* has been seen to suggest the survival of an ancient hamlet/farmstead and many such farms occupy the sites of even earlier settlements. The moorlands of the South-West appear to have been less intensively settled than the surrounding lowlands. Anne Preston-Jones has noted the absence of early name forms on Bodmin Moor.[22]

Yet, as noted above, the apparent antiquity of this pattern hides many changes. In Somerset, many individual farmsteads were once hamlets and there are indications that this was true for much of the South-West. According to Aston:

> The process of the growth of a single farmstead into a small hamlet and its subsequent disintegration back to a farmstead, perhaps through several cycles, can be expected to have been a widespread phenomenon as population grew and then declined and as the economic activity of such settlements changed through the Middle Ages.[23]

Plate XX 'Ancient countryside' in Devon near Fingal's Bridge: looking northwards from the valley of the River Teign, Drewsteignton.

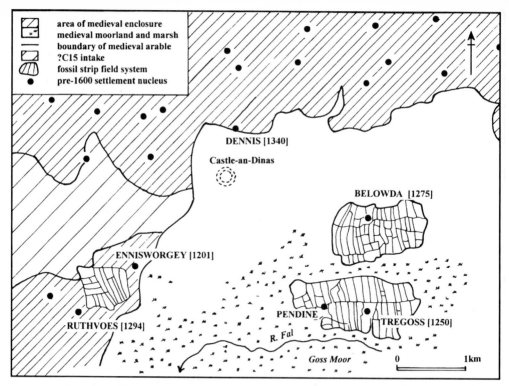

Fig. 73 Field patterns and medieval settlement on Goss Moor, Cornwall.

Fox has noted that there were few true medieval villages in the South-West apart from the hundredal centres and that 'isolated farmsteads and small hamlets were the rule'.[24] But many of today's isolated farmsteads appear earlier to have been hamlet clusters. He notes the amalgamation of holdings in the fourteenth century whereby single farms often replaced the tiny smallholdings and quotes examples from the Devon parish of Hartland showing how this came about.[25] This also led to the decay of their open field systems. Even the associated outfield had been subdivided in the same manner and survivals of such a practice are documented as late as the nineteenth century long after the infield had been enclosed. In Cornwall, the origin of such hamlets is less clear but charter evidence for Cornwall clearly shows that common fields were present at Trerice in the eleventh century.[26] These seem to have been subdivided before the Norman Conquest and fossilized strip systems can still be identified.[27] The number of villein tenants recorded on even the tiniest Domesday manors seems to support the view that the hamlet was already a common settlement form everywhere by the end of the Anglo-Saxon period.

Figure 73 shows a field pattern surrounding the hamlet of Tregoss in the parish of Roche which lies at the northern edge of the granitic moorland of central Cornwall to the north of St Austell. The place-name may contain

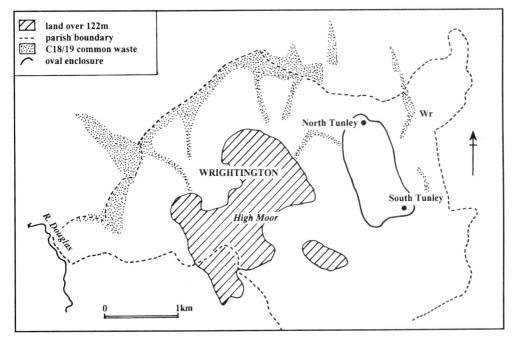

Fig. 74 Medieval vaccaries in Lancashire.

the ancient Cornish *tre*, 'estate, farmstead', with *cors*, 'reeds, fen', and the settlement lies on an island of higher land which is surrounded by low-lying marshy moorland. The present fields again appear to fossilize an earlier strip pattern which remains undated. These seem to have been similar to the unenclosed strips noted by Fox on a late seventeenth-century map of Predannack Wollas, a hamlet on Mount's Bay in the remote far western coastlands of the Lizard peninsula in that county.[28] Investigations in Cornwall and Devon have confirmed that strip cultivation often continued in outfield locations taken into permanent cultivation in medieval times after it had been abandoned on the old infield core.[29]

It may be useful to complete this rapid circuit of early regional characteristics with an example of an early settlement form from the north of England. Mary Atkin[30] believes that she can identify the demesne lands of several townships and that these are reflected in surviving field patterns (Figure 74) which are not unlike those of the hall farms described by Warner in Suffolk. Very often a strong lynchet bounds the oval enclosures she has identified, as around part of the margins of the Tunley holding in Wrightington, Lancashire. Other hedges and fences beyond obviously belong to later enclosure. The original 'hall' often seems to have lain within an enclosure used as demesne pasture in medieval times, while a second oval remained the subdivided arable worked from a number of farms established around its fringe. Stock would be led away from these home pastures onto the common moor on a seasonal basis. These were medieval vaccaries maintaining large herds of cattle by utilizing the resources of both enclosed holdings and open moorland, but such a pattern may be rooted in antiquity (see Chapter 8).

There is a wealth of information to be gained from detailed local studies and the evidence has by no means been exhaustively studied. Hopefully, this book has suggested approaches which may be investigated further, especially through the medium of the living countryside. A palimpsest produced by thousands of years of man's activity, the landscape today is still full of clues to its gradual evolution through time and will undoubtedly reward the informed observer with greater understanding and enjoyment.

Notes

1. de la Blache, *Tableau de la Géographie de la France*, p.3.
2. Fox, 'Peasant farmers', pp.58–9.
3. Jones, 'The distribution of bond settlements'.
4. Dyer, *Warwickshire Farming*, p.10.
5. Day, 'History and palaeography'.
6. Rackham, *The History of the Countryside*, Fig. 1.3, p.3.
7. Beresford and St Joseph, *Medieval England*, Figs 13, 36, 37, pp.44, 99, 101.
8. Hooke, *Warwickshire's Historical Landscape*.
9. Hall, 'The origins'.
10. Preston-Jones and Rose, 'Medieval Cornwall', pp.141–5; Thomas, 'A cultural–ecological model'.
11. Everitt, *Continuity and Colonization*.
12. Ibid., p.199.
13. Ibid., p.205.
14. Witney, *The Jutish Forest*, pp.256–9.
15. Hooke, 'Pre-Conquest woodland', pp.115–16.
16. Hooke, *Warwickshire's Historical Landscape*.
17. Hooke, *The Landscape of Anglo-Saxon Staffordshire*, pp.34–7.
18. Rackham, *The History of the Countryside*, Plate XIII.
19. Williamson, 'Settlement chronology'.
20. Warner, *Greens, Commons and Clayland Colonization*.
21. Roberts, 'Townfield origins'.
22. Preston-Jones and Rose, 'Medieval Cornwall'.
23. Aston, 'The development of medieval rural settlement', p.21.
24. Fox, 'Peasant farmers', p.48.
25. Ibid., pp.50–2.
26. Sawyer, *Anglo-Saxon Charters*, S 1019; Hooke, *The Pre-Conquest Charter-Bounds of Devon and Cornwall*.
27. Hooke and Herring, 'Interrogating Anglo-Saxons in St Dennis'.
28. Fox, 'Tenant farming and farmers', pp.731–2.
29. Herring, 'Prehistory and history of land-use'; for an actual example on Bodmin Moor, see Rose, 'The historic landscape', pp.107–9.
30. Atkin, 'Some settlement patterns in Lancashire'.

Bibliography

Reference is occasionally made to the most accessible sources rather than to the academic texts.

Ælfric, Abbot of Eynsham, *The Homilies of the Anglo-Saxon Church, Vol. 2: Colloquium ad pueros lingua latinæ locutione exercendos ab Ælfrico compilatum Analecta Anglo-Saxonica*, (ed.) B. Thorpe (Ælfric Society, London, 1846).

Albarella, U. and Davis, S. J. M., 'The Saxon and medieval animal bones excavated 1985–1989 from West Cotton, Northamptonshire', *Ancient Monuments Laboratory Report 17/94* (English Heritage, London,1994).

Aldsworth, F. G., 'Parish boundaries on record', *The Local Historian* 15 (1982), pp.34–40.

Allen, J., Henderson, C. and Higham, R., 'Saxon Exeter', in Haslam, J. (ed.) *Anglo-Saxon Towns* (1984), pp.385–411.

Anglo-Saxon Chronicle, (ed.) M. Swanton (Dent, London, 1996).

Anglo-Saxon Poetry, trans. R. K. Gordon (Dent, London, 1954), includes Anglo-Saxon Charms.

Anglo-Saxon Riddles of the Exeter Book, trans. P. F. Baum (Duke University Press, Durham, NC, 1963).

Aston, M., 'The development of medieval rural settlement in Somerset', in Higham, R. (ed.) *Landscape and Townscape in the South West* (1989), pp.19–40.

Atkin, M. A., 'Stock tracks along township boundaries', *J Engl Place-Name Soc* 15 (1982–3), pp.24–31.

Atkin, M. A, 'Early territorial organisation in the Hundred of Leyland in Lancashire' (unpublished University of Leicester M. Phil. thesis,1985).

Atkin, M. A., 'Some settlement patterns in Lancashire', in Hooke, D. (ed.) *Medieval Villages* (1985), pp.171–86.

Atkyns, R., *Notes on the Fens of Cambridgeshire* (1604) Harl 5011.

Attenborough, F. L., *The Laws of the Earliest English Kings* (Cambridge University Press, Cambridge, 1922).

Austin, D., 'Dartmoor and the upland village of the south-west of England', in Hooke, D. (ed.) *Medieval Villages* (1985), pp.71–9.

Bailey, K., 'The Middle Saxons', in Bassett, S. (ed.) *The Origins of the Anglo-Saxon Kingdoms* (1989), pp.108–22.

Baker, A. R. H. and Butlin, R. A. (eds), *Studies of Field Systems in the British Isles* (Cambridge University Press, Cambridge, 1973).

Barker, K., 'Institution and landscape in early medieval Wessex: Aldhelm of Malmesbury, Sherborne and Selwoodshire', *Dorset Nat Hist and Archaeol Soc Proc* 106 for 1984 (1985), pp.33–42.

Barker, P. and Lawson, J., 'A pre-Norman field system at Hen Domen, Montgomery', *Medieval Archaeology* 15 (1971), pp.58–72.

Barrow, G. W. S., *The Kingdom of the Scots: Government, Church and Society from the Eleventh to the Fourteenth Century* (Edward Arnold, London, 1973).

Bassett, S., 'In search of the origins of the Anglo-Saxon kingdoms', in Bassett, S. (ed.) *The Origins of Anglo-Saxon Kingdoms* (1989), pp.3–27.

Bassett, S. (ed.) *The Origins of Anglo-Saxon Kingdoms* (Leicester University Press, Leicester, 1989).

Bede, The Venerable, *A History of the English Church and People*, trans. L. Shirley-Price, revised by R. E. Latham (Penguin Books, Harmondsworth, 1968).

Beresford, M., *History on the Ground* (Methuen, London, 1957).

Beresford, M. W. and St Joseph, J. K. S., *Medieval England: An Aerial Survey*

(Cambridge University Press, Cambridge, 1st edn, 1958, 2nd edn, 1979).

Biddle, M., 'Towns', in Wilson, D. M. (ed.) *The Archaeology of Anglo-Saxon England* (Cambridge University Press, Cambridge, 1976), pp.99–150.

Biddle, M., 'The study of Winchester, archaeology and history in a British town', *Proc Br Academy* 69 (1983), pp.93–135.

Biddle, M., 'Archaeology, architecture, and the cult of saints in Anglo-Saxon England', in Butler, L. A. S. and Morris, R. K. (eds) *The Anglo-Saxon Church*, Counc Br Archaeol Res Rep 60 (London, 1986), pp.1–31.

Birch, W. de Grey, *Cartularium Saxonicum* (Whiting & Co., London, 1885–99; reprinted Johnson Reprint Co., New York and London, 1964).

Bishop, T. A. M., 'Assarting and the growth of the open fields', *Econ Hist Rev*, 1st ser 9.1 (1935), pp.38–44.

de la Blache, V., *Histoire de France depuis les origines jusque la Révolution, Vol. 1: Tableau de la Géographie de la France* (Hachette, Paris, 1911).

Blair, J., 'Secular minster churches in Domesday Book', in Sawyer, P. H. (ed.) *Domesday Book: A Reassessment* (Edward Arnold, London, 1985), pp.104–42.

Boke of St Albans, The, Dame Juliana Berners, facs edn. (London, 1881).

Bonney, D., 'Pagan Saxon burials and boundaries in Wiltshire', *Wiltshire Archaeol and Nat Hist Mag* 61 (1966), pp.25–30.

Bonney, D., 'Early boundaries in Wessex', in Fowler, P. J. (ed.) *Archaeology and the Landscape: Essays for L. V. Grinsell* (John Baker, London, 1972), pp.169–86.

de Bont, C., 'Reclamation patterns of peat areas in the Netherlands as a mirror of the medieval mind', in Bideau, A. (ed.) *L'Avenir des Paysages Ruraux Européens*, Standing European Conference for the Study of the Rural Landscape (Lyons, 1994), pp.57–64.

Bourdillon, J., 'Countryside and town: the animal resources of Saxon Southampton', in Hooke, D. (ed.) *Anglo-Saxon Settlements* (1988), pp.176–96.

Bowman, P., 'Contrasting pays: Anglo-Saxon settlement in Langton Hundred', in Bourne, J. (ed.) *Anglo-Saxon Landscapes in the East Midlands* (Leicestershire Museums Arts and Records Service, Leicester), pp.121–46.

Brooks, N., 'Romney Marsh in the early Middle ages', in Eddison, J. and Green, C. (eds) *Romney Marsh: Evolution, Occupation,* *Reclamation*, Oxford University Comm Archaeol, Monogr No. 24 (1988), pp.90–104.

Brooks, N., 'The creation and early structure of the kingdom of Kent', in Bassett, S. (ed.) *The Origins of Anglo-Saxon Kingdoms* (1989), pp.5–74.

Brooks, N., Gelling, M. and Johnson, D., 'A new charter of King Edgar', in Clemoes, P. (ed.) *Anglo-Saxon England* 13 (Cambridge University Press, Cambridge, 1984), pp.137–55.

Bruce-Mitford, R., *The Sutton Hoo Ship-Burial*, 3 vols (British Museum Publications, London, 1975, 1978, 1983).

Cam, H. M., *Liberties and Communities in Medieval England: Collected Studies in Local Administration and Topography* (Cambridge University Press, Cambridge, 1944).

Cameron, K., 'The meaning and significance of Old English *walh* in English place-names', *J Engl Place-Name Soc* 12 (1979–80), pp.1–46.

Cameron, M. L., 'Bald's *Leechbook*: its sources and their use in its compilation', in Clemoes, P. (ed.) *Anglo-Saxon England* 12 (Cambridge University Press, Cambridge, 1983), pp.153–82.

Campbell, A., *Charters of Rochester*, Anglo-Saxon Charters i (R Hist Soc, London, 1973).

Campbell, E. M. J., 'Berkshire', in Darby, H. C. and Campbell, E. M. J. (eds) *The Domesday Geography of South-East England* (Cambridge University Press, Cambridge, 1971), pp. 239–86.

Campbell, G., 'The preliminary archaeobotanical results from Anglo-Saxon West Cotton and Raunds', in Rackham, J. (ed.) *Environment and Economy in Anglo-Saxon England* (1994), pp.65–82.

Campbell, J., 'Observations on English government from the tenth to the twelfth century', *Trans R Hist Soc* 25 (1975), pp.39–54.

Campbell, J., 'The lost centuries: 400–600', in Campbell, J. (ed.) *The Anglo-Saxons* (Book Club Associates, London, 1982), pp.20–44.

Campbell, J., 'The late Anglo-Saxon state: a maximum view', *Proc Br Acad* 87 (1995), pp.39–65.

Chaplais, P., 'The authenticity of the royal Anglo-Saxon diplomas of Exeter', *Bull Inst Hist Res* 39 (1966), pp.1–34.

Charles-Edwards, T. M., 'Kinship, status, and the origins of the hide', *Past and Present* 56 (1972), pp.3–33.

Charles-Edwards, T. M., 'Boundaries in Irish law', in Sawyer, P. H. (ed.) *Medieval Settlement, Continuity and Change* (Edward Arnold, London, 1976), pp.83–90.

Chronicle of Æthelweard, The, ed. and trans. A. Campbell (Nelson's Medieval Texts, London, 1962).

Cockayne, O., *Leechdoms, Wortcunning and Starcraft of Early England, Herbarium Apuleii Platonici*, Vol. 1, Rolls Series (London, 1864).

Cole, A., 'The origin, distribution and use of the place-name element *ora* and its relationship to the element *ofer*', *J Engl Place-Name Soc* 22 (1989–1990), pp. 26–41.

Coles, J. M. and Goodburn, D. M. (eds), *Wet Site Excavation and Survey, Proceedings of a Conference at the Museum of London* (Wetlands Archaeology Research Project, Exeter, 1991).

Costen, M., 'Some evidence for new settlements and field systems in late Anglo-Saxon Somerset', in Carley, J. and Abrams, L. (eds) *The Archaeology and History of Glastonbury Abbey* (Boydell Press, Woodbridge, 1991), pp.39–55.

Costen, M., *The Origins of Somerset* (Manchester University Press, Manchester, 1992).

Costen, M., '"Huish and worth": Old English survivals in a later landscape', *Anglo-Saxon Studies in Archaeology and History* 5 (Oxford, 1992), pp.65–84.

Cox, B., 'The place-names of the earliest English records', *J Engl Place-Name Soc* 8 (1975–6), pp.12–66.

Crabtree, P. J., 'The faunal remains', in West, S. (ed.) *West Stow: The Anglo-Saxon Village, Vol 1: Text*. East Anglian Archaeology 24 (1985), pp.85–96.

Crabtree, P. J., 'Animal exploitation in East Anglian villages', in Rackham, J. (ed.) *Environment and Economy in Anglo-Saxon England* (1994), pp.40–54.

Cunliffe, B., 'Saxon and medieval settlement-pattern in the region of Chalton, Hampshire', *Medieval Archaeology* 16 (1972), pp.1–12.

Cunliffe, B., 'The evolution of Romney Marsh: a preliminary statement', in Thompson, F. H. (ed.) *Archaeology and Coastal Change* (Soc Antiq London, London, 1980), pp.37–55.

Dahlman, C. J., *The Open Field System and Beyond* (Cambridge University Press, Cambridge, 1980).

Darby, H. C., *Domesday England* (Cambridge University Press, Cambridge, 1977).

Darby, H. C., *The Changing Fenland* (Cambridge University Press, Cambridge, 1983).

Davis, R. H. C., 'Domesday Book: Continental parallels', in Holt, J.C. (ed.) *Domesday Studies* (Boydell Press, Woodbridge, 1987), pp.15–39.

Day, S. P., 'History and palaeography of woodlands in the Oxford region' (unpublished University of Oxford D. Phil. thesis, 1990).

Day, S. P., 'Reconstructing the environment of Shotover Forest, Oxfordshire', *Medieval Settlement Res Group Ann Rep* 3 for 1989 (1990), p.6.

Dixon, P., *Barbarian Europe* (Phaedon, Oxford, 1976).

Dodgshon, R. A., *The Origin of British Field Systems: An Interpretation* (Academic Press, London, 1980).

Dumville, D., 'The origins of Northumbria: some aspects of the British background', in Bassett, S. (ed.) *The Origins of the Anglo-Saxon Kingdoms* (1989), pp.212–22.

Dyer, C., *Warwickshire Farming, 1349– c. 1520: Preparations for Agricultural Revolution*, Dugdale Soc Occ Pap, 27 (1981).

Dymond, D., *The Norfolk Landscape* (Hodder and Stoughton, London, 1985).

Earle, J., *A Hand-Book to the Land-Charters and Other Saxonic Documents* (Clarendon Press, Oxford, 1888).

Ekwall, E., *English River-Names* (Clarendon Press, Oxford, 1928).

Ekwall, E., *The Concise Oxford Dictionary of English Place-Names* (4th edn, Oxford University Press, Oxford, 1960).

Esmonde-Cleary, A. S., *The Ending of Roman Britain* (Batsford, London, 1989).

Everitt, A., *Continuity and Colonization: The Evolution of Kentish Settlement* (Leicester University Press, Leicester, 1986).

Exeter Book, The, Part II, (ed.) W. S. Mackie, Early English Text Soc, original ser no. 194 (London, 1934).

Extent of Merioneth, 1284, pr. in *Archaeologia Cambrensis*, 3rd ser, 13 (1867).

Eyton, R. W., *Antiquities of Shropshire*, Vol. 9 (John Russell Smith, London 1859).

Fairbrother, J. R., 'Faccombe Netherton', *Archaeol and Hist Res* 1 (City of London Archaeol Soc, London, 1984).

Faull, M. L., 'Place-names and the kingdom of Elmet', *Nomina* 4 (1980), pp.21–3.

Finberg, H. P. R., *Gloucestershire Studies* (Leicester University Press, Leicester, 1957).

Finberg, H. P. R., *The Early Charters of Wessex* (Leicester University Press, Leicester, 1964).

Finberg, H. P. R., 'Ayshford and Boehill', *Rep Trans Devonshire Assoc* 103 (1971), pp.19–24.

Finberg, H. P. R., *The Early Charters of the West Midlands* (Leicester University Press, Leicester, 2nd edn, 1972).

Finberg, H. P. R., 'Anglo-Saxon England to 1042', in Finberg, H. P. R. (ed.) *The Agrarian History of England and Wales, A.D. 43–1042, Vol. I.II., Part II* (Cambridge University Press, Cambridge, 1972).

Fleming, A., 'Swadal, Swar (and Erechwydd?): early medieval polities in Upper Swaledale', *Landscape History* 16 (1994), pp.17–30.

Foard, G. and Pearson, T., 'The Raunds area project: first interim report', *Northamptonshire Archaeology* 20 (1985), pp.3–21.

Ford, W. J., 'Anglo-Saxon cemeteries along the Avon valley, Warwickshire', *Trans Birmingham and Warwickshire Archaeol Soc* 100 (1995), pp.59–98.

Fowler, P. J., 'Agriculture and rural settlement', in Wilson, D. M. (ed.) *The Archaeology of Anglo-Saxon England* (1976), pp.23–48.

Fox, H. S. A., 'Field systems of east and south Devon, Pt. 1', *Trans Devonshire Assoc* 104 (1972), pp.81–135.

Fox, H. S. A., 'Approaches to the adoption of the Midland system', in Rowley, T. (ed.) *The Origins of Open-Field Agriculture* (1981), pp.64–111.

Fox, H. S. A., 'Peasant farmers, patterns of settlement and pays: transformations in the landscapes of Devon and Cornwall during the later Middle Ages', in Higham, R. (ed.) *Landscape and Townscape in the South West* (1989), pp.41–73.

Fox, H. S. A., 'Tenant farming and farmers: Devon and Cornwall', in Miller, E. (ed.) *The Agrarian History of England and Wales, Vol. III, 1348–1500* (Cambridge University Press, Cambridge, 1991), pp.722–3.

Fox, H. S. A., 'The bounds of Paignton on Dartmoor: a new identification of an Old English boundary perambulation of circa 1050' (forthcoming).

Gallyon, M., *The Early Church in Wessex and Mercia* (Dalton, Lavenham, 1980).

Gascoyne, J., *Map of the County of Cornwall 1699*, reprint in facsimile with an introduction by W. L. D. Ravenhill and O. J. Padel, Devon & Cornwall Record Soc, new ser 34 (Devon & Cornwall Record Office, Exeter, 1991).

Gelling, M., *The Place-Names of Oxfordshire, Part I*, Engl Place-Name Soc, Vol. 23 (Cambridge University Press, Cambridge, 1953).

Gelling, M., 'Further thoughts on pagan place-names', *Otium et Negotium: Studies in Onomatology and Library Science presented to Olaf von Feilitzen* Acta Bibliothecae Regiae Stockholmiensis 16 (Kungl Boktrycheriet, P. A. Norstedt & Soner, Stockholm, 1973), pp.109–28.

Gelling, M., 'Some notes on Warwickshire place-names', *Trans Birmingham and Warwickshire Archaeol Soc* 86 (1974), pp.59–79.

Gelling, M., *The Place-Names of Berkshire, Part II*, Engl Place-Name Soc, Vol. 50 (Cambridge University Press, Cambridge, 1974).

Gelling, M., *The Place-Names of Berkshire, Part III*, Engl Place-Name Soc, Vol. 51 (Cambridge University Press, Cambridge, 1976).

Gelling, M., *Signposts to the Past* (Dent, London, 1978).

Gelling, M., *Place-Names in the Landscape* (Dent, London, 1984).

Gelling, 'Anglo-Saxon eagles', in Turville-Petre, T. and Gelling, M. (eds) *Leeds Studies in English, XVIII: Studies in Honour of Kenneth Cameron* (University of Leeds, Leeds, 1987), pp.173–8.

Gelling, M., *The Place-Names of Shropshire, Part 1*, Engl Place-Name Soc, Vols 62/63 (Cambridge University Press, Cambridge, 1990).

Gelling, M., *The West Midlands in the Early Middle Ages* (Leicester University Press, London, 1992).

Gildas, *The Ruin of Britain and other Works*, ed. and trans. M. Winterbottom, Arthurian Period Sources, Vol. 7 (Phillimore, Chichester, 1978).

Gnomic Verses, in *A Choice of Anglo-Saxon Verse*, trans. R. Hamer (Faber & Faber, London, 1970), pp.109–15.

Goodburn, D., 'Fragments of a 10th-century timber arcade from Vintner's Place on the

London waterfront', *Medieval Archaeology* 37 (1933), pp.78–92.

Goodier, A. J., 'The formation of boundaries in Anglo-Saxon England: a statistical study', *Medieval Archaeology* 28 (1984), pp.1–21.

Gover, J. E. B., Mawer, A. and Stenton, F. M., *The Place-Names of Devon, Part 2*, Engl Place-Name Soc, Vol. 9 (Cambridge University Press, Cambridge, 1932).

Gover, J. E. B., Mawer, A. and Stenton, F. M., *The Place-Names of Warwickshire*, Engl Place-Name Soc, Vol. 13 (Cambridge University Press, Cambridge, 1936).

Green, F. J., 'Iron Age, Roman and Saxon crops: the archaeological evidence from Wessex', in Jones, M. and Dimbleby, G. (eds) *The Environment of Man: The Iron Age to the Anglo-Saxon Period* (1981), pp.129–54.

Grigson, G., *The Englishman's Flora* (Paladin, St Albans, 1975).

Grundy, G. B., 'Saxon charters of Worcestershire', *Birmingham Archaeol Soc Trans and Proc* 52 (1927), pp.1–183; 53 (1928), pp.18–131.

Hall, D., 'The changing landscape of the Cambridgeshire silt fens', *Landscape History* 3 (1981), pp.37–50.

Hall, D., 'The origins of open-field agriculture: the archaeological fieldwork evidence', in Rowley, T. (ed.) *The Origins of Open-Field Agriculture* (1981), pp.22–38.

Hall, D., 'The Late Saxon countryside: villages and their fields', in Hooke, D. (ed.) *Anglo-Saxon Settlements* (1988), pp.99–122.

Hall, D. and Coles, J., *Fenland Survey: An Essay in Landscape and Persistence*, English Heritage Archaeol Rep 1 (London, 1994).

Hall, R., 'The making of Domesday York', in Hooke, D. (ed.) *Anglo-Saxon Settlements* (1988), pp.233–47.

Hamerow, H., 'Mucking: the Anglo-Saxon settlement', *Current Archaeology* 111 (Sept. 1988), pp.128–31.

Harvey, M., 'The origin of planned field systems in Holderness, Yorkshire', in Rowley, T. (ed.) *The Origins of Open-Field Agriculture* (1981), pp.184–201.

Harvey, M., 'Planned field systems in eastern Yorkshire: some thoughts on their origin', *Agric Hist Rev* 31 (1983), pp.91–103.

Harvey, P. D. A., '*Rectitudines Singularum Personarum* and *Gerefa*', *Engl Hist Rev* 108 (1993), pp.1–22.

Hase, P. H., 'The development of the parish in Hampshire' (unpublished University of Cambridge Ph.D thesis, 1952).

Haslam, J. (ed.), *Anglo-Saxon Towns in Southern England* (Phillimore, Chichester, 1984).

Havinden, M., *The Somerset Landscape* (Hodder and Stoughton, London, 1981).

Hayes, P. P., 'Roman to Saxon in the south Lincolnshire fens', *Antiquity* 62 (1988), pp.321–6.

Heighway, C., *Ancient Gloucester* (Gloucester City Museums Pub, Gloucester, 1976).

Heming, *Hemingi Chartularium Ecclesiae Wigorniensis*, ed. T. Hearne (Oxford, 1723).

Herring, P. C., 'Prehistory and history of land-use and settlement on north-west Bodmin Moor, Cornwall' (unpublished University of Sheffield M. Phil. thesis, n.d.).

Hickin, N. E., *The Natural History of an English Forest* (Country Book Club, Newton Abbot, 1972).

Higham, N. J, 'Settlement, land use and Domesday ploughlands', *Landscape History* 12 (1990), pp.33–44.

Higham, N. J., 'Old light on the Dark-Age landscape: the description of Britain in the *De Excidio Britanniae* of Gildas', *J Hist Geogr* 17 (1991), pp.363–72.

Higham, N. J., *Rome, Britain and the Anglo-Saxons* (Seaby, London, 1992).

Higham, R. (ed.), *Landscape and Townscape in the South West*, Exeter Studies in History No. 22 (University of Exeter, Exeter, 1989).

Hill, D., *An Atlas of Anglo-Saxon England* (Basil Blackwell, Oxford, 1981).

Hill, D., *Offa's and Wat's Dykes* (forthcoming).

Hill, D., *The Turning Year* (forthcoming).

Hodges, R., *The Anglo-Saxon Achievement* (Duckworth, London, 1989).

Hodges, R., *Wall-to-Wall History: The Story of Roystone Grange* (Duckworth, London, 1991).

Holt, J. C., *Robin Hood* (Thames & Hudson, London, 1982).

Hooke, D., 'Llanaber: a study in landscape development', *J Merioneth Hist Rec Soc* 7 (1975), pp.221–30.

Hooke, D., 'Early Cotswold woodland', *J Hist Geogr* 4 (1978), pp.333–41.

Hooke, D., 'Anglo-Saxon landscapes of the West Midlands', *J Engl Place-Name Soc* 11 (1978–79), pp.3–23.

Hooke, D., 'Burial features in West Midland charters', *J Engl Place-Name Soc* 13 (1980–81), pp.1–40.

Hooke, D., 'The Droitwich salt industry: an examination of the West Midland charter evidence', in Campbell, J., Brown, D. and Hawkes, S. (eds) *Anglo-Saxon Studies in Archaeology and History*, Br Archaeol Rep, Br ser 92 (Oxford, 1981), pp.123–69.

Hooke, D., *Anglo-Saxon Landscapes of the West Midlands: The Charter Evidence*, Br Archaeol Rep, Br ser 95 (Oxford, 1981).

Hooke, D., 'Open-field agriculture – the evidence from the pre-Conquest charters of the West Midlands', in Rowley, T. (ed.) *The Origins of Open-Field Agriculture* (1981), pp.39–63.

Hooke, D., 'Pre-Conquest estates in the West Midlands: preliminary thoughts', *J Hist Geogr* 8 (1982), pp.227–44.

Hooke, D., 'The Anglo-Saxon landscape', in Slater, T. R. and Jarvis, P. J. (eds) *Field and Forest: A Historical Geography of Warwickshire and Worcestershire* (Geo Books, Norwich, 1982), pp.79–103.

Hooke, D., *The Landscape of Anglo-Saxon Staffordshire: The Charter Evidence* (University of Keele, Keele, 1983).

Hooke, D., 'Cada's minster, Broadway, Worcs.', *Bull Counc Br Archaeol Churches Committee* 18 (1983), pp.2–6.

Hooke, D., *The Anglo-Saxon Landscape: The Kingdom of the Hwicce* (Manchester University Press, Manchester, 1985).

Hooke, D., 'Village development in the West Midlands', in Hooke, D. (ed.) *Medieval Villages* (1985), pp.125–54.

Hooke, D. (ed.), *Medieval Villages: A Review of Current Work*, Oxford University Comm Archaeol Monogr 5 (Oxford, 1985).

Hooke, D., *Anglo-Saxon Territorial Organization: The Western Margins of Mercia*, Dep Geogr Occ Pap 22 (University of Birmingham, Birmingham, 1986).

Hooke, D., 'Territorial organization in the Anglo-Saxon west Midlands: central places, central areas', in Grant, E. (ed.) *Central Places, Archaeology and History* (Dep Archaeology and Prehistory, University of Sheffield, Sheffield, 1986), pp.79–93.

Hooke, D., 'Two documented pre-Conquest Christian sites located upon parish boundaries: "Cada's minster", Willersey, Gloucs., and "the holy place", Fawler in Kingston Lisle, Oxon.', *Medieval Archaeology* 31 (1987), pp.96–101.

Hooke, D., 'Regional variation in southern and central England in the Anglo-Saxon period and its relationship to land units and

settlement', in Hooke, D. (ed.) *Anglo-Saxon Settlements* (1988), pp.123–52.

Hooke, D. (ed.), *Anglo-Saxon Settlements* (Blackwell, Oxford, 1988).

Hooke, D., 'Early forms of open-field agriculture in England', *Geografiska Annaler* 70 B (1) (1988), pp.123–31.

Hooke, D., 'Pre-Conquest woodland: its distribution and usage', *Agric Hist Rev* 37 (1989), pp.113–29.

Hooke, D., 'A note on the evidence for vineyards and orchards in Anglo-Saxon England', *J Wine Res* 1, No.1 (1990), pp.77–80.

Hooke, D., *Worcestershire Anglo-Saxon Charter-Bounds* (Boydell Press, Woodbridge, 1990).

Hooke, D., 'Early units of government in Herefordshire and Shropshire', *Anglo-Saxon Studies in Archaeology and History* 5, Oxford University Comm for Archaeol (Oxford, 1992), pp.47–64.

Hooke, D., 'The use of early medieval charters as sources for the study of settlement and landscape evolution', in Verhoeve, A. and Vervloet, J. A. J. (eds) *The Transformation of the European Rural Landscape: Methodological Issues and Agrarian Change 1770–1914* (Standing European Conference for the Study of the Rural Landscape, Brussels, 1992), pp.39–47.

Hooke, D., *Warwickshire's Historical Landscape, 1: The Arden* (Self-published, Birmingham, 1993).

Hooke, D., 'The administrative and settlement framework of early medieval Wessex', in Aston, M. and Lewis, C. (eds) *The Medieval Landscape of Wessex*, Oxbow Monograph 46 (Oxbow Books, Oxford, 1994), pp.83–96.

Hooke, D., *The Pre-Conquest Charter-Bounds of Devon and Cornwall* (Boydell Press, Woodbridge, 1994).

Hooke, D., 'The mid-late Anglo-Saxon period: settlement and land use', in Hooke, D. and Burnell, S. (eds) *Landscape and Settlement in Britain AD 400–1066* (University of Exeter Press, Exeter, 1995), pp.95–114.

Hooke, D., 'The Anglo-Saxons in England in the seventh and eighth centuries: aspects of location in space', in Hines, J. (ed.) *The Anglo-Saxons from the Migration Period to the Eighth Century: An Ethnographical Perspective* (Boydell Press, Woodbridge, 1997), pp.65–85.

Hooke, D., 'Names and settlement in the Warwickshire Arden', in Hooke, D. and Postles, D. (eds) *Names, Time and Place,*

Festschrift for R. A. McKinley (Leopard's Head Press, Oxford and London, forthcoming), pp.32–45.

Hooke, D., *The Anglo-Saxon Charter-Bounds of Warwickshire* (Boydell Press, Woodbridge, forthcoming).

Hooke, D., *Anglo-Saxon England: An Historical Geography* (Blackwell, Oxford, forthcoming).

Hooke, D., 'Saxon conquest and settlement', in Kain, R. and Ravenhill, W. (eds) *An Historical Atlas of the South-West* (forthcoming).

Hooke, D. and Herring, P., 'Interrogating Anglo-Saxons in St Dennis', *Cornish Archaeology* 32 (1993), pp.67–75.

Hooper, M., 'Dating hedges', *Area* No.4 (1970), pp.63–5.

Hooper, M., 'Hedges and history', *New Scientist* 31 Dec (1970), pp.598–600.

Hope-Taylor, B., *Yeavering: An Anglo-British Centre of Early Northumbria*, Dep Env Archaeol Rep 7 (HMSO, London, 1977).

Hoskins, W. G. *Fieldwork in Local History* (Faber & Faber, London, 1967).

Hoskins, W. G., *English Landscapes* (BBC, London, 1974).

Hoskins, W. G. and Dudley Stamp, L., *The Common Lands of England and Wales* (Collins, London, 1963).

Humble, R., *The Saxon Kings* (Book Club Associates, London, 1980).

Hunter Blair, P., *Northumbria in the Days of Bede* (Gollancz, London, 1977).

James, S., Marshall, A. and Millett, M., 'An early medieval building tradition', *Archaeol J* 141 (1984), pp.182–215.

Johansson, C., *Old English Place-Names Containing Leah* (Almqvist and Wiksell Int., Stockholm, 1975).

Jolliffe, J. E. A., 'Northumbrian institutions', *English Hist Rev* 41 (1926), pp.1–42.

Jones, G. R. J., 'The distribution of bond settlements in north-west Wales', *Welsh History Revue* 2 (1964), pp.19–36.

Jones, G. R. J., 'Post-Roman Wales', in Finberg, H. P. R. (ed.) *The Agrarian History of England and Wales* (1972), pp.283–382.

Jones, G. R. J., 'Continuity despite calamity', *J Celtic Stud* 3 (1981), pp.1–30.

Jones, G. R. J., 'Celts, Saxons and Scandinavians', in Dodgshon, R. A. and Butlin, R. A. (eds) *An Historical Geography of England and Wales* (Academic Press, London, 2nd edn, 1990), pp.49–52.

Jones, M., and Dimbleby, G. (eds), *The Environment of Man: The Iron Age to the Anglo-Saxon Period*, Br Archaeol Rep, Br ser 87 (Oxford, 1981).

Jones, M. U. and Jones, W. T., 'The crop-mark sites at Mucking, Essex, England', in Bruce-Mitford, R. (ed.) *Recent Archaeological Excavations in Europe* (Routledge and Kegan Paul, London, 1975), pp.133–87.

Keen, L., 'The towns of Dorset', in Haslam, J. (ed.) *Anglo-Saxon Towns* (1984), pp.203–48.

Kemble, J. M., *Codex Diplomaticus Aevi Saxonici*, 6 vols (1839–48).

Kemble, J. M., 'Notices of heathen internment in the Codex Diplomaticus', *Archaeol J* 14 (1857), pp.119–39.

Kerr, N. and Kerr, M., *A Guide to Anglo-Saxon Sites* (Granada, London, 1982).

Kerridge, E., *The Common Fields of England* (Manchester University Press, Manchester, 1992).

Klingelhöfer, E. C., *Manor, Vill, and Hundred: The Development of Rural Institutions in Early Medieval Hampshire*, Studies and Texts 112 (Pontifical Institute of Mediaeval Studies, Toronto, 1992).

Langdon, J., 'Agricultural equipment', in Astill, G. and Grant, A. (eds) *The Countryside of Medieval England* (Blackwell, Oxford, 1988), pp.86–107.

Liber Eliensis, ed. E. O. Blake (Royal Hist Soc, London, 1962).

Liebermann, F., *Die Gesetze der Angelsachsen* (Leipzig, 1903).

Losco-Bradley, S. and Wheeler, H., 'Anglo-Saxon settlement in the Trent Valley: some aspects', in Faull, M. L. (ed.) *Studies in Late Anglo-Saxon Settlement* (Oxford University Dep External Studies, Oxford, 1984), pp.101–14.

Mackie, W. S., *The Exeter Book, Part II: Poems IX-XXXII*, Early English Text Society 194 (London, 1934).

Maltby, M., 'Iron Age, Romano-British and Anglo-Saxon animal husbandry: a review of the faunal evidence', in Jones, M. and Dimbleby, G. (eds) *The Environment of Man* (1981), pp.155–203.

Mawer, A. and Stenton, F. M., *The Place-Names of Worcestershire*, Engl Place-Name Soc, Vol. 4 (Cambridge University Press, Cambridge, 1927).

McCloskey, D., 'English open fields as behavior towards risk', in Uselding, P. (ed.) *Research in Economic History, Vol. 1* (J.A.I. Press, Greenwich, CN, 1976), pp.124–70.

McGurk. P., 'The labours of the months', in Dumville, D. M., Godden, M. R. and

Knock, A. (eds) *An Eleventh-Century Anglo-Saxon Illustrated Miscellany: British Library Cotton Tiberius B. V, pt 1*, Early English MSS in Facsimile, ed. G. Harlow, no. 21 (Rosenkilde & Bagger, Copenhagen, 1983), pp. 40–3.

Medieval Settlement Res Rep 2 (1987); 4 (1989).

Metz, W., 'Das "gehagio regis" der Langobarden und die deutschen Hagenortsnamen', in *Beitrage zur Namenforschung in Verbindung mit Ernst Dickenmann, herausgegeben von Hans Krahe*, Band 5 (Winter, Heidelberg, 1954).

Miles, D., 'Appendix' to M. Gelling, 'Anglo-Saxon eagles', (1987), pp.178–9.

Miles, D. and Palmer, S., 'White Horse Hill', *Current Archaeology* 142 (1995), pp.372–8.

Miles, H. and Miles, Y., 'Excavations at Trethurgy, St Austell: interim report', *Cornish Archaeology* 12 (1973), pp.25–30.

Millett, M., 'Excavations at Cowdery's Down, Basingstoke, 1978–1981', *Archaeol J* 140 (1983), pp.151–279.

Mills, A. D., *A Dictionary of English Place-Names* (Oxford University Press, Oxford, 1991).

Morgan, P. (ed.), *Domesday Book, 5, Berkshire* (Phillimore, Chichester, 1979).

Murphy, P., 'The Anglo-Saxon landscape and rural economy: some results from sites in East Anglia and Essex', in Rackham, J. (ed.) *Environment and Economy in Anglo-Saxon England* (1994), pp.23–39.

Napier, A. S., and Stevenson, W. H., *The Crawford Collection of Early Charters and Documents* (Bodleian Library, Oxford, 1895).

Nennius, *Nennius, British History and The Welsh Annals*, ed. and trans. J. Morris (Philimore, Chichester, 1980).

Noble, F. *Offa's Dyke Reviewed*, Br Archaeol Rep 114 (Oxford, 1983).

Olson, B. L., *Early Monasteries in Cornwall*, Studies in Celtic History (Boydell Press, Woodbridge, 1989).

Ordnance Survey, *Map of Dark Age Britain* (HMSO, London, 1966).

Orwin, C. S. and Orwin, C. S., *The Open Fields* (Clarendon Press, Oxford, 3rd edn, 1967).

Padel, O., 'The Cornish background of the Tristan stories', *Cambridge Medieval Celtic Stud* 1 (1981), pp.53–81.

Padel, O., *Cornish Place-Name Elements*, Engl Place-Name Soc, Vols 56/57 (Cambridge University Press, Cambridge, 1985).

Peake, H. J., *Trans Newbury and District Field Club*, 7 (1934–7), pp.175–80.

Pesez, J. M., 'The emergence of the village in France and in the West', *Landscape History* 14 (1992), pp.31–5.

Phœbus, Gaston, *The Hunting Book*, ed. G. Bise (Regent Books, London, 1984).

Phythian-Adams, C., *Land of the Cumbrians* (Scolar Press, Aldershot, 1996).

Prescott, A., 'Manuscripts', in Webster, L. and Backhouse, J. (eds) *The Making of England* (1991), pp.39–41.

Preston-Jones, A. and Rose, P., 'Medieval Cornwall', *Cornish Archaeology* 25 (1986), pp.135–84.

Pritchard, F. A., 'Late Saxon textiles from the city of London', *Medieval Archaeology* 28 (1984), pp.46–71.

Quinnell, H., 'Cornwall during the Iron age and the Roman period', *Cornish Archaeology* 25 (1986), pp.135–85.

Rackham, J. (ed.), *Environment and Economy in Anglo-Saxon England*, Counc Br Archaeol Res Rep No 89 (York, 1994).

Rackham, J., 'Economy and environment in Saxon London', in Rackham, J. (ed.) *Environment and Economy in Anglo-Saxon England* (1994), pp.126–35.

Rackham, O., *Ancient Woodland: Its History, Vegetation and Uses in England* (Edward Arnold, London, 1980).

Rackham, O., *The History of the Countryside* (Dent, London, 1986).

Rahtz, P., *The Saxon and Medieval Palaces at Cheddar*, Br Archaeol Rep, Br ser 65 (Oxford, 1979).

Reaney, P. H., *The Place-Names of Cambridgeshire and the Isle of Ely*, Engl Place-Name Soc, Vol. 19 (Cambridge University Press, Cambridge, 1943).

Reece, R. M., 'Town and country: the end of Roman Britain', *World Archaeology* 12.1 (1980), pp.77–92.

Rivet, A. L. F. and Smith, C., *The Place-Names of Roman Britain* (Batsford, London, 1979).

Roberts, B. K., 'Settlement, land use and population in the western portion of the Forest of Arden, Warwickshire, between 1086 and 1350' (unpublished University of Birmingham Ph.D thesis, 1965).

Roberts, B. K., 'Townfield origins – the case of Cockfield, County Durham', in Rowley, T. (ed.) *The Origins of Open Field Agriculture* (1981), pp.145–61.

Roberts, B. K., *The Making of the English Village* (Longman, Harlow, 1987).

Robertson, A. J., *Anglo-Saxon Charters* (Cambridge University Press, Cambridge, 2nd edn, 1956).

Romilly Allen, J., 'Early Christian art', in *The Victoria History of the Counties of England, Worcestershire*, Vol. 2 (Inst Hist Res, London, 1906).

Rose, P. 'The historic landscape', in Johnson, N. and Rose, P., *Bodmin Moor: An Archaeological Survey, Vol 1: The human landscape to c. 1800* (Cornwall Archaeology Unit, English Heritage and RCHME, London, 1994), pp. 77–115.

Rose, P. and Preston-Jones, A., 'Changes in the Cornish countryside AD 400–1100', in Hooke, D. and Burnell, S. (eds) *Landcape and Settlement in Britain* (1995), pp.51–68.

Round, J. H., 'Introduction to the Worcestershire Domesday', in *The Victoria History of the County of Worcester*, Vol. 1 (Inst Hist Res, London, n.d.), pp.235–81.

Rowley, T., *The Shropshire Landscape* (Hodder and Stoughton, London, 1972).

Rowley, T. (ed.), *The Origins of Open-Field Agriculture* (Croom Helm, London, 1981).

Rutherford Davis, K., *Britons and Saxons: The Chiltern Region 400–700* (Phillimore, Chichester, 1982).

Sawyer, P. H., *Anglo-Saxon Charters: An Annotated List and Bibliography* (R Hist Soc, London, 1968).

Sawyer, P. H., 'The royal Tun in pre-Conquest England', in Wormald, P. (ed.) *Ideal and Reality in Frankish and Anglo-Saxon Society* (Blackwell, Oxford, 1983), pp.273–99.

Scherr, J., 'Names of some English holy wells', *Proc of XVIIth Int Congress of Onomastic Sciences*, Vol. 2 (University of Helsinki and Finnish Res Centre for Domestic Language, Helsinki, 1990), pp.318–23.

Scott, A. F., *The Saxon Age* (Book Club Associates, London, 1979).

Seebohm, F., *The English Village Community examined in its relations to the manorial and tribal systems and to the common or open field system of husbandry* (Longmans, Green, and Co., London, 1890, 4th edn, 1905).

Shennan, S., *Experiments in the Collection and Analysis of Archaeological Survey Data: The East Hampshire Survey* (Dept Archaeol and Prehist, University of Sheffield, Sheffield, 1985).

Shoesmith, R., *Hereford City Excavations, II, Excavations On and Close to the Defences*, Counc Br Archaeol Res Rep 36 (1982).

Slade, C. F. (ed.), *The Great Roll of the Pipe for the Twelfth Year of the Reign of King John, Michaelmas 1210, Pipe Roll 56*, Pipe Roll Soc, new ser 26 (1949).

Silvester, R., *The Fenland Project, 3: Marshland and the Nar Valley, Norfolk*, East Anglian Archaeology, 45 (Norwich, 1988).

Smith, A. H., *The Place-Names of Gloucestershire, Part I*, Engl Place-Name Soc, Vol. 38 (Cambridge University Press, Cambridge, 1964).

Smith, A. H., *The Place-Names of Gloucestershire, Part III*, Engl Place-Name Soc, Vol. 40 (Cambridge University Press, Cambridge, 1964).

Stenton, F. M. (ed.), *The Great Roll of the Pipe for the Thirteenth Year of the Reign of King John, Michaelmas 1211, Pipe Roll 57*, Pipe Roll Soc, new ser 28 (1951–52).

Stenton, F. M., *The Latin Charters of the Anglo-Saxon Period* (Clarendon Press, Oxford, 1955).

Stenton, F. M., *Anglo-Saxon England* (Oxford University Press, Oxford, 3rd edn, 1971).

Storms, G., *Anglo-Saxon Magic* (Martinus Nijhoff, The Hague, 1948).

Swanton, M. (ed. and trans.), *Anglo-Saxon Prose* (Dent, London, 1975).

Tatton-Brown, T. 'The towns of Kent', in Haslam, J. (ed.) *Anglo-Saxon Towns* (1984), pp.1–36.

Taylor, C., *Fields in the English Landscape* (Dent, London, 1975).

Taylor, C., *The Cambridgeshire Landscape* (Hodder and Stoughton, London, 1973).

Taylor, C., *Village and Farmstead* (Book Club Associates, London, 1983).

Tebbutt, C. F., 'A Middle Saxon iron-smelting site at Millbrook, Ashdown Forest, Sussex', *Sussex Archaeological Collections* 120 (1982), pp.19–36.

Thirsk, J., 'The common fields', *Past and Present* 29 (1964), pp.3–25.

Thirsk, J., 'The origin of the common fields', *Past and Present* 33 (1966), pp.142–7.

Thomas, C., 'Social organisation and rural settlement in medieval North Wales', *J Merioneth Hist Rec Soc*, 6 (1970), pp.121–31.

Thomas, C., 'A cultural–ecological model of agrarian colonisation in upland Wales', *Landscape History* 14 (1992), pp.37–50.

Thorn, C., and Thorn, F. (eds), *Domesday Book, 6, Wiltshire* (Phillimore, Chichester, 1979).

Thorn C., and Thorn, F. (eds), *Domesday Book, 9, Devon* (Phillimore, Chichester, 1985).

Trinder, B., *A History of Shropshire* (Phillimore, Chichester, 1983).

Turner, J., 'The vegetation', in Jones, M. and Dimbleby, G. (eds) *The Environment of Man* (1981), pp.67–73.

Unwin, P. T. H., 'Townships and early fields in north Nottinghamshire', *J Hist Geog* 9, (1983), pp.341–6.

Victoria History of the County of Worcester, Vol 2, ed. W. Willis-Bund, (Inst Hist Res, London, 1906).

Victoria History of the County of Wiltshire, Vol. 3, ed. R. B. Pugh (Inst Hist Res, London, 1956).

Vince, A., *Saxon London: An Archaeological Investigation* (Seaby, London, 1990).

Vince, A., 'Saxon urban economies: an archaeological perspective', in Rackham, J. (ed.) *Environment and Economy in Anglo-Saxon England* (1994), pp.108–19.

Wade, K., 'A settlement site at Bonhunt Farm', in Buckley, D. (ed.) *Archaeology in Essex to A.D. 1500*, Counc Br Archaeol Res Rep 34 (London, 1980), pp.96–103.

Wade-Martins, P., 'Excavation in North Elmham Park 1967–72', *East Anglian Archaeology* 9 (1980), pp.1–661.

Warner, P., *Greens, Commons and Clayland Colonization*, University of Leicester Dep Engl Local Hist Occ Pap, 4th ser, no.2 (Leicester University Press, Leicester, 1987).

Watkins, C., *Woodland Management and Conservation (Britain's Ancient Woodland)*, Nature Conservancy Council (David & Charles, Newton Abbot and London, 1990).

Webster, L., 'Metalwork, ivory and textiles', in Webster, L and Backhouse, J. (eds) *The Making of England* (1991), pp.184–5.

Webster, L., and Backhouse, J. (eds), *The Making of England: Anglo-Saxon Art and Culture, AD 600–900* (British Museum and British Library, London, 1991).

Welch, M., 'The kingdom of the South Saxons', in Bassett, S. (ed.) *The Origins of the Anglo-Saxon Kingdoms* (1989), pp.75–83.

Welch, M., *Anglo-Saxon England* (Batsford/English Heritage, London, 1992).

West, S., *West Stow: The Anglo-Saxon Village*, 2 vols, East Anglian Archaeol 24 (Ipswich, 1985).

Whitelock, D., *English Historical Documents, I, c. 500–1042* (Eyre and Spottiswoode, London, 1955, 1979).

Wickham, C., 'European forests in the early Middle Ages: landscape and land clearance', *L'Ambiente Vegetale Nell'Alto Medioevo, Settimane di studio del Centro italiano di studi sull'alto medioevo* 37 (Centro Italiano di Studi Sull'alto Medioevo Spoleto, 1990), pp.399–548.

Williams, A., Smyth, A. P. and Kirby, D. P., *A Bibliographical Dictionary of Dark Age Britain* (Seaby, London, 1991).

Williamson, T., 'Settlement chronology and regional landscapes: the evidence from the claylands of East Anglia', in Hooke, D. (ed.) *Anglo-Saxon Settlements* (1988), pp.153–75.

Wilson, D. M., 'Craft and industry', in Wilson, D. M. (ed.) *The Archaeology of Anglo-Saxon England* (1976), pp.253–81.

Wilson, D. M. (ed.), *The Archaeology of Anglo-Saxon England* (Cambridge University Press, Cambridge, 1976).

Wilson, D. M., 'The Viking adventure', in Wilson, D. M. (ed.) *The Northern World* (Thames & Hudson, London, 1980), pp.159–82.

Winchester, A. J. L., *Landscape and Society in Medieval Cumbria* (John Donald, Edinburgh, 1987).

Winchester, A. J. L., *Discovering Parish Boundaries* (Shire, Haverfordwest, 1990).

Witney, K. P., *The Jutish Forest: A Study of the Weald of Kent from 450 to 1380 A.D.* (Athlone Press, London, 1976).

Woodward, A. and Leach, P., *The Uley Shrines: Excavation of a Ritual Complex on West Hill, Uley, Gloucestershire: 1977–9* (English Heritage/British Museum Press, London, 1993).

Wormald, P., 'Bede, *Beowulf* and the conversion of the Anglo-Saxon aristocracy', in Farrell, R. T. (ed.) *Bede and Anglo-Saxon England*, Br Archaeol Rep, Br ser 46 (Oxford, 1978), pp.32–95.

Index

Reference to figures and plates are shown in *italics*; individual places referred to only once are not entered by name but will be found under their respective counties.